The Lost Life of
Horatio Alger, Jr.

The Lost Life

—⬦of⬦—

Horatio Alger, Jr.

Gary Scharnhorst

with Jack Bales

Bloomington

To Herbert R. Mayes,

who urged us to set the record straight

Library of Congress Cataloging in Publication Data

Scharnhorst, Gary.
    The lost life of Horatio Alger, Jr.

    Bibliography: p.
    Includes index.
    1. Alger, Horatio, 1832–1899. 2. Authors, American—
19th century—Biography. I. Bales, Jack. II. Title.
PS1029.A3Z84 1985   813'.4 [B]   84-48295
ISBN 0-253-14915-0

1 2 3 4 5   89 88 87 86 85

Only fools laugh at Horatio Alger, and his poor boys who make good. The wiser man who thinks twice about that sterling author will realize that Alger is to America what Homer was to the Greeks.

—NATHANAEL WEST AND BORIS INGSTER
(1940)

Contents

PREFACE

We once doubted this book could be written. Horatio Alger, Jr., was an intensely private man who shunned publicity throughout his life, fearing his reputation would be tarnished if an intimate secret, an unsavory incident in his early adulthood, was publicly exposed. He referred inquisitive correspondents to brief, often inaccurate biographical sketches and feigned surprise that others were curious about him, protesting to a friend in 1896 that "I really feel very little interest in my own biography."[1] Over eighty-five years after his death, Alger's story deserves to be told at last.

The compilation of this story posed both a challenge and a question: Can a historical figure be both significant yet virtually unknown? Consider the possibility that a person who is otherwise a suitable subject for biography, in order to guard his privacy, leaves no personal papers for researchers to sift and weigh. Consider the possibility that such a figure becomes the subject of intense public interest only many years after his death. In the mirror of historical hindsight, might not the life of this figure be hidden in a biographical blind spot?

Such has been the case with Alger. Upon his death in 1899, his sister Augusta, in accordance with his instructions, destroyed all his private papers.[2] Nary a letter he received or a single page of a diary was preserved. Other members of the family followed Augusta's lead. As late as 1942, Anna Alger Richardson warned a researcher she "might resent your going prying in Natick" into her late Uncle Horatio's hometown affairs.[3] Over the years, some sources have disappeared without a trace, like cowed witnesses before an inquest. For example, a letter in which the Reverend William Rounseville Alger may have discussed his cousin's aborted ministry was removed long ago from the archives of the American Unitarian Association and presumably destroyed.[4] In all, fewer than two hundred letters from Horatio's hand, nearly half of them addressed to the same correspondent over a period of only four years, are extant. For many years, these precautions against publishing scoundrels seemed unnecessary. No one cared.

Only in the 1920s, after Alger's name became a shibboleth invoked by the American cult of success, did anyone notice the paucity of sources about his life. In this climate of ignorance, his first biographer perpetrated an incredible hoax.[5] In 1927, Herbert R. Mayes, a young journalist who would later become editor of *Good Housekeeping*, a director of the *Saturday Review*, and president of the McCall Corporation, contracted to write the first full-length life of Alger. He spent a few days researching his subject but, as he subsequently observed, "the more of the little I read and heard" the more difficult the task seemed, given the dearth of biographical data. A friend suggested an alternative: "Why not do a take-off on Alger, a parody?" Unable to write the biography he had planned, Mayes changed his plans. He would fabricate a life from whole cloth.

> Here was a project that with scant trouble I felt I could handle in a matter of months or even weeks. All I had to do was come up with a fairy tale. No research required. Nothing required but a little imagination. . . . Thus I began, and the going was easy, particularly when I decided to quote copiously from Alger's diary. If Alger ever kept a diary, I knew nothing about it. In any case, it was more fun to invent one. I had no letters ever written by Alger, which was fortunate. Again, it was more fun to make them up, as it was with letters presumably sent *to* Alger, none of which I had ever seen.

Mayes's publisher, George Macy, who at first doubted a tongue-in-cheek approach would work, "was not merely satisfied, but pleased" after "I put together a few chapters. . . . He thought I might pull off a delightful spoof." That Mayes did, in spades. The bluff succeeded for nearly half a century with implications neither he nor his publisher nor anyone else had anticipated.

"Because there had to be a *few* facts," Mayes later explained, "I corresponded with a handful of people, interviewed a few, and made a visit to South Natick," Alger's hometown in Massachusetts, "for all of two days. The project was undertaken with malice aforethought—a take-off on the debunking biographies that were quite popular in the

20's, and a more miserable, maudlin piece of claptrap would be hard to imagine, though I surely could not have considered it so bad then as I did later." That Mayes's work would not be recognized immediately as an exercise in histrionics seems curious today. A passage from one of the diaries he invented, in which Alger mentions having read *Moby-Dick*, is particularly transparent: The biography appeared in the spring of 1928 at the height of the Melville revival.

Mayes was genuinely surprised when the biography, upon its publication, was regarded as authoritative.

> As anyone who has read my book is aware, I made Alger out to be a pathetic, quite ridiculous character. I provided him with mistresses. I had him adopt and become attached to a little Chinese boy, and then had the boy killed by a runaway horse. I credited to him as a child essays and verses—never existent—that a child of ten might have written. I had Alger dreaming of a great novel that some day he would write. I put in the mind of the character I created the delusion that some day he might be President of the United States.

With few facts but a surfeit of *chutzpah*, Mayes depicted Alger as a philandering neurotic obsessed with personal success, and he would fool reviewers, historians, and would-be biographers with the tale for over forty years. None of Alger's surviving friends or family objected overtly to his treatment because, apparently, Mayes at least had not revealed the truth. A more conscientious researcher might have discovered even more embarrassing skeletons in the closet. "Unfortunately—how unfortunately!—the book when it appeared was accepted pretty much as gospel," Mayes later lamented. "Why it was not recognized for what it was supposed to be baffled the publisher and me."

Notices of Mayes's *Alger: A Biography Without a Hero*, though mixed, were generally favorable.[6] "Don't miss it," Harry Hansen adjured the readers of the old *New York World*. Malcolm Cowley, in the *New Republic*, concluded that "Mr. Mayes' biography of Alger . . . is a little better than the average of its class." Mark Van Doren in the *Nation* and Allan Nevins in the *Saturday Review of Literature* were not as impressed, though neither questioned the reliability of Mayes's work. "What can be said for this volume," wrote Nevins, a one-time president of the American Historical Association, "is that it has collected, together with much which might better have been omitted, some facts which the future writer of a magazine essay or a chapter in a history of juvenile fiction will put to good use." Edwin Blanchard of the old *New York Sun* leveled the harshest criticism: Mayes, he asserted, had let "a second-rate vocabulary and a fifth-rate imagination loose on the few known facts" about Alger's life. Mayes later recalled he was flabbergasted by the accusation he lacked imagination.

Not surprisingly, most readers ignored Harry Hansen's advice. Fewer than fifteen hundred copies of Mayes's book were sold, and the author never received a penny in royalties. But late in 1928, the work acquired a type of immortality. It became the primary source for the Alger entry in the *Dictionary of American Biography*, and, ordained by that canon, its veracity was virtually above reproach. To this day, entries about Alger in every major reference work, every encyclopedia from the *Britannica* up and down, contain "facts" first concocted by Mayes which through reiteration have obtained the force and luster of truth.

In this respect, Hansen's review had both unfortunate and unforeseen consequences. Hansen and George Macy were good friends, "which put Macy in a dilemma," as Mayes has explained. "How was he to announce that the book was a hoax without making Hansen look silly? As a publisher, and a fairly new one, Macy felt he was in no position to offend a critic." At length, Macy decided "to let the book ride, to try to dispose of the print order to get back his publication costs, and then forget about it." So as not to embarrass Hansen, with whom he too "became fairly friendly as the years went by," Mayes continued to stonewall until the early 1970s. Occasionally a few people, including Cowley, contacted him through the years to inquire about the sources he used to write the book. On all such occasions, Mayes replied that the diary "together with all other 'research' material had been turned over to the Newsboys' Home in New York. . . . The original decision to perpetuate the myth was never changed."

To his credit, Cowley was unconvinced by Mayes's easy assurances. In 1945, he became the first person to dispute publicly the reliability of Mayes's *Alger*.[7] Working on assignment from *Time*, Cowley sent several Time-Life staffers to the offices of the Children's Aid Society to search for the Alger material Mayes claimed he had donated to the Newsboys' Lodging House—to no avail, of course. Cowley subsequently observed in print that "Mayes says that much of his own account was based on Alger's private diary, a black, clothbound volume; but in view of his other errors you can't help wondering whether he copied it correctly or whether it ever existed—for the diary has vanished since Mayes used it, and nobody else remembers having seen it." Not until 1958, in private correspondence, did Mayes respond to Cowley's insinuation, and then only to insist with a brave front that he had faithfully reproduced excerpts from Alger's diaries in his biography. "There were a number of books, not merely one, in which Alger made his entries," he asserted. Had he not died only the year before, Mayes added, George Macy doubtless would have verified their existence. Macy

> was familiar with the diaries, because in one of our original meetings, and before any contract was signed, he had them in his office. I think it not unreasonable to suppose therefore that other individuals in his firm, among others, were familiar with them. . . . I had no use for the Alger books I had collected—they were worth practically nothing then—and it was Mr. Macy's suggestion that they and my manuscript and Alger's letters and all the other supporting material be given to the Brace Memorial Newsboys' Home. That seemed like a good idea, and though I wasn't present—I don't know why—I recall clearly that this plan was carried out and that Mr. Macy arranged some kind of ceremony to suit the occasion.[8]

Cowley replied with admirable tact: "I'm glad to learn that there was— or rather were—Alger diaries, and if you succeed in tracking them down, I'd be most grateful for a chance to see them, though you know, to make a confession, I would have admired the kid that you once were if he'd had the nerve to make them up."[9] Fifteen years later, Cowley would privately remark less circumspectly that Mayes's letter to him contained "fabrications amounting in some cases to pretty barefaced lies."[10]

By then, however, Mayes had decided on his own to make a clean breast of the affair. He acknowledged, first in private correspondence and later in print, that he had deliberately perpetrated the hoax, that his *Alger* had been a "complete fabrication, with virtually no scintilla of basis in fact. Any word of truth in it got in unwittingly. I made it up out of nothing. Most of the few facts I uncovered were intentionally distorted." No American writer had been so misrepresented by a biographer since Edgar Allan Poe suffered the peculiar stings and arrows from the quiver of the Reverend Rufus Griswold a century before. When Mayes reread in the spring of 1976 the cheeky letter he had written Cowley in 1958, he too was struck by the "gall and nonsense! What it demonstrates, probably, is that a fellow, by going on the offensive, indulging in enough bluff, can help sustain a myth. In any case, it was a presumptuous letter, wholly uncalled for. Cowley deserved better."[11] Unfortunately, the brazen tactic worked. Cowley observed in print as late as 1970 that Mayes's biography of Alger was the best available work on the subject.[12]

Mayes's bogus biography was long regarded as factual, apparently because it served to reinforce Alger's popular image, coined during the prosperous 1920s, as a prophet of business success. "All of Horatio Alger's heroes started poor and ended up well-to-do," Mayes had written.[13] For the most part, the accuracy of his biography was not questioned because it presented a view of Alger's life which was compatible with the popular impression of his work. Much as no one had troubled to investigate Alger's life before Mayes, almost no one sensed any real discrepancies in Mayes's biography later. "Nobody bothered to do any digging," as Mayes subsequently observed.[14] His hoax, paradoxically, both distorted the record of Alger's life and mirrored perfectly the prevailing opinion of Alger's books, which were by then mostly out of print and no longer read. Ironically, his account is a revealing source, as well as an entertaining story, not about Alger's life but about his reputation as a pumping station on the pipeline/pipe dream of success. The triumphs of his heroes, as Mayes portrayed Alger, were less rewards for faithful service than the means by which a neurotic storyteller repeatedly compensated for his personal failings. In the 1950s, students of Alger were still plucking Freudian fruit from the orchard Mayes had planted. In 1955, for example, Kenneth S. Lynn claimed that by "Sublimating a lifetime which Alger himself judged to be ignominiously unheroic, he created the 'Alger hero,' and thereby became one of the great mythmakers of the modern world."[15] In 1959, Norman N. Holland concluded from Mayes's biography that Alger suffered from intense Oedipal conflict. Alger's "pathetic life," he argued, was "one long attempt to replace his father. . . . Writing books enabled Alger to surpass his father, yet avoid competing directly with him. Both in the pages themselves and in the fame they brought, he outdid his father, whom, in later life, he either squabbled with or ignored."[16] Obviously, Mayes's admission of hoax undermines these too-tidy interpretations.

In a sense, Mayes originated the two schools of Alger biography, one distinguished by its Mayes-like diagnosis of the problem faced by the biographer, the other by its Mayes-like solution. All Alger biographers to date have grappled with the same problem of meager sources that first beset Mayes. At best, they have cursorily sketched a life on the basis of skimpy evidence. Most have cited without question Mayes's fabricated documents. At worst, they have borrowed and embellished those sources with their own fabrications. Writing an authoritative biography of Alger now is a task akin to disproving a conspiracy theory.

In 1961, Frank Gruber, a writer of B-western screenplays and pulp detective fiction, published at his own expense a brief monograph designed to correct Mayes's more outlandish claims. Gruber began his essay by repudiating the earlier work: "Mayes' book is studded with such a vast number of factual errors and flights of the imagination that I am compelled to discard virtually everything in the book with one single exception, the date of his birth. Even the date of his death is wrong."

Unfortunately, however, Gruber did not so carefully insulate himself from Mayes's mistakes as he supposed. In fact, he perpetuated many of Mayes's fabrications and spiced the record with a few flights of his own fancy. "In plot, in incident material, in the characterizations of minor characters, Alger was unsurpassed in his day and scarcely equalled in the present time," he asserted. "His misers can be compared to the best of Dickens, his drunken harridans were not surpassed by Dickens or Victor Hugo or Eugene Sue. His villains are frequently more vivid and villainous that the villains of Robert Louis Stevenson." In all, Gruber's *Horatio Alger, Jr.: A Biography and a Bibliography* protested the Mayes myth in a feeble and unconvincing voice. Its print run was limited to 750 copies. Though Gruber was the first person to research systematically the events of Alger's life, he unearthed little relevant information. His biographical sketch of Alger covered but thirty-five pages. "I must say," he confessed, in extenuation of Mayes, "if I had to write a full-length biography of Horatio Alger, Jr., I would myself be compelled to invent even more romantic and glamorous incidents than [he did] to fill out the pages."[17] Alger's next three biographers failed to diagnose the problem in such dour terms largely because they relied upon Mayes to document their works.

The most transparently derivative of these studies appeared in 1963 from the pen of a biographer with scholarly credentials. Ironically, John Tebbel, professor and chairman of the Journalism Department at New York University, failed to verify his sources. Despite critical questions about the reliability of Mayes's work raised by both Cowley and Gruber, Tebbel prefaced his Alger biography, entitled *From Rags to Riches*, with a startling acknowledgment:

> It is a tribute to the research [Mayes] did at twenty-eight to note that it can hardly be improved upon nearly four decades later. The primary sources of Alger material are meager, indeed, but Mr. Mayes appears to have examined all of them, and no new original material has turned up in the intervening decades. . . . Mr. Mayes' research was definitive and I have drawn upon it freely.

Nearly ten years later, when queried about the location of the putative diary on which both he and Mayes had based their accounts, Tebbel glibly asserted that it reposed in the Marlborough, Connecticut [*sic*], Public Library. The situation is all the more ripe with irony in light of a personal credo Tebbel has articulated:

> From the time my own career began, at 14, I have tried to write as well and clearly and accurately as I can, so that I could best inform people who read

> my books and articles about the world they live in. To me it is the obligation
> of every writer to recognize the responsibility his talent imposes on him,
> and understand that he is one of the transmitters of knowledge upon whom
> the world depends for advancement and the betterment of human society.

Tebbel repeated the Mayes myth as late as 1974, in a biographical sketch of Alger he prepared for the *Encyclopedia of American Biography*.[18]

Normally, of course, biographers of the same figure will differ in their interpretations, especially as additional letters and other records are exhumed. But in Alger's case, an original biography, purposely spurious, was succeeded by others that not only failed to correct obvious distortions but multiplied them. Alger's biographers, like a fraternity of fishermen, wink at each other's deceits. If Mayes told a whopper which, to his credit, he never expected to be believed, then Ralph Gardner, Alger's next biographer, caught a carp he pretended in the telling was a rainbow trout. Peculiarly, the adversarial role once played by Cowley in correspondence with Mayes was later played by Mayes in correspondence with Gardner. In the spring of 1975, Gardner asked Mayes to write an introduction to a reprint of his own biography, entitled *Horatio Alger, or the American Hero Era* and first issued in 1964. Mayes agreed and proposed to draw in his introduction "some parallels between [Gardner's] approach in [his] 1964 book, and my approach in my 1928 book." Gardner objected. "I'll appreciate it very much if you don't refer to any parts of my book as 'fiction,'" he wrote Mayes, "because no parts are untrue." Like Cowley seventeen years before, Mayes was unpersuaded by such protests. "What has me stymied is your suggestion that I not refer to any portions of your book as fiction," he replied, "as it is impossible for me to have any conclusion other than that much of it *is* fiction."[19] He was uniquely qualified to judge, after all. Not surprisingly, the project fell through.

Lest this comment seem like a case of the potboiler calling the kettle black, Gardner's biography deserves even stronger censure than Mayes accorded it. In a prefatory note to the original edition, Gardner admitted he undertook the biography with apologetic purpose: "Critics finding this treatment of the subject to be highly sympathetic are reminded it is done by an unabashedly enthusiastic admirer of the author."[20] Inexperienced as a researcher and untrained as a historian—Gardner owned a small advertising agency—he committed fundamental methodological and hence factual mistakes. In order to entertain his audience of book collectors, he invented dialogue, incidents, and even documentation much as Mayes had done. Gardner described Alger's acquaintance with such eminent nineteenth-century figures as Harriet Beecher Stowe, P. T. Barnum, Mark Twain, Bret Harte, Oliver Wendell Holmes, and Ulysses Grant. There is not a scrap of evidence Alger ever so much as spoke with any of these people. When queried about particular sources used in the preparation of his biography, Gardner has replied that to keep his insurance premiums to a minimum he has stored his Alger material away.[21] It is a tactic reminiscent of Mayes's old response that his sources had been donated to the Newsboys' Lodging House. To this day, Gardner continues to insist his biography was dramatized but not fictionalized. His distinction seems analogous to the nice one between fabrication and distortion. Perhaps, in time, like Mayes, he will own to the truth.

Because the biographies by Tebbel and Gardner were published within the span of a few months, they were often reviewed together and, inevitably, compared. The reviewers who squared off in sometimes acrimonious debate over the merits of these works could hardly have understood they had been presented with a Hobson's choice. Though some of them, like the novelist Harvey Swados, excoriated both biographies, most of them preferred Tebbel's account. It was at least stylistically superior. Hal Borland concluded in the *New York Times* that Tebbel's study was more realistic than Gardner's account. He noted that "According to Tebbel (and the major biographical references agree) Horatio Alger, Jr., was harried and repressed for years by his bigoted, indigent preacher-father." In other words, Borland preferred Tebbel's biography for a most unfortunate reason—because it echoed the "major biographical references" he checked. He failed to attribute the unanimity of all Alger studies to their reliance on Mayes's original biography. Similarly, Brooks Atkinson complained that Gardner was so steeped in the Alger stories that he wrote his biography "in the same mawkish and pedestrian style." Cecil Williams, late professor of English at Texas Christian University, in a review of the biographies for *American Literature*, agreed that Tebbel had written a readable book though one "verging on the cynical" and that Gardner's was "not as well written," in part because he ignored the past-perfect tense. Even the playwright S. N. Behrman, who confessed to an addiction to Alger books in his boyhood, concluded that in Gardner's biography "Alger remains elusive. He is a ghost."

Nevertheless, Gardner had his partisans, most notably John Seelye, currently a professor of English at the University of North Carolina. In late 1964, in the *American Quarterly*, Seelye surveyed the sorry litter of Alger biographies published to that time and reached a surprising conclusion:

> Ignorant of the facts of Alger's life, impressed perhaps by Tebbel's credentials, put off perhaps by Gardner's lack of them, reviewers took style for content and gave Tebbel's rehash of Mayes' debunking biography full credit as truth. . . . Ironically, it was only where the "truth" is traditionally revered—in the academy and the critical establishment—that Tebbel's book passed as authoritative while Gardner's carefully researched study was discredited.

In all, the story of the Alger wars of the mid-1960s is a grim sidebar in the history of American scholarship.[22]

The most recent full-length biography of Alger, Edwin P. Hoyt's *Horatio's Boys*, which appeared in 1974, attempted to exploit the prurient trend toward detailing sexual episodes in the lives of public figures. Hoyt did virtually no firsthand research for his book, a curious blend of iconoclasm and apology, but merely rehashed Gardner much as Tebbel had rehashed Mayes. "According to Ralph Gardner," whose "exhaustive study is the most complete book about Alger and his works," Hoyt wrote, "Alger was lionized in Massachusetts and accepted by Harriet Beecher Stowe and others of the literary community as one of them."[23] Except for his sensational treatment of Alger's sexual peccadillo, Hoyt followed Gardner's lead so closely that he compounded the biographical problem. By deferring to Gardner in virtually all matters, he left the unfortunate impression that virtually all light had been shed on Alger's life. Hoyt's biography is in fact a collection of misinformation.

It is difficult to leaf through any of these biographies without wincing. Readers of all five may never trust a biographer again. Some librarians may decide to remove them from the nonfiction shelves. As Herbert Mayes, who hardly could have dreamed what he was starting in 1927, wrote to Ralph Gardner in the summer of 1977, "Somewhere along the way somebody is bound to undertake a definitive biography that would make everything previously published seem silly if not downright, deliberately misleading."[24] We hope, at least, we have proved him right.

While it does not fall within the province of biographers to declare their own work definitive, we are confident this biography will not soon be superceded. It is the culmination of several years of research, and no other investigators seem to be trailing in our wake. Every clue in what may be fairly deemed a complicated missing-person case has been painstakingly pursued. Alger's note in one letter that he had acted as a foreign correspondent for the *New York Sun* during his first tour of Europe in 1860–61, for example, led to the discovery of thirteen travel letters printed in that newspaper under a previously unsubstantiated pseudonym. His casual reference in another letter to an interview with him printed in the *Boston Advertiser* led first to the discovery of several essays and sketches contributed under the same pseudonym to the *Boston Yankee Blade* forty years earlier and eventually to the discovery of over eighty previously unknown poems and stories he wrote during the same period for the *Boston True Flag* and *American Union*. Some letters that mention Alger were unearthed almost by accident at the Harvard Divinity School and the New-York Historical Society. A holograph in which Alger's father details his dire financial condition was literally rescued by a child from a trash heap in suburban Boston. We scanned hundreds of reels of microfilm, searching for overlooked contributions from his pen or for his name on published passenger lists and hotel registers. Of course we wrote hundreds of letters of inquiry over the years. The preparation of this biography has been nothing less than a labor of love. It was undertaken to set straight the record of a lost life.

The tale told in these pages is one of thwarted ambition. It is a characteristically American story. Ironically, the writer most often credited with popularizing a rags-to-riches mythology failed to realize his own early promise and vaunted ambition. Much of his life reads like a case study in frustration. In middle age, when circumstances conspired to dictate his decision, he became a writer for juveniles. The differences between the Alger portrayed here and the characters invented by his debunkers and apologists should be obvious to those readers who compare versions and/or who turn to the bibliographical sections of the end notes. Admittedly, had the phrase "Horatio Alger hero" not obtained popular, if inflated, currency in the language—and had Alger not been so profoundly misrepresented by his earlier biographers—his life would probably command little attention. But because his name, for better or worse, became the countersign of American dreamers, and because his experience was so dramatically at odds with his own dream, the events of his life, reliably reconstructed, merit modern review. As Willy Loman's wife declares in Arthur Miller's *Death of a Salesman*, "Attention, attention must finally be paid to such a person." Ironically, the last Alger story to be told is Alger's own, and it should give pause to those who take the others too seriously.

GARY SCHARNHORST
JACK BALES

ACKNOWLEDGMENTS

Many people have helped us complete this book. We especially wish to thank Harley P. Holden, curator of the Harvard University Archives, and Margaret M. Grassby, assistant director of the Marlborough, Massachusetts, Public Library. Both patiently tracked down obscure references and answered our many questions. Bob Bennett, Gilbert K. Westgard II, Paul Miller, Stanley Pachon, and Eddie LeBlanc each opened his private files to us. The late Harriet Stratemeyer Adams provided copies of Alger's letters to her father, Edward Stratemeyer. Professor Jerry Soliday deciphered Joseph Seligman's idiosyncratic German script. Vickie Bullock of the interlibrary loan office at the University of Texas at Dallas tolerated, even expedited orders of esoterica over these past several years with no more reward from me than the vague promise, now kept, that I would put her name in my next book. Brenda Sloan of the Mary Washington College library dispatched requests with equal efficiency. Alan Seaburg of the Andover-Harvard Theological Library; Carl Seaburg, archivist of the Unitarian Universalist Association; Lynn Pedigo Robison of the Library of Congress; and Michael Schroeder patiently replied to our appeals for help. Dennis Cooper reproduced some of the Alger photographs we located. Professors Cole Dawson, Keith Byerman, and Charles Trainor each saved us legwork. Herbert Cahoon of the Pierpont Morgan Library sent, unsolicited, a copy of an Alger letter so recently acquired it had not yet been catalogued. Nancy Burkett and Joyce Tracy of the American Antiquarian Society were both cordial and resourceful during our visits there. In all, librarians from twenty-four public institutions provided us with copies of holographs either about Alger or in his hand. The task of retrieving even a small fraction of the letters Alger wrote during his life has seemed tantamount at times to pasting leaves back onto trees on a windy autumn day, and we deeply appreciate the cooperation we have received from these librarians. Our ledger of debts could be extended almost indefinitely. Suffice it here to note that we thank all from whom we received assistance.

I wish especially to thank Sandy, as ever; the editors of the *Markham Review* for permission to quote in the Afterword excerpts from my article "Demythologizing Alger," which first appeared in the pages of their magazine; and Jack Bales, my friend and collaborator, for his tireless assistance as a researcher and for criticizing the manuscript at various stages of its preparation.

G. S.

*The Lost Life of
Horatio Alger, Jr.*

INTERLUDE

At the age of thirty-four, the midpoint of his life, Horatio Alger, Jr., lost his way. One day in mid-March 1866, he beat a hasty retreat from the village of Brewster, on Cape Cod, where he had pastored the Unitarian flock since December 1864. Some of his parishioners had threatened to prosecute him to the full extent of the law—or worse—if he remained longer in the community. He promptly boarded the next train for Boston and soon reached the safe haven of his parents' home, the Unitarian parsonage in South Natick, Massachusetts.[1]

At first, unsure how best to break the news, he said nothing of the brewing scandal. On March 19, he posted a letter "written in deep sadness" to the committee charged with investigating his conduct in Brewster, begging them to consider the shame his family would suffer if they chose to publicize his transgressions.[2] Then, delaying no longer, he confessed to his father that he had been charged with pedophilia, engaging in sexual acts with boys in his congregation.

The patriarch of the Alger clan was in the thirty-seventh year of his ministry that somber day in March when his namesake returned home in disgrace. His own career had been blemished by an unfortunate circumstance which at least enabled him now to sympathize with his son. In 1844, he had slipped into bankruptcy and, humbled before his neighbors, he had resigned the pulpit in Chelsea, Massachusetts, and left town. When his son finished his story, the elder Horatio drew on this sad experience. He recommended that his son resign from the ministry discreetly, attracting as little attention as possible to the events which had forced his departure from Brewster. So Horatio, Jr., addressed a letter to the general secretary of the American Unitarian Association in Boston, explaining that "from physical necessity" he was "obliged to leave his position in Brewster & the profession and to take some more healthful occupation."[3] In light of the threat of violence against him during his final hours in the village, he expressed a pale version of the truth.[4] Thus ended the short-lived ministry of the Reverend Horatio Alger, Jr.

On March 22, the elder Alger also wrote the general secretary, Charles Lowe, to plead for a special dispensation of mercy on his son. "I presume you have already received from my son Horatio a note announcing that he has resigned his parish and all intention of ever again entering a pulpit," he began.

> It is not unlikely that you may have learned from other sources something of the unfortunate circumstances under which his ministry has closed. I am naturally anxious that no unnecessary publicity should be given to the matter. The only desirable end to be gained by such publicity would be to prevent his further employment in the profession, and that I will guarantee that he will neither seek nor desire. His future, at the best, will be darkly shaded. He will probably seek literary or other employment at a distance from here, and I wish him to be able to enter upon the new life on which he has resolved with as little as possible to prevent his success.[5]

The senior Alger did not mention another likely consequence of publicizing his son's problems in Brewster. His own ministry would certainly be complicated. After all, they shared the same name. If blackened for one, how could it fail but be blackened for both?

Alger *père* had guessed correctly. Lowe had already received letters about the events which had transpired in Brewster, and he had decided on his own to suppress the distressing news. A stalwart named Solomon Freeman had written to complain that their late pastor had willfully "remained with us to serve the Devil by writing novels,—leading boys to destitution" while "receiving pay as a minister." Not even the younger Alger's remorseful letter appeased his anger.

> I have a letter before me from him dated the 19th inst. full of compunction of feeling for the disgrace he has bro[ugh]t on himself and the consequent grief of his parents and family, but not one feeling properly expressed of that remorse and penitence which ought to be consequent on the commission of such crime against God and the injury he has done to the cause of religion, to our society, and youth in particular. It is all too selfish to be sincere,—it is all in consequence of detection, and not in consequence of guilt.[6]

Another parishioner in Brewster was more sympathetic, though he did not doubt the minister's culpability. Upon reading young Alger's appeal for mercy on behalf of his family, George Copeland, the only lawyer in the village, wrote to ask Lowe "to exercise all the forebearance you can consistently." The revelation of Alger's misconduct had come "like a thunderbolt upon us," he added. He had hitherto "thought him the very purest and best of young men."[7]

Lowe agreed the matter should be handled discreetly. "It is a serious injury to the church & to the ministry that such a thing should occur," he admitted, but "the injury is greater the wider it is known. Consequently I think that since Mr Alger has absolutely taken himself from the ministry, & is never to bear its name or try to exercise its functions, it will not be necessary for us as an Association to take any action."[8] Even the more irate churchgoers in Brewster were calmed by such "cool considerate and truly Christian" counsel,[9] and Lowe pressed his advantage. "I think very decidedly that some passage of resolutions for your own record—not to be published, but only to stand as assurance of your own clear views of the case—is all that your duty to the cause requires," he advised the congregation on March 22, the very day the elder Alger wrote him to appeal for discretion.[10]

Thus the scandal was contained. Horatio Alger, Jr., would be allowed to resign from the ministry unmolested so that "he may have a chance in some other walk of life to redeem his character." So long as he left quietly, so long as he did not attempt to parade under a Unitarian banner or ever again claim the title of Reverend, the young man need not fear reprisal from denominational headquarters.

A few days later, young Alger packed his bags and fled his native New England for New York. Over the preceding fifteen years he had written dozens of poems and hundreds of tales for adults, and more recently he had tried his hand at writing for juveniles. He was determined now to earn his living with his pen. A one-sentence announcement of his resignation from the pastoral charge of the Society at Brewster was buried in the March 24 issue of the *Christian Register*, a Unitarian weekly published in Boston.[11]

1.

The Odds Against Him

(1832–1860)

I

I wish I could send you to college, Guy," said Mr.
Fenwick, as they sat in the library. . . . The speaker was
the Rev. Mr. Fenwick, the pastor of a church in Bayport, a
few miles from New Bedford, Massachusetts. . . . "When I
was your age, . . . I was already a student of Harvard. You
are ready for college, but my means are not sufficient to
send you there.

—HORATIO ALGER, JR.,
In Search of Treasure

Alger sprang from hardy Puritan stock. He counted among his ancestors three of the Plymouth pilgrims who reached the shores of the New
World aboard the *Fortune* on November 10, 1621: Robert Cushman, a
wool carder and one of the leaders of the Separatist colony; his son
Thomas; and William Bassett, a gunsmith and metalworker. However,
according to William Bradford, the governor and historian of Plymouth
plantation, Cushman retreated with his family to England after his
"heart and courage" were spent within a few months of his arrival. A
branch of the Alger clan was transplanted to New England in about
1665, when one Thomas Alger set down roots on a farm near Taunton,
Massachusetts. One of his great-great-grandsons, Sylvanus Lazell,
marched with the Minutemen from Bridgewater to Lexington and rose
to the rank of brigadier general in time for the War of 1812. Another

great-great-grandson, Edmund Lazell, was a member of the Constitutional Convention in 1788. Yet another, James Alger, was a devoted Unitarian, an occasional contributor to the pages of the *Christian Register*, and the father of the first Horatio, born on the family homestead near Bridgewater on November 6, 1806.[1]

His life was unremarkable, though by all accounts this Horatio was a tolerable scholar and public servant.[2] He was fitted for Harvard College at the academy in Bridgewater, matriculated in Cambridge at the age of fourteen, and graduated at eighteen. He then opened a private academy in Beverly, Massachusetts, which lasted but a year. In the fall of 1826, he entered the Theological School at Cambridge, and, three years later, still only twenty-two, he completed the ministerial course there. On September 2, 1829, only six months after Ralph Waldo Emerson was installed across the bay as the associate minister of the Second Church in Boston, Alger was ordained over the First Congregational Church and Society in Chelsea, a parish organized over a century before by Cotton Mather.[3] Among the participants in the service were Joseph Tuckerman, Alger's predecessor in the Chelsea pulpit, who later became well known for his program of social outreach in the Boston slums; James Walker, a future professor of moral philosophy and president of Harvard; and Francis Parkman, pastor of the North Church in Boston and the father of the author of *The Oregon Trail*. A week later, the *Christian Register* editorially congratulated the "ancient Church and Society upon their new prospects." Well versed in the nuances of liberal theology, Alger contributed four exegetical exercises to the short-lived *Unitarian Advocate* between September 1831 and October 1832.[4] The career of the young minister seemed fairly launched.

Unfortunately, though he served the parish for fifteen years, the Reverend Mr. Alger's early prospects there were never realized. One reason was Chelsea's local reputation as a backwater to the mainstream of Brahmin culture. A few miles northeast of the hub of Boston, the coastal village contained fewer than eight hundred residents. It was best known in the area for its cemetery and was the butt of jokes throughout New England. A doornail was as dead as Chelsea, the saying went. The parish was neither large nor prosperous nor primed to grow. Nine years after his ordination, the Reverend Mr. Alger still drew a salary of only fifty dollars a month.[5]

The pittance simply was not adequate to cover his expenses, especially after he became a husband and father. Within a few months of settling in the village, Horatio Alger began to court homely, twenty-two-year-old Olive Augusta Fenno, youngest child and only unmarried daughter of Charlotte and John Fenno, a substantial land-owner, local businessman, and distant cousin of the Knickerbocker writer Charles Fenno Hoffman. In 1804, Deacon Fenno had built a general store on Commercial Street near the Boston station of the Chelsea Ferry, and, in 1829, he had multiplied his talents with the purchase of a hundred and twenty acres of farmland in the unincorporated district of North Chelsea. In January 1830, he moved his family across the bay, and, with the blessing of his pastor, Francis Parkman, he transferred his membership from the New North Church in Boston to the First Church in Chelsea. He built a slaughterhouse on his land and, a few years later, erected another general store on the southeast corner of the intersection of the old County Road and the Salem Turnpike—a site long afterwards known simply as Fenno's Corner.[6] The Reverend Mr. Alger and Olive Fenno each brought to their union a considerable asset: the former his prospects, the latter her birthright. Lamentably, each would be disappointed.

They were married on March 31, 1831, and to them a son and namesake was born barely ten months later, on Friday the 13th of January 1832. The blessed event occurred in the squat parsonage still standing near Fenno's Corner on Beach Street. The modest cottage had been built for the young couple by Deacon Fenno, who charged them nominal rent. Young Horatio later would reminisce in verse about this

> cottage, by the sea,
> By the ever-rolling sea;
> Where the surges rage and roar,
> As they dash along the shore,
> With their foaming crests of white,
> Sparkling with reflected light;
> Where the winds are moaning low
> To the water's ebb and flow;
> In the pleasant days gone by,
> Fled—alas! how silently![7]

To supplement his strained ministerial allowance, the elder Horatio successfully campaigned to establish the first post office in the village, and, on July 6, 1832, he was appointed its first postmaster, a position he would hold for a decade. In November 1832, moreover, he was elected to represent the village in the state legislature during its next term—indeed, he was one of the youngest of the six hundred members of that body in 1833.[8] Yet as his family continued to grow—with the births of Olive Augusta (after her mother) on November 19, 1833, and James (after his grandfather) on March 11, 1836—his income seemed all the more inadequate.[9] As early as 1834, he began to speculate in land around Chelsea without, however, measurably improving his fortunes.[10]

By the autumn of 1838 he was desperate. His father-in-law, who had once seemed a safe harbor against straitened circumstances, had recently died. On November 5, the Reverend Mr. Alger submitted his letter of resignation to the standing committee of the church. "The reason of my taking this step is readily & cheerfully given," he explained.

> On some accounts my situation here has been quite pleasant & desirable. I have esteemed it quite an advantage to be so near to Boston & to Cambridge, so near to public libraries,—& connected with such a ministerial association as that of Boston and the vicinity. But this advantage has been attended with great disadvantages. All the expenses of living (except house-rent) are as great here as in the city. But while my brethren in the city are receiving from fifteen to twenty five hundred dollars a year, I have only six hundred. I find this sum quite inadequate to the wants of my family. Those wants are more likely to increase than to diminish; and I feel that my duty to my family requires me to seek some place where my income will better correspond with my expenses. I do not take this step hastily or without due consideration. For more than two years past it has

The parsonage in Chelsea, Massachusetts, birthplace of Horatio Alger, Jr.
Courtesy of the Marlborough Public Library.

been with me a subject of frequent thought. I have felt for some time past that I was making a sacrifice in staying here. I have been repeatedly assured by my friends out of town, and especially by my brethren in the ministry that without being less useful, I might do much better in a pecuniary point of view elsewhere than here. Moreover, it would not be consistent with my ideas of integrity to remain in a situation where I must incur expenses without any adequate means to defray them.[11]

Perhaps the threat of departure chastened the deacons and prompted them to raise his salary, or at least to collect a special subscription on his behalf. Perhaps Alger was unable to make good his threat to land a more lucrative position. Whatever the reason, his resignation was refused or withdrawn, and he remained in Chelsea nearly six more years.

There must have been moments during those years when he wished he had left, however, for he only slipped further into debt. Some fifteen years later, Horatio, Jr., obliquely discussed his father's plight in a story, "Robert Lawson, or A Minister's Fortunes." As he explained, parishioners often fail to appreciate

that a minister's expenses are naturally increased by his position—that it requires him and his family to dress better than they would if, for instance, they were engaged in mechanical employment—that they are called upon to exercise a freer hospitality—that his expenses for books and stationery must be considerable, and that his riding on exchanges forms no unimportant item.[12]

When the grammar schoolmaster unexpectedly resigned in November 1839, the Reverend Mr. Alger turned his largely ceremonial post as moderator of school committee meetings to account by filling the post until the following March, when a permanent replacement was hired.[13]

Unfortunately, such opportunities to augment his ministerial stipend were at best temporary expedients. Despite the extra jobs, his expenses continued to outstrip his income, in part because his father had joined his family in North Chelsea. The Reverend Mr. Alger at last turned to farming to pay his bills. In the spring of 1840, with his wife pregnant with their fourth child, he began to cultivate a hundred-acre tract near the village, meanwhile continuing to serve as both pastor and postmaster.[14] With the births of his invalid daughter, Annie, in October 1840 and son Francis in August 1842,[15] the shortfall in income became acute, and he quit the post office to have more time to farm. On April Fools' Day, 1844, he unloaded a lot he had owned for nearly a decade.[16] The sale failed to stave off bankruptcy. On April 3, his embarrassment imminent, he once more tendered his resignation from the Chelsea pulpit. Though his contract stipulated that he could remain in office for three months after serving notice, he asked for immediate release. "I know that no such delay is desired by you," he allowed in an open letter to the church membership,

> and as for myself, I cheerfully waive my right, and put wholly out of view all considerations of personal convenience, and thereby resign to you from this day all charge of the pulpit and all connexion with you as a minister.
>
> I cannot take this step without returning my heartfelt thanks to those among you whose faithful friendship and many kindnesses have cheered me amid many trying and disheartening circumstances and whose kind regard, it will, I hope, be my privilege to retain. I now take my leave of you, brethren, with the sincere hope & prayer that under other ministrations you will be more prosperous as individuals & as a society than you have been under mine.[17]

The next day, his resignation was accepted. On April 13, his remaining property was assigned by law to a creditor, a local magnate named Carpenter Staniels, who years later would figure as the sinister squire in the juvenile fiction of Alger *fils*. In his thirty-eighth year, at the midpoint of his life, the Reverend Horatio Alger was publicly humiliated and left town under a cloud. A generation later, his son and namesake would follow in his footsteps.[18]

To make matters worse, Horatio, Jr., was a sickly child, near-sighted and almost certainly afflicted with bronchial asthma. "My near-sightedness was born with me, and it is likely to last me through my lifetime," the narrator declares in a tale young Alger wrote in 1859.[19] "Being of delicate health it was deemed expedient to defer my introduction into the world of 'letters,'" he reminisced upon his graduation from college in 1852. "I had accordingly attained the age of six before I was initiated into the mysteries of the alphabet."[20] Unfortunately, asthma was considered by most physicians of the day a medical curiosity, an illness with no discernable organic cause. They failed to appreciate fully the psychosomatic factors which complicate it, though increasing numbers of them were reporting that nervous influences or intense stress seemed to play a part in provoking and aggravating attacks. Joshua Bicknell Chapin, an American physician, summarized prevailing medical opinion on the subject in 1843, when young Horatio was barely eleven years old: "Extreme nervous irritability not only invites the attack, but aggravates the symptoms and prolongs continuance." All cases of asthma, he reported, owe "their origin to certain mental impressions, or emotions." There were no universally effective methods of treatment, though emetics and enemas were often administered, especially to children, to throw their fragile nervous systems into slight shock and so arrest the attacks. An ounce of prevention was worth a hundredweight of such treatments. Asthmatics seemed to suffer less severe and fewer attacks when breathing the "air of low situations" like that of sea coasts than when exposed either to mountain breezes or to the miasma of cities.[21] For the sake of an asthmatic son, the Reverend Mr. Alger may have remained in Chelsea longer than he otherwise would have preferred.

Though delicate, Horatio, Jr., was undeniably precocious, once he learned to read. After his father began to tutor him, at home, at the age of six—the regularity of the instruction "being much disturbed by my father's engagements"—young Alger's progress was, by his own testimony, "more than ordinarily rapid." With no false modesty, he recalled in his college Class Book how "At eight years of age I commenced the study of Latin and Algebra, which were rather premature as it will easily be believed that I was not at that time any too familiar with the common branches of an English education." A prodigy of classical learning, he began to read voraciously "whatever came in my way, from Josephus' History of the Jews and works of theology to the Arabian Nights' Entertainments and the wonderful adventures of Jack the Giant Killer." In 1842, at the age of ten, he finally entered the grammar school in Chelsea where his father had taught briefly and

> where I remained for about a year and a half pursuing English studies exclusively with a greater degree of method and regularity than at any time previous.... I can recall without much difficulty the general appearance of the school-house where first I was a regular attendant. It was a square brick edifice on whose walls the storms of more than a century had beaten without producing any decided effect. Through panes incrusted with dirt—the accumulation of many years—whose smallness indicated their antiquity, the light streamed in upon a scene which might well have furnished employment for the pencil of Hogarth.[22]

The bankruptcy of his father and the removal of his family from Chelsea soon closed this chapter in his education. Though "very uneventful," his childhood in the village "had been very happy, partly I suppose because I had been so little subjected to the restraints of school-life." Ironically, had his father not been forced by financial exigency to abandon his ministry in the village, young Alger might have continued "this desultory mode of instruction" indefinitely, to his eventual distress.

In August, four months after he resigned his post in Chelsea, the Reverend Mr. Alger surfaced as supply-minister of the Second Congregational Society or the West Church in Marlborough, a town of about twenty-five hundred souls twenty-five miles west of Boston.[23] The assignment was evidently a congenial one, for in December, a few weeks after his invalid father died, Alger moved his wife and children there.[24] He bought a twelve-room clapboard house with a cellared stable situated on a half-acre of land at the corner of West Main and Broad streets.[25] On Wednesday, January 22, 1845, with his ministerial colleagues Francis Parkman and Joseph Allen in attendance, the elder Alger was installed as regular pastor of the congregation.[26] In his charge to the society, the Reverend Alonzo Hill of Worcester referred indirectly to Alger's bankruptcy in Chelsea: "Never let your Minister be diverted from his appropriate work—a work for which the strongest are found all too weak—by worldly cares," he adjured his audience. "I say it for you and the Gospel's sake, that if he looks upon his young and dependent

The Alger home in Marlborough, Massachusetts.
Courtesy of the Marlborough Public Library.

family, he be not haunted by apprehensions of future embarrassments." As young Horatio later remembered, the area was "chiefly noted" for the orchards of fruit trees which grew on the "numerous hills" encircling the homes. "The manufacture of shoes which is carried on to a considerable extent," he added, gave "a business air to" an otherwise "quiet agricultural town."[27]

Though diversified, the local economy was not immune to the cyclical fluctuations which plagued the shoe industry at large. As one of young Alger's characters would complain years later in the novel *Bound to Rise*, "the worst of the shoe trade" is that it "isn't steady. When it's good everybody rushes into it, and the market soon gets overstocked. Then there's no work for weeks."[28] Automation, especially the introduction of the steam-powered pegging machine in the 1860s, would eventually rationalize production in the industry. In the 1840s and 1850s, however, dozens of New England factory towns suffered recurrent booms and busts. Fortunately, many of the Marlborough parishioners were farmers.[29] While they rarely attended evening services at the church, at least their incomes did not wax and wane with the sales of shoes. Though the village was no font of prosperity, in the short run the Reverend Mr. Alger was probably secure against another bankruptcy. Though his family still lived in genteel poverty, his ministerial allowance in Marlborough was sufficient to cover his expenses. He even could afford a few luxuries, such as preparatory schooling for his eldest son.

II

Tom is now at Harvard College, a good student and a promising young man. . . . He promises to grow up into an upright and honorable man.

—Horatio Alger, Jr.,
Tom Brace

"Though the idea had long been entertained," young Alger later recalled, "now for the first time I commenced a course of study preparatory to entering college."[30] Not only could his father at last afford his tuition but also the town of Marlborough boasted a preparatory school. "There was in this place," as he wrote, "a small academy in successful operation, under the superintendence of Mr. O. W. Albee, a graduate of Brown, and quite a respectable scholar."

Obadiah Wheelock Albee was only thirty-seven years old in the fall of

1845, when he began to direct young Alger's studies. He had earned a master's degree from Brown in 1832, graduating Phi Beta Kappa, and he had been hired the next year to serve as principal of Gates Academy, founded in 1826 and located on the Marlborough public common. "Though his tastes inclined him rather to mathematics and the physical sciences than to the classics"—the opposite of his own predilections, Alger later admitted—"possibly this was of advantage to me as it tended to equalize the time which I devoted to these various branches" of instruction. Albee subsequently represented the district around Marlborough in the state legislature—three terms in the lower house and one in the Senate—and served as the first principal of the local public high school for a decade before he retired from teaching in 1860 to become a deputy collector of internal revenue.[31]

Young Alger flourished under Albee's tutorage. "Beneath the elm trees in front of Gates Academy," as he wrote later, "I have conned many a lesson in Latin, Greek, and mathematics." During his first year in Marlborough, he began to contribute poems and stories to local papers which "won him considerable distinction" in the area.[32] ("When I was young," the narrator of one of his stories later reflects, "I had written a few silly verses, and had them printed in a village newspaper.")[33] Unfortunately, none of these works have been found, if indeed any are extant. At the age of thirteen, Alger even began to learn French.[34] During his three-year course at the academy, "I suppose my time was occupied in about the same way that others have passed it when placed in similar circumstances." He completed his preparatory studies at the age of fifteen, "a year before I actually entered college." For several months in late 1847 and early 1848, a pleasant period, "which approached as nearly to the famous *dolce far niente* as could be desired," he read at leisure in "several of the modern languages," specifically French, German, Spanish, and Italian.[35] Like his later hero Ragged Dick, he studied alone, confident he would later reap dividends from the investment.

In July 1848, at the tender age of sixteen, Horatio Alger, Jr., was examined for admission to the freshman class at Harvard College. He was expected to demonstrate proficiency in four subjects—Latin (the whole of Virgil and Caesar's *Commentaries*, plus selected orations of Cicero), Greek (mostly grammar), mathematics (Alger's weakest subject), and history (including geography). Despite the ominous tone of the college catalogue, according to the jurist Joseph H. Choate, Alger's classmate, the exams "were not formidable." Alger passed with a creditable score and was admitted to the Class of 1852—the "Toodles," as they came to be known. Among the other young men admitted to the same class were William Choate, Joseph's brother, later a federal judge of the southern New York district; William Ware, who became a respected architect and helped design Memorial Hall at Harvard; David Cheever and Charles Ellery Stedman, both of them later eminent Boston physicians; and Chauncey Wright, a laborious if not brilliant student who subsequently gained renown as a scientist and philosopher.[36]

With about ninety classmates, Alger began to attend lectures at Harvard in late August 1848. He pompously observed a few years later that the rite of matriculation "has for the Sub Freshman an indescribable charm. To him it is in very truth the grand portal of the Temple of Knowledge, the calm retreat of wisdom and philosophy."[37] The hyperbole, if not pardonable, at least is understandable. Though they numbered but fourteen, the full-time Harvard College faculty—especially Louis Agassiz and Asa Gray, the leading natural scientists in America; C. C. Felton, the foremost classicist; Henry Wadsworth Longfellow, the eminent poet and professor of belles-lettres; and James Walker, professor of religion and philosophy and the elder Alger's old friend—were distinguished figures in their respective disciplines. Edward Everett, a Greek scholar, early editor of the distinguished *North American Review*, former governor of Massachusetts and Ambassador to the Court of St. James, served as president of the university. Everett later became a U.S. senator and secretary of state, though he would be best remembered, or forgotten, as the long-winded speaker who preceded Abraham Lincoln at Gettysburg. Little wonder that the lad from Marlborough was overwhelmed by these stars in the American firmament!

Though it was the oldest college in the country, Harvard in 1848 still consisted of about a dozen brick and stone buildings clustered around the Yard adjacent to Harvard Square. The entire campus was ringed by dirt roads and a low fence, a barrier more symbolic than real. Visitors from Boston traveled to the school by horsecar. "Harvard College at the time I entered it was a comparatively small affair, and as provincial and local as could well be imagined," Joseph Choate would recall seventy years later. "I call it provincial and local because its scope and outlook hardly extended beyond the boundaries of New England; besides which it was very denominational, being held exclusively in the hands of Unitarians." The college was growing, albeit erratically, with fewer than three hundred students in attendance. Most of them, like Alger, lived within a day's journey of Boston. Many were the scions of the old-monied elite. Still, it was the second-largest undergraduate college in the nation, behind Yale.[38]

Though evangelical Christians scorned the Unitarian bent of the school, its standards of discipline were severe. Recitations began at eight in the morning and continued through the day until six in the evening. All students were required to attend prayers twice a day— morning chapel was scheduled at seven in the winter and six in the summer—and that was but one rule in a handbook of nearly forty pages given every student when he entered. Choate, who once was repri- manded for failing to tip his hat to Everett, carped that compulsory prayers "served merely as contrivances for getting the boys out of bed in the morning and preventing their leaving the college before night." Even the mild-mannered Alger complained later that "the inexorable college-bell" had been "in the habit of summoning us, unfortunate wights, at a most uncomfortable hour in the morning, to a chapel, the atmosphere of which savored of concentrated frost," to "listen to the long-drawn prayers of a devotional divine."[39] The evangelicals at Yale and Princeton doubtless considered such asceticism a sop to con- science. The story soon went around among the undergraduates that once an absent-minded prayer-maker had petitioned the Almighty to make the intemperate temperate, the insincere sincere, and the indus- trious 'dustrious.

Alger incurred modest expenses while at college. Because of his father's poverty, he was selected his first year to serve as the President's Freshman—in effect, Everett's errand boy.[40] In return, he received a stipend of forty dollars and a rent-free room—number 18 in Holworthy Hall, a so-called "senior room" he shared with George Lovell Cary, years later the president of Meadville Theological School. He also received financial support as a student from his father's cousin Cyrus Alger, a prosperous iron founder in South Boston. His bill for tuition was only seventy-five dollars annually, the rent of his room each of his final three years but fifteen dollars. By way of comparison, full professors at Har- vard lived comfortably on a salary of only fifteen hundred dollars. As a freshman, moreover, Alger could take his meals at the college commons for two dollars a week. The repasts were not extravagant—"we had meat one day and pudding the next," Joe Choate recalled—but they were wholesome and abundant. After the commons was closed at the end of his first year, Alger arranged to eat at a boardinghouse near the campus.[41]

In that era, a generation before the innovative curriculum introduced during the presidency of Charles W. Eliot, Harvard undergraduates were fed a high-protein diet of classics, mathematics, and physical sciences. To graduate, a student was obliged to complete six semesters of Greek, six of Latin and Roman literature, and four each of math, physics, and philosophy, including a capstone seminar in moral philosophy in the senior year. Required texts for this course, which James Walker taught when Alger was a senior, were William Whewell's *Elements of Morality*, Joseph Butler's *Analogy of Religion*, and William Paley's *Evidences of Christianity*, works which celebrate the rational God Who beneficently governs the universe through natural law.[42] In later years, incredible as it may seem, Alger occasionally betrayed his erudition in his formulaic juvenile fiction by alluding, for example, to such works as Xenophon's *Anabasis* and to such ideas as the doctrine of probabilities promulgated by the French philosopher Pierre Simon Laplace.[43] Though undergraduates at Harvard followed a rigidly prescribed curriculum of study—chiefly classics and mathematics the first year, those subjects plus French the second—they were allowed to register for a few optional courses in their final two years. Alger's senior electives, for example, were Greek and German.[44] After Jared Sparks assumed the presidency of the university on February 1, 1849, succeeding Everett, even this modest elective system came under fire. Students enrolled in recitation courses such as rhetoric were soon divided into sections alphabetically.

Though unaccustomed to regimentation, Alger prospered in this disciplined academic environment. At the close of his sophomore year, he received the traditional mark of scholastic achievement, the *detur digniori*, with the upper third of his class. In the junior exhibition of October 1850, he delivered a Greek version of "Lacy's Address in Behalf of the Greeks." The following spring, he received two prestigious Bowdoin awards. He won first prize of forty dollars for an English exercise entitled "Athens in the Time of Socrates," an essay he wrote "with ease, *con amore*," according to his roommate Addison Brown. Admittedly, competition was not stiff: Only one other student submitted an entry. Alger won another prize of fifteen dollars for a composition in Greek on "The State of Athens before the Legislation of Solon."[45] Professor Felton, who judged the submissions, commented on the final page of Alger's manuscript that "There are several errors in this, partly in the use of words, and some in inflections; but it is, on the whole, deserving of the prize."[46] In the senior exhibition of October 1851, Alger delivered a dissertation on "The Poetry of the Troubadors," and, later that year, he won yet another Bowdoin prize for Greek composition.

He also excelled at the prescribed course of study, however incidental to his education the lectures and recitations may have seemed. "Too much of our work," especially during the first two years, "was routine work, studying the texts of prescribed volumes and reciting by rote," Joseph Choate complained later. "Our examinations did not amount to much, and I think never did until long after we left college."[47] Instead, the instructors graded each recitation on a scale of zero to eight, and students were assigned rankings in their class on the basis of these marks. Class rank in turn determined the sequence in which students performed at the periodic exhibitions and, eventually, at commencement. To his credit, at the end of four years Alger stood eighth in a class of eighty-eight scholars, and he graduated with Phi Beta Kappa honors. William Choate ranked first. Addison Brown, who transferred from Amherst as a sophomore and who years later succeeded Choate as a federal judge in New York, ranked second. In comparison, Chauncey Wright, a genius at math but a dullard at Greek and Latin, ranked twenty-seventh.[48] "In common with the rest of my class," Alger wrote in the Class Book on Commencement Day in July 1852, "the various phases of college life have successively presented themselves to my view, and have, I suppose, produced upon me the same effects as upon them. I have been a stranger neither to the verdancy of the Freshman, the self-conceit of the Sophomore, the lazy indifference and patronizing air of the Junior, nor to the dignified philosophy and spirit of independence which eminently distinguish the Senior."[49]

Yet a catalogue of Alger's academic acquirements at Harvard College merely silhouettes his life over four years. This was also a crucial period in his literary apprenticeship. In 1849, at the age of seventeen, he published his first works—essays on medieval chivalry and Cervantes and a poem about imperial Rome—in a magazine with national distribution, the Boston *Pictorial National Library*.[50] According to the charging lists at the Harvard library, Alger began to read modern fiction in abundance—Washington Irving's *Bracebridge Hall*, Sir Walter Scott's Waverley romances, novels by Tobias Smollett and Charles Brockden Brown. He also read *Redburn*, "one of the fascinating narratives of Herman Melville" as he later termed it, about this time. Alger developed an especial fondness during his freshman year for the novels of G. P. R. James, since consigned to that hell, the footnote, reserved for writers who scribble away their talents pandering to popular taste. Between August 30, 1848, a few days after the beginning of classes, and the following March, Alger borrowed at least seven of James's books from the Harvard library.[51] "In my college days I read many of James' novels with pleasure and profit," he reflected forty years later. "While the author has some peculiarities that provoke a smile, his novels are well worth reading," he added.[52] He hoped the same might be said of his stories.

In the course of his undergraduate career, Alger also genuflected at the altars of James Fenimore Cooper, the eminent if aging American novelist, and Longfellow, the poet and professor. A remarkable letter, dated September 12, 1850, written by Alger when he was eighteen and posted from Cambridge where he was beginning his junior year, survives among Cooper's papers. In it, the fledgling writer announced he was "about forming a collection of the autographs of American authors of distinction," and he solicited the signature of the venerable Cooper, whom he addressed as "the first of American Novelists." "Permit me to take this opportunity to express to you, Sir," he wrote, "the great gratification with which I have perused many of your works—more especially the Leatherstocking Series." He concluded his letter with "the hope that your life may long be spared to add to the works with which you have already enriched American literature."[53] Not surprisingly, Alger would often allude later in his juvenile fiction to Cooper stories he had enjoyed in his own adolescence.

On another occasion, Alger chanced to breach an unwritten rule of Harvard etiquette by visiting Henry Wadsworth Longfellow at Craigie House, his home near campus. Traditionally, members of the faculty discouraged students who sought informal contact or association. Mingling of teachers and students outside the classroom was rare. However, probably while enrolled in the German course he elected as a senior, Alger once made a social call on Longfellow, the teacher of modern languages. As he wrote Longfellow in 1875, "Years since, when at college, I remember calling upon you with a classmate, and I shall not forget the kindness with which you received the two impertinent boys whose visit might have been regarded as an intrusion."[54] The incident, though trivial, left a deep impression on Alger. He would praise Longfellow and his works without stint until the end of his life. In fact, a few weeks after Longfellow died in the spring of 1882, Alger paid homage in a stanza of unpublished verse to the teacher whose example had influenced him over the years. The tribute opened with a couplet from Longfellow's "The Building of a Ship":

> "It is the heart and not the brain
> That to the Highest doth attain."

So sang the bard whose rhythmic strain
We shall not hear on earth again.
Yet higher than his tuneful Art
We prize the kindness of his heart.[55]

As in the case of Cooper, Alger occasionally modeled his own works, especially his ballads, after Longfellow's verse and often alluded to him in his fiction.

While at Harvard, Alger was also touched by the social and political ferment agitating the entire nation. After Daniel Webster, in an apparent bid to appease the South and win the presidency, endorsed the Compromise of 1850 in a famous speech in Congress on March 7 that year, he returned to an enthusiastic reception in the street outside the Revere House in Boston which masked deep hostility to his personal compromise with the slave power.[56] Many students, including Joseph Choate and Addison Brown, took the cars from Cambridge to Boston to be present. Alger likely was among their number, though his attendance at the rally is not a matter of record. Certainly Alger understood the ramifications of Webster's shift of policy *vis-à-vis* the peculiar institution. In a juvenile biography of Webster written in 1882 and dedicated to his friend Brown, Alger noted the New England statesman had been charged by such abolitionists as John Greenleaf Whittier and William Lloyd Garrison "with falling from honor and making undue concessions to slavery. Upon this last point I shall express no opinion. I only claim that Mr. Webster's motives were pure, and that though he may have gone too far in his concessions, he was influenced thereto by the depth of his devotion to the Union."[57]

At the invitation of college authorities, moreover, the Hungarian revolutionary Louis Kossuth attended the senior exhibition in the spring of 1852. Kossuth was campaigning throughout the United States to garner funds and public support for his cause, eventually lost, to liberate his country from Austrian domination. In the midst of the program, he was ushered into the college chapel by Governor James Boutwell and, before its close, he appealed to the assembly for its support "in as perfect English as I have ever heard from any English or American orator," as Joseph Choate recalled.[58] Alger subtly expressed a different opinion of Kossuth's pitch in a story written fifteen years later. The protagonist of "Count von Heilbrun" is an "adroit swindler" who purports to "belong to one of the noblest Hungarian families." Because he served the revolution, he claims, he had been "compelled by the proud tyrants" in power to flee his native land. "Since then, I have lived in England, in America—where have I not lived?" he rhetorically asks a spinster under his spell. He offers to make her a countess if she will but loan him a thousand dollars so that they can return to Hungary and "take possession of the estates of my father." Fortunately, as Alger told the story, he is arrested before his crude confidence game succeeds.[59]

Alger was undeniably popular among the students at Harvard, though his middle-class lineage and poverty precluded his entry into the Brahmin class of undergraduates. He was a member of neither the Hasty Pudding Club nor the even more exclusive Porcellian. But he was, as Addison Brown wrote in his autobiography, "bright, active, and jocose; an intelligent, faithful, industrious, and quick scholar; a ready and rapid writer, with natural literary aptitudes, and sound critical judgment. He was kind, affable, good-tempered and companionable."[60] He joined the Natural History Society, whose rolls included the names of Charles Ellery Stedman and Chauncey Wright. As a sophomore, he was among the students in his class invited to join the Institute of 1770, a pseudo-literary club and the oldest secret society at the college, whose members assembled each fortnight to enjoy facetious lectures and mock debates.[61] Later, he depicted a meeting of such an organization in his novel *Walter Sherwood's Probation*, after first taking the elaborate caution of changing the name of the school to Euclid College. "If the reader does not find Euclid in a list of American colleges," he explained, "it is because for special reasons I have thought it best to conceal the real name of the college, not wishing to bring the institution into possible disrepute. There are some who might misjudge the college, because it contained some students who made an unprofitable use of their time."[62] For the record, Alger joined in the fun. At the meeting of September 7, 1850, he delivered a disquisition "On the Immortality of Boot Soles."[63] On a "pleasant September evening" the same year, to judge from his pseudonymous sketch "Frightening a Tutor: A College Scrape," Alger was partying with several classmates in Hollis Hall, playing cards and drinking port in flagrant violation of college rules, when they were suddenly surprised by "tutor N." "Luckily for us," however, as Alger added, the tutor tripped over a chair and "never ascertained through whose instrumentality his fall was brought about, and he never will, unless he happens to read the veracious account which I have just given."[64]

As a senior, Alger also pledged membership in the Alpha chapter of Psi Upsilon, one of the first Greek letter societies at the school, with meeting rooms overlooking Harvard Square.[65] Addison Brown, a founding member of the chapter the previous year, was charged with initiating him. After living alone in Stoughton Hall as a sophomore, Alger began to room with Brown at the beginning of their junior year. For a few months, they lived in room 29 (fourth floor, rear) of Hollis Hall, but they were reassigned in midyear to "an excellent senior room," number 7 of Holworthy Hall (fourth floor, fronting the Yard), "which we kept till we graduated." The roommates "never had the least falling out," Brown recalled. Later, in his juvenile *Sam's Chance*, Alger burlesqued the hazing he had received from his friend a quarter-century before. The hero of this novel comes to Harvard and is initiated into the so-called "Alpha Zeta Society":

> He was blindfolded by Brown and seated in the center of the room. He heard various movements, lasting for perhaps five minutes. Then the bandage was removed, and Sam saw that his three companions were metamorphosed. All wore masks. The light of day had been shut out, and four candles were burning on the table. In the center was a skull, and beside it was a large book. . . . "Barker," said one of the masked figures in a sepulchral voice, "do you desire to join our mystic band? . . . Before you are admitted you must swear solemnly not to divulge the secrets of the association." . . . Brown proceeded to read a chorus from Euripides.[66]

Despite the inanities of the ceremony, Alger was a loyal fraternity brother. He subsequently composed the lyrics to the Alpha chapter greeting song. Sung to the tune "Fair Harvard," the first stanza alludes to the secrets of the society:

> We have gathered once more in our mystical hall,
>   To strengthen the ties that of old,
> Cemented by friendship and brotherly love,
>   Have bound us with fetters of gold.
> The glance of the eye and the grasp of the hand,
>   Though silent, still loudly proclaim
> That the union of hearts and the union of hands
>   With us shall be ever the same.[67]

It was an infestation of anapests which limped on truncated feet, but the lyricist was nonetheless celebrated. As late as 1941, a historian of the national fraternity noted Alger's contributions to the illustrious past of the Alpha chapter.[68]

In all, Alger earned a reputation on campus over the years as a student of letters and the rhymster laureate of occasional verse. He penned the forgettable lyrics of a rally song for the local chapter of Phi Beta Kappa (e.g., "A night of festive joy and pleasure / May well succeed a day of toil, / In delving deep for Learning's treasure / Tonight we'll burn no midnight oil").[69] Alger ridiculed his doggerel style a few years later in a story about a tallow chandler who thinks he is a poet: "It was his custom to select a certain number of rhymes, place them in their required position at the end of the line, and then fill up."[70] As a testimony to his versifying facility, however, Alger was selected Class Odist. On Class Day, June 25, 1852, he delivered an utterly conventional ode, a predictable paean to Fair Harvard which, despite its hackneyed stanzas and elevated sentiment, at least betrayed his genuine affection for his *alma mater*:

> As we turn our last gaze on the time-honored courts
>   That have echoed our footsteps for years,
> That have witnessed full many a scene in the Past
>   Which fond recollection endears,
> A shadow of sadness we cannot dispel
>   O'er the prospect will silently steal,
> And the sigh and the tear which unbidden escape
>   The heart's deep emotions reveal.[71]

He echoed the thought in his inscription that day in the Class Book. "No period of my life has been one of such unmixed happiness as the four years which have been spent within college walls," he wrote. "Whatever may be the course of my life hereafter, I shall never cease to regard it with mingled feelings of pleasure and regret—pleasure which the recollection of past happiness never fails to excite—regret that it is gone forever."[72] Similarly, during commencement exercises on July 21,[73] he delivered an oration on "Cicero's Return from Banishment" which seems in retrospect partly personal comment: "It was with a heavy heart that Cicero turned his back upon the city which he had loved so well," Alger declared. "The Past and the Present! his mind turned from the one to contemplate the other, but the contrast was too violent, and he burst into tears."[74] His sympathy for Cicero was as pronounced as the expression of it was prophetic.

The men who attended Harvard during this era often struck a nostalgic chord in their memoirs later. "No friendships of after-life begin to equal in ardor and intensity those of college days, and no names ever become so familiar as those of the associates of that early period of life," Joseph Choate wrote in 1916.[75] Even at that late date, Choate displayed in his bedroom the daguerreotypes of his Harvard classmates "in all the beauty and freshness of youth, just as they appeared on Commencement Day in 1852, when we graduated and parted, never to meet again in full ranks." In his graduation portrait, Alger appears fair complexioned, like his father, and he sports long hair on his disproportionately large head, a fashionably high collar, and a neckkerchief. Sixty-five years after Alger faced the camera that day, after of a life of inestimable public service, Choate confessed he often lulled himself to sleep by reciting "the roll of my classmates, whose names are as familiar now as then." Alphabetically, at least, Alger's name led all the rest.

III

When I began to write for publication it was far from my
expectation that I should devote my life to writing stories
for boys. I was ambitious, rather, to write for adults.
                                   —HORATIO ALGER, JR.,
                                   "Writing Stories for Boys"

On the Tuesday after graduation, as one of Alger's classmates later remembered, "Cambridge looked like another place. Men were at work in all directions upon the rooms, and groups of dirty paddies lying at full length were desecrating the grass yet warm with the impress of our hallowed bums." Alger, David Cheever, and other graduates of the Class of '52 were packing. "If you had seen the fervor with which we rushed into one another's arms," George Norris wrote Joseph Choate, "you would have thought that our affection, like some children, was too heavenly to live long."[76] Unlike many of his friends, however, Alger was packing to return to his parents' home. He had been unable to find a job, and he was unprepared for a career in law or medicine.

Muse-struck, he was determined to become a writer, if possible a poet in the Longfellow mold. However, at the age of twenty—standing only five feet two inches and weighing but a hundred and twenty pounds with his Harvard diploma in his pocket—Alger was barely an adult.[77] For several months after graduation, he placed almost nothing with publishers. For a time, at the instigation of his cousin William Rounseville Alger, he even tried writing for the religious press. Son of the elder Horatio's brother Nahum, William had graduated from the Cambridge Theological School in 1847 at the age of twenty-five and accepted a call to settle over the Mount Pleasant Congregational Society (later All Souls' Unitarian Church) in Roxbury, a few miles southeast of Marlborough.[78] In fact, the elder Horatio had delivered a prayer at his ordination. William's writing began to appear regularly in the *Monthly Religious Magazine*, a Unitarian journal of fiction, poetry, and biblical exegesis, in early 1849, and in the *Christian Register* a year later.[79] His success in placing articles prompted his uncle Horatio, after a long retirement from scholarship, to submit an essay about the Old Testament prophecies regarding the Messiah to the *MRM*, where it appeared in April 1851.[80]

Emboldened by their example, young Horatio soon followed suit. His Dickensian tale, "Bertha's Christmas Vision," appeared in the February 1853 issue of the *MRM*. The next month, he contributed a brief obituary ode to the *Christian Register* which recounted in sophomoric style the life and death of a child:

> In the quiet grave we laid her;
>   There, we trust, she sleepeth well;
> And we hope, when life is over,
>   We shall meet our Gabrielle.

In a topical sketch, "The Vacant Chair"—a title he borrowed from a poem by Longfellow—in the *MRM* for April 1853, he sympathized with

Daguerrotype of Horatio Alger, Jr., Commencement Day, July 21, 1852.
Courtesy of the Harvard University Archives.

the new President, Franklin Pierce, whose eleven-year-old son had been killed in a train wreck the previous winter. "Not many weeks hence," Alger wrote, "our hearts were saddened and our sympathies called forth by the sudden and melancholy bereavement of one who has just been elected to the highest office in the nation's gift." Barely past his own adolescence, he was already writing about children, albeit with morbid fascination. He would contribute one more slight story to the *MRM* and a poem written on the occasion of an elm-tree planting in Marlborough to the *Christian Register*, then abandon the experiment with the religious press. In all, Alger contributed three prose works to the *Monthly Religious Magazine* and two poems to the *Christian Register* over a period of seventeen months. For them he probably received no payment.[81]

By the spring of 1853, he was searching with special determination for literary employment. Still living with his parents, he had been commissioned to prepare a history of Middlesex County, but that project bored him.[82] In March, he began to send manuscript verse and fiction to the editors of *Peterson's*, the *Boston Daily Evening Transcript*, and several Boston literary weeklies—with mixed results at best. The editors of *Peterson's* accepted only one poem and one story. The editors of the *Transcript* printed one of his poems—"A Chant of Life," strongly reminiscent of Longfellow's "A Psalm of Life"—in the April 11, 1853, issue, then accepted nothing else from his pen for nearly two years.[83]

He enjoyed greater success with the weeklies. In April 1853, Alger's work began to appear regularly in the Boston *True Flag*, edited by William U. Moulton. Over the next nine years, ninety of his poems and stories would appear in its pages. At first, he specialized in translations of Spanish, German, Latin, and Greek verse, but soon he was contributing humorous sketches to its pages.[84] In May, his work also began to appear in a less distinguished weekly, the *American Union*, conducted by William E. Graves.[85] William T. Adams ("Oliver Optic"), a young Bostonian descended from the Presidential Adamses, was another frequent contributor to both magazines, and Alger tried to emulate his style. Originally, Alger signed his own name to his contributions, but, in a bow to literary fashion, he adopted in June 1853 the *nom de plume* "Carl Cantab," short for "Cantabrigian," the Latinate nickname given university students in both Cambridges. In March 1854, he began to write sentimental romances for *True Flag* under a second pseudonym, "Charles F. Preston." He would reserve his own signature for his best pieces—a tacit admission of his compromised ambition. He normally

wrote under his real name only for Frederick Gleason, a Boston entrepreneur who published *Gleason's Pictorial Drawing-Room Companion*, one of the first illustrated weeklies, and *Flag of Our Union*. Each of
these magazines claimed a circulation of about 100,000. Alger published several poems in these magazines in 1853, and he was writing
fiction under his own name for the two leading papers in Gleason's
stable regularly by early 1854.[86]

Alger had returned to Cambridge in June 1853 to attend Class Day
festivities and to read an interminably long and wretched poem at the
first annual reunion of the Class of '52. A blend of equal parts nostalgia
and apprehension, it also hints at the poet's frustration since graduating:

> Twelve months with varying light and shade
>   On Time's swift course have rolled along,
> Since we with faltering hearts and tongues
>   Breathed out our farewell song.
> . . .
>
> 'Twas on a tranquil summer day,
>   With hearts brimful of earnest yearning,
> We left behind the dusty streets
>   That still hem in the haunts of learning.
> For we had wondered, hand in hand,
>   Within the shadows of the trees,
> Which, rising in their stately strength,
>   Will stand, we trust, for centuries.
> But now, alas! our ways divide,—
>   The mystic Future silent stands
> And beckons us with outstretched hands
> To cast ourselves upon the tide
>   That bears us—who shall say how far?[87]

Ironically, Alger later published excerpts of this poem in *True Flag*
under the "Cantab" pseudonym. It seems he was not particularly
pleased with this expression of his discontent.

However poor the pieces "Cantab" signed, Alger meant no disrespect
to the Cantabrigians. Harvard remained the hub of his world, Marlborough road but a spoke. In September 1853, he abandoned the
history of Middlesex County, moved back to Cambridge, and entered
the Theological School.[88] The same month, he began to contribute
under the "Cantab" pseudonym a series of brief sketches to another
Boston literary weekly, the *Yankee Blade*, edited by William Mathews.
These sketches were little more than homespun homilies on common-
place themes, moral in tendency but without the dullness of didactic

exhortations, published under such titles as "Selling an Antiquary," "Having His Hair Dyed," and "Some More of Them 'Ere Beans."[89] Alger would serve as a contributing editor to the magazine, as he later noted, "for 2 years nearly."[90] However, he was paid almost nothing for his sketches. During "my early struggles" to become a writer, he reported in 1897, "I wrote for a dollar a column, and was glad to get it."[91] He obviously could not earn a living at that rate.

His decision to move back to Cambridge may have been prompted by personal considerations quite apart from proximity to publishers. He referred in several poems written during his fifteen-month exile in Marlborough to "an absent friend," presumably a companion he had left behind in Cambridge. In a poem addressed to this friend and published under his own name in the April 9, 1853, issue of *True Flag*, for example, Alger apparently depicted an autoerotic reverie:

> When the twilight darkens all the hills
>   And shadows all the sea,
> A while I pause from other cares
>   To think, dear friend, of thee.
>
> And soon into my darkened room
>   Thy image seems to glide,
> And, as in old familiar times
>   Thou'rt seated by my side.
>
> Again I clasp thy friendly hand
>   That throbs within my own;
> Again I look upon thy face
>   Nor deem I am alone.

Alger published a similar lyric, "I Think of Thee," in *True Flag* for September 10, 1853, only a few days after he returned to Cambridge.

> I think of thee
> Through all the livelong day, and in my dreams
> Thy image brightens all my way with sunny gleams,
>   When thinkest thou of me?
>
> Wilt thou, too, think of me,
> That our two hearts may mingle into one,
> And our two lives in one calm current run?
>   Then, dear one, think of me.[92]

It seems, on the basis of this admittedly circumstantial evidence, that Alger returned to Cambridge not so much to attend divinity school as to rejoin a friend.

Though he matriculated, in any case, he had not decided either to

attend classes or enter the ministry. After a few weeks in the thralldom
of theological studies, he concluded he was no more eager to pursue a
ministerial course than he had been ready to write a county history.
When Charles Hale, whom he had known at Harvard, offered him a job
with the family-owned *Boston Daily Advertiser*, Alger leaped at the
opportunity.[93] Like the aspiring *littérateur* in Bayard Taylor's novel *John
Godfrey's Fortunes*, he was persuaded that "reporting was the surest
resource for a young man who was obliged to earn his living by his
pen."[94] When he read the novel later, Alger detected the similarity. The
story of John Godfrey "was very real to me—I suppose it was [Taylor's]
own story, but it was mine also."[95] In November 1853, he withdrew from
the seminary and entered the employ of Messrs. Hale.

Unfortunately, again like John Godfrey, he only lasted there a few
months.[96] Though his official title was assistant editor, he was assigned,
if not the most onerous, at least the most pedestrian of duties: writing
brief announcements of scheduled events, codifying local gossip, and
"condensing the miscellaneous" which he gleaned from other papers
sent to the *Advertiser* office on exchange. He did not earn a single
byline during his brief tenure on the editorial staff. "When I left" after
half a year, he later confessed, "they did not urge me to remain. I do not
think I was adapted for newspaper work."[97]

He apparently took to heart the adage that "those who can't, teach,"
for he next took a job as a schoolmaster. To be sure, in his Class Book he
had expressed envy of his classmates, including Addison Brown, who
had spent vacations from college teaching school:

> I have never known what it is to be looked up to as the teacher of a country
> school. I have not the satisfaction of knowing that some of the future
> orators, statesmen, and poets of America will become such through the
> profound impressions made upon them by my instructions. It is said that
> when he believed the liberties of his country in imminent danger, Milton
> opened a common village school, conceiving that in no other way could he
> do so much towards averting the danger. I admire the patriotism of Milton
> but cannot follow it. Those of my classmates who have done so are suf-
> ficiently recompensed by the thanks of a grateful country, saved through
> their means.[98]

However high-flown his rhetoric, however unsuited he may have been
to the profession, Alger accepted his first teaching post when, in the
spring of 1854, he was broke and out of work. He would have preferred
to earn his living as a writer but teaching, with its regular salary,
seemed at the time a more viable alternative. In "The Disguised Schoolmaster," a story written in 1858, Alger described his own predicament

in the spring of 1854: "Edward Livingston was a young man of fine natural abilities. Two years since, he had graduated, with high honors, at a leading New-England college. Since his graduation, however, it must be confessed, he had done little or nothing."[99] The hero finally accepts a teaching job. "I resisted the infection till the last moment," writes the narrator of another sketch, "Keeping a District School."[100] In June, Alger, contracted to join the faculty of the Grange, a private boarding school for boys in the Potowome district of Rhode Island, under the supervision of Charles Winston Greene. Beginning with the fall term, Alger's official title was assistant teacher.[101]

No doubt it was accommodation to necessity. Yet, to his credit, Alger still was determined to write professionally. His decision to teach was at once tactical and expedient: It allowed him the leisure to write while it subsidized his writing. During the year 1854 alone he published stories and occasional poems in five different Boston weeklies under three different names. A cynic might argue that he had become a hack, that he had yielded to the temptation to gorge the masses with tasteless pablum. It might be said in his defense, on the other hand, that he was merely serving his apprenticeship.

His frequent appearance in these magazines certainly boosted his career, however facile his fiction. He was a member of a literary cadre which included such popular writers as William T. Adams, John T. Trowbridge, T. S. Arthur, Sylvanus Cobb, Jr., the poets Alice and Phoebe Cary, and Ellen Louise Chandler, who after her marriage in 1855 to the editor of *True Flag* earned modest fame under the name Louise Chandler Moulton. Despite the aspersions Emerson, among others, cast upon the "yellow-covered literature of the Sylvanus Cobb, Jr. stamp,"[102] Louisa May Alcott, no less, wrote under a pseudonym for *Flag of Our Union* a decade later. The chief engraver for *Gleason's Pictorial Drawing-Room Companion*, a brazen imitation of the *Illustrated London News*, was a young English emigre named Henry Carter, alias "Frank Leslie," who would soon found his own publishing empire. Its editor was Maturin Ballou, the son and grandson of eminent New England divines. In November 1854, a few weeks after Alger left Boston for Rhode Island, Ballou bought both *Gleason's Pictorial* and *Flag of Our Union* from Frederick Gleason. He retained Alger as a contributor and even reprinted several of his earliest stories in his own *Ballou's Dollar Monthly*. He also printed in the retitled *Ballou's Pictorial* some early unsigned illustrations by an unknown artist named Winslow Homer.

In short, Alger served his apprenticeship during the heyday of the

Boston weeklies. Trowbridge reflected later that he "found the Boston weeklies ready to accept about everything I had to offer."[103] Unfortunately, the magazines were not so ready to pay for stories. Alger received little money for his work—only two dollars per column from Gleason and Ballou, although he confessed years later that "I thought that magnificent pay."[104] The other weeklies paid him only half that amount. Yet even at those paltry prices, competition was keen. "I achieved fair success" as a contributor to the weeklies, he once wrote, "but I could see that I had so many competitors that it would take a long time to acquire a reputation."[105]

The predominant theme of the formulaic stories and poems Alger wrote during this period was sexual subterfuge, as if he were dramatizing his own sexual uncertainties. These works are not literal autobiography, of course, but they reveal the author's ambivalence toward normal adult heterosexuality and suggest he was ill-at-ease depicting common courtship and romance. "Cantab," who admits he is "a bachelor in lodgings" though he sometimes invites male friends over to his room to smoke "some choice Havanas," specialized in farcical sketches—almost always written in first-person—about mock marriages and mistaken sexual identities.[106] He typed women as deceptive lynxes, ostensibly for humorous effect. In one sketch, for example, "Cantab" nearly marries by mistake a black maidservant whose face is concealed behind a veil; in another, he pays court to a mysterious lady who, upon removing her veil, exposes "a face scarred with the wrinkles of seventy years." A subtitled "story for gentlemen" in the *American Union* seems an especially transparent parable of the author's anxieties, despite his attempt to bury them beneath two fictional personae: Alger alias "Cantab" writes the tale from the point of view of one "A. Green," a "victimized bachelor" who must pack his carpetbag in haste and catch a train in the dead of night to escape the clutches of an ugly spinster and her designing mother. In one of the rare poems Alger wrote under a pseudonym, the bashful bachelor "Cantab" describes how he became the butt of a joke with ambiguous sexual overtones. On the first day of April, he explains,

> I was sitting in my chamber,
> —— House, No. 20,
> Enjoying what Italians call
> The "*dolce far niente*."

Suddenly he hears the knock of a post-boy, who delivers a letter addressed to him personally.

> A perfumed envelope of white
>   Directed in a female hand!
> Aha! here lies some mystery
>   I fain would understand.
> It cannot be some lady fair
>   Has looked on me with favoring eyes,
> And knowing my great bashfulness,
>   Has planned a sweet surprise.
> The very thought my face suffused,
>   Awhile the note in doubt I held,
> Then opened it. Alas, my dreams
>   Were all too cruelly dispelled.
> I saw—now, while I write of it,
>   My feelings I can scarcely school—
> These words in staring capitals,
>   "I'VE MADE ONE APRIL FOOL!"[107]

Read as autobiographical gloss, the poem contains more pathos than humor.

To accept the authority of another poem published in the October 14, 1854, issue of *True Flag*, Alger was jilted by his companion in Cambridge about the same time he left town to teach in Rhode Island. Though signed with Alger's own name, the poem was written, significantly enough, from the point of view of a woman scorned—the first time, in fact, that Alger had assumed the voice of a woman in any of his published verse:

> They told me thou wert false, Jamie,
>   And did na care for me;
> I heeded not their voice, Jamie,
>   I thought it could na be,
> So loving were thy words, Jamie,—
>   So winsome was thy smile,
> I did not think that *it*, Jamie,
>   Could veil one thought of guile.
>
> Dost thou recall the hawthorn glade,
>   Where we sat side by side,
> When on a summer's night, Jamie,
>   Thou sued me for thy bride?
> My heart was very full, Jamie,
>   As in the pale moonshine,
> I promised to be thine, Jamie,
>   To be forever thine.
>
> Thegither then we knelt, Jamie,
>   We bent a reverent knee,
> And prayed our Heavenly Father's love

> Might rest on thou and me.
> So radiant seemed thy path, Jamie,
>   My cup so full of bliss,
> How could I ever dream, Jamie,
>   That it would come to *this*?
>
> I never see thee now, Jamie,
>   Thou comest not to me,—
> 'Tis said thou seek'st another's love—
>   Ah, Jamie, can it be?
> They tell me she is rich, Jamie,
>   And of a lordly line;
> Not twice her rank and wealth, Jamie,
>   Could buy a love like mine.[108]

Read as autobiographical gloss, this "Jamie" poem apparently documents an instance of Alger's unrequited love.

Alger served on the faculty of C. W. Greene's boarding school near Warwick, Rhode Island, for nearly two years[109]—from the opening of the fall term 1854 until the close of the spring term 1856, when Greene's failing health forced him to suspend operations.[110] Alger's life there was singularly uneventful. He might have said, like John Godfrey, that "For months I strictly performed my appointed duties, increasing my circle of acquaintances but slightly, and acquiring no experiences which seem worthy of being recorded."[111] Though his routine during these months was dull and monotonous, Alger would remember fondly his tenure on the faculty. In 1865, nine years after the school closed, he would dedicate his second juvenile novel "to the boys whose memory goes back with me to the Boarding School at Potowome."[112]

Though he was not yet able to earn a living by writing, he was able, like one of his later juvenile heroes, to lay up a few dollars, as his hero might say, in relief of his pecuniary anxieties. He was sufficiently flush in November 1854 that he could spare three dollars in response to an appeal from Joseph Choate. Jared Sparks had recently resigned the Harvard presidency for reasons of health, to be succeeded by James Walker, and Choate was soliciting contributions from members of the Class of '52 to help commission a marble bust of Sparks for the library gallery. "I am quite of the opinion that our worthy ex-President should have a place among the dignitaries of Gore Hall," Alger added in a note he enclosed with the money.[113] It is his only extant correspondence dating from this period. The bust was subsequently executed by Hiram Powers, a prominent American expatriate sculptor, and sits today in Memorial Hall.[114]

In the spring of 1855, after a lapse of two years, Alger's verse once more began to appear in the *Boston Transcript*.[115] On September 24, 1855, for example, the editors printed his poem "My Castle" with its ever-so-faint echoes of Coleridge's "Kubla Khan":

> I have a beautiful castle,
>   With towers and battlements fair;
> And many a banner, with gay device,
>   Floats in the outer air.
>
>   . . .
>
> For when clouds and darkness are round me,
>   And my heart is heavy with care,
> I steal me away from the noisy crowd,
>   To dwell in my castle fair.[116]

On November 8, 1885, the editors of the *Transcript* announced the imminent publication of a collection of poetry and fiction from the same pen.[117] Over the preceding five years, a period F. O. Matthiessen has called the "American Renaissance," Emerson had published *Representative Men*, Hawthorne both *The Scarlet Letter* and *The House of Seven Gables*, Melville *Moby-Dick* and *Pierre*, Thoreau *Walden*, and Whitman the first edition of *Leaves of Grass*. On his part, Alger compiled *Bertha's Christmas Vision: An Autumn Sheaf*, an anthology of eleven stories and eight of his poems, all probably reprinted from other sources. Alger hardly would have consigned a work to this volume which he might have first sold elsewhere, though prior publication of four of the pieces has not yet been discovered. He dedicated the collection to his mother, "but for [whose] sympathy and encouragement, much would still remain unwritten."[118] It was issued by a new Boston firm—Brown, Bazin and Co., which had recently published a juvenile novel, *The Boat Club*, by "Oliver Optic." It was copyrighted by Alger, suggesting the likelihood that he subsidized its printing costs. The subtitle notwithstanding, the book appeared in early December in time for Christmas sales.

There were few. "Whether strikingly and immediately successful, or the reverse," John Godfrey rationalizes upon the publication of his first book, "it would at least serve a purpose by bringing my name before the reading public."[119] Still only twenty-three years old, Alger must have shared this sanguine attitude. Notices, even unfavorable ones, would at least advertise his name and work. Ironically, the notices were generally favorable. On December 7, the *Boston Transcript* ballyhooed the book "from the pen of Horatio Alger, Jr., with whose poetical pieces the readers of the Transcript are familiar." The reviewer predicted that the stories "will be perused by young and old readers with great interest" and pronounced the poems "gracefully written; the versification is easy, and the sentiments are such as alone proceed from a writer distinguished for the purity of his thoughts, and his genial sensibilities." The *Boston Post* plugged his "graceful and interesting productions in prose and verse" on December 17, and the *Advertiser*, Alger's former employer, echoed the praise on December 19, adding that the volume "is very suitable for a gift book to a young person." A week later, the *Providence Daily Journal* described it as "a varied collection of tales, sketches, and poems, all in good taste." In January, it was puffed in the *Monthly Religious Magazine*, where two of the tales had originally appeared, as a "collection of stories and verses, written in an uncommonly pure spirit and graceful style, by Horatio Alger, jun., a literary gentleman of high promise." Mathews plugged it in the *Yankee Blade* as "tastefully published" and "a most acceptable" present for young readers. In February, the *Christian Register*, where two of the poems had first appeared, commended the didactic tone of the book as though it were one of Alger's later juveniles: ". . . whoever is in search of a book for children which they will be likely to read and be profited by, will do well to select this little volume." There was no adverse criticism, no discriminating comment, in any of these reviews.[120] Similarly, John Godfrey "was accredited with 'tender sentiment.' 'sweetness of versification,' and 'much promise.'"[121] Such praise was cheap. Alger may have been cheered by the generous notices—he even donated a copy of *Bertha* to the Harvard library in April 1856[122]—but he could not eat favorable notices.

Though his reputation had spread and he was now able to command larger payments from better magazines for his work, he still was unable to live solely by writing. He needed to supplement his income by teaching. He left Rhode Island in May 1856, when Greene closed the school, and moved to Deerfield, Massachusetts, where he served as principal of the local academy and supervised a staff of three teachers during the summer term. "Mr. A. comes satisfactorily recommended as a thorough and accomplished scholar, and an experienced teacher," the local newspaper reassured parents of prospective students. On August 7, Alger received a stipend of seventy-five dollars for his services, and he returned to Boston out of work.[123]

It was not so triumphant a return as Cicero's to Rome, but it was a homecoming nonetheless. During the next year, Alger was engaged as a private tutor around the city.[124] Many of his old chums—Mathews, Moulton, and Cheever, for example—still resided in Boston, and William Alger had recently settled over the Bulfinch Street Society there.

The two cousins lived in the same town for the first time, and they sometimes met socially.[125]

Meanwhile, of course, Horatio continued to write, though with a difference: He was determined to improve the caliber of periodical in which his work appeared. Predictably, he began to reach print less often, yet his stories also began to evince genuine promise. He still wrote under the "Cantab" pseudonym for *True Flag*, to be sure, and he serialized under the "Preston" pseudonym a lurid and sensational romance entitled "Hugo, the Deformed" in the *New York Sun* early in 1857.[126] But he took little pride in these stories. In his more serious work, he played variations on conventional literary formulae. In his early fiction for Gleason, a genteel hero had sometimes married a seemingly penniless seamstress who is actually an heiress-in-disguise. However, he ignored such fairy-tale devices in the stories he wrote during 1857–58 for such journals as the original *Putnam's*, which boasted Herman Melville among its other contributors. His fiction was still sentimental—for example, in "Love," published in *Putnam's* in March 1857, an aging spinster finally meets her *beau ideal*—but it was more creditable.[127] Alger also reworked some of the old "Cantab" material in such first-person comic confessions as "Five Hundred Dollars" in the January 1858 issue of *Graham's Illustrated* and "An Affair of Honor" in the December 1858 issue of *Harper's Monthly*, though he developed these plots with greater finesse than before.[128]

In the summer of 1857, Alger also published his second book, *Nothing to Do: A Tilt at Our Best Society*, an unsigned satirical poem of nearly three hundred lines. In it, he mimicked a popular burlesque of high society, *Nothing to Wear*, by William Allen Butler, a prominent New York lawyer-businessman. Of the swift sales of Butler's poem, W. D. Howells later wrote that "The prairie fire suggests but a feeble image."[129] Its success spawned a number of pale imitations. In Alger's version, respectfully dedicated to Butler, the ostentatious son of a vulgar millionaire, an early version of the prissy snob he later caricatured in his juvenile stories,

> . . . cherishes deep and befitting disdain
> For those who don't live in the Fifth Avenue,
> As entirely unworthy the notice or thought
> Of the heir of two millions and nothing to do.

The poem lampoons the idle rich, all the more vulnerable and inviting a target in the wake of the stock market panic of 1857 and the economic depression which followed, and it rises to a rhetorical flourish in the final stanza:

O, ye who in life are content to be drones,
And stand idly by while your fellows bear stones
To rear the great temple which Adam began,
Whereof the All-Father has given each man
A part in the building—pray look the world through,
And say, if you can, you have nothing to do!
Were man sent here solely to eat, drink, and sleep,
And sow only that which himself hoped to reap,—
If, provided his toil served to gain his subsistence,
He had answered in the full the whole end of existence,—
Where then would be poets, philanthropists, sages,
Who have written their names high on History's pages?
They stood not aloof from the battle of Life,
But, placing themselves in the van of the strife,
Marching manfully forward with banner unfurled,
Left their deeds and their names a bequest to the world.
Have you ever (forgive me the bold impropriety)
Reckoned up your outstanding debt with society,
Or considered how far, should your life close tomorrow,
You would merit her real and genuine sorrow?
If, in dying, the world be no wiser or better
For your having lived there, then you are her debtor;
And if, as Faith, Reason, and Scripture, all show,
God rewards us in heaven for the good done below,
I pray you take heed, idle worldling, lest you
With that better world should have nothing to do![130]

Like most didactic verse, the poem consists of little more than an anecdote and a sermon on the same theme.

Though Alger evidently wrote the piece on assignment from its publisher, James French & Co. of Boston, it was more than a hackwork-manlike potboiler, quickly tossed off for a few easy dollars. Though Alger "fancied my poem 'Nothing to Do' quite forgotten" in 1869,[131] he wistfully referred to it in correspondence as late as 1896, nearly forty years after he submitted the manuscript to the publisher.[132] It went on sale in Boston bookstores on July 30, 1857,[133] and, like *Bertha*, it attracted immediate and favorable, if indiscriminate attention in the press. In early August, the *Boston Transcript* urged readers "who have 'nothing to do' at this time" to read "this pleasant 'tilt at our best society.'" The *Christian Register* added that "It carries on the fun" of Butler's poem "with light pleasantry, revealing incidentally a serious moral, and manifests uncommon facility of versification and fertility in odd rhymes." The *Portland Transcript* agreed that the poet "has done his theme with great ease," and the *New York Sun*, a working-class paper, averred that the poet had offered "a reasonably fair portrait" of a young snob habituated to Fifth Avenue fashion. From his privileged position on the editorial staff, Alger managed to insert into an early number of *True Flag* an announcement of the poem's publication, complete with excerpts, a recommendation, and a bit of self-serving gossip: "The poem is written in a sparkling and lively style, and indulges in much well-deserved satire upon what is generally called 'our best society.' We confidently predict for it a wide popularity. The author's name is not apprehended, but, if rumor be correct, he is already known as a contributor to our best periodicals."[134] Ironically, a modern reader would claim there is "reason to doubt that Alger wrote *Nothing to Do*" because it "is substantially better than any poem" he ever signed.[135] Though at the time the joke went around that it was just "another nothing book," Alger certainly considered it more than a facile exercise of wit. He submitted the final sermon-stanza, under the title "Something to Do," to the *Christian Register*, where it appeared in early September.[136]

The style of those lines suggests the bent of young Alger's mind in mid-1857. For years he had been by vocation a teacher, by avocation a writer. His moral exhortations, whether in the classroom or in fiction, always were first cousins to the sermon. And his combined income as a teacher and writer was neither reliable nor substantial, especially during hard times. Why not try another tack? A minister, Alger well knew, was hardly insulated from lean years, but he usually enjoyed a regular competence. Though he had tried once before to attend divinity school, perhaps now he was ready for the regimen. If his income as a teacher-writer was insufficient, he would become a minister-writer, even though his classmate Addison Brown believed "He was not in the least adapted to the Ministry."[137] In retrospect, "Something to Do" seems nothing less than an unemployed poet's self-admonition. About the same time it appeared in the *Register*, Alger again entered the Cambridge Theological School, and this time he stayed. On September 15, as if to ratify his decision, he donated a copy of *Nothing to Do* to the Harvard Library.[138]

During the next three years, he lived alone in Divinity Hall, at the time a severe two-story brick structure with three-story wings perched in a wooded lot nearly half a mile north of the Yard. His chamber, like the others in the building, consisted of a room about sixteen feet square with a fireplace and a gas stove, an alcove with an iron bedstead, and a closet.[139] Later, the building was refurbished, plumbing installed, and his room 22 converted into a restroom. If, as one wag declared, a typical Harvard Divinity School class in Alger's day consisted of "three mystics, three skeptics, and three dyspeptics,"[140] Alger doubtless would have been counted among the dyspeptics. Yet he persevered in the theological course, in part because Frederic Henry Hedge, the old Transcendentalist, his father's college classmate and his cousin William's good friend, joined the faculty of the school as professor of ecclesiastical history the same year young Alger reenrolled.

In the short run, his program of self-improvement entailed some personal sacrifice. Because he had to rely on savings and income from his writing to pay tuition and expenses, he could no longer afford to tailor his stories to fit the fashionable magazines. Indeed, publication of *Putnam's*, which had long floundered in a sea of red ink, was suspended in a splash the same month he reentered the School at the nadir of the depression. Alger hastily abandoned his faltering efforts to stylize his stories and once more embraced the conventional fiction formulae. He submitted work to offices where he was known, where it would be accepted with little hesitation and rewarded on scale.

During his years of ministerial preparation, in brief, he did not exactly cast his bread upon the waters. He turned instead to the democratic editors of the *New York Sun*, a dreadful penny paper for the unwashed masses, who had accepted the grisly tale of Hugo the hunchback a few months before. Between August 1857 and June 1860, Alger published eight more sensational serials, with such titles as "The Cooper's Ward," "Manson the Miser," "The Gipsy Nurse," and "The Mad Heiress," in the *feuilleton* of the *Sun*.[141] They usually appeared unsigned or under the "Preston" pseudonym. He still wrote occasional "Cantab" stories for *True Flag*, and, in addition, he rejoined Frederick Gleason's corps of writers. In November 1858, Gleason launched a lavishly illustrated, if frail and ephemeral, miscellany in Boston. Alger's work appeared in *Gleason's Weekly Line-of-Battle Ship* over thirty times during its fourteen months of life.[142] In March 1860, moreover, he began to contribute to *Gleason's Literary Companion*, a more robust successor which reunited the publisher-editor team of Gleason and Maturin Ballou.[143]

Back in Marlborough, the elder Horatio once more faced his own shaky financial future. His salary had been ample at first, a welcome relief from the straits of Chelsea. Despite an intense intradenominational rivalry with the crosstown East Church,[144] he had been elected by the voters of the entire village to the school committee and, in his leisure time, he labored on behalf of the Sons of Temperance.[145] In December 1853 he had helped organize a local Mechanics' Institute chiefly composed of the young men in the town who wished to sponsor a winter series of lectures by prominent men. The series of 1885 was especially noteworthy: On successive evenings in early December, Samuel Johnson, a liberal minister from Lynn, Massachusetts, and Ralph Waldo Emerson addressed the Institute.[146] As chief organizer of the lyceum, the Reverend Mr. Alger claimed the privilege of hosting Emerson overnight in the parsonage on Broad street. Horatio, Jr., away teaching in Rhode Island, missed the Wednesday lecture, but he boasted forty years later that the Concord sage once had been "a guest at our house."[147]

For over a decade, the elder Alger had held the wolf of want at bay. In August 1855, in fact, he had contributed sixty dollars to a fund to subsidize Yankee emigration to "bloody Kansas" in the hope that territory would be admitted to the Union as a free state.[148] As a shoe manufacturing town, however, Marlborough was particularly vulnerable to the depression that gripped the nation in the late 1850s.[149] In March 1858, Alger *père* privately groused that "Manufacturing towns like this feel the pressure of the times with peculiar severity."[150] Amid hints of a growing schism between the farmers and the townsfolk in the parish, he resigned the pulpit in April 1859.[151] The congregation, which numbered about 135 when he was installed, actually had shrunk during his fourteen-year ministry. He had buried more parishioners than he had attracted to membership.[152]

Still, he retained the confidence of a majority of the congregation, who first urged him by vote to withdraw his resignation and finally accepted it with reluctance.[153] His separation from the society occurred in July, and the church, still squabbling, still was searching for a replacement over a year later.[154] The elder Alger continued to reside with his family in the town for several months, supplying a vacant pulpit in the neighboring village of Stow and contemplating his prospects. Many of his former parishioners subscribed to a special offering on his behalf shortly after his resignation, and, as the local paper allowed, "his porridge-dish was right side up at the time."[155] Though two of his sons—Horatio, Jr., and James—had moved from under his roof to make their own way, he still provided for a wife and three other children. In November 1859, still an official resident of Marlborough, he was elected to represent the town in the state assembly the following spring.[156] After all, he was experienced as a legislator and had nothing better to do. He subsequently served as House chairman of the Joint Standing Committee on the Library and was cited in the local press as an attentive assemblyman ("He speaks only at the right time, and when he does speak, he says something").[157] Neither a pedant nor a tyrant, the Reverend Horatio Alger was a "good scholar" and "an active, benevolent, and highly esteemed citizen" with a "gentle manner."

His eldest son, meanwhile, cultivated a taste for travel. In the summer of 1858, young Alger railed west to Niagara for a few days of sightseeing.[158] Goat Island, he later reported, "affords, from the extremity, excellent views of the Falls." In August 1859, he vacationed with three friends in Montreal and Quebec. The party spent an entire day on an excursion to the Falls of Montmorenci outside Quebec City. "If I had never seen Niagara I should no doubt have been more impressed," Alger admitted in a sketch he prepared for the *Marlborough Mirror*. As it was, "I found them both beautiful and striking, and did not soon tire of looking at them."[159] If the trip whetted his appetite for foreign travel, the sketch piqued his interest in another literary genre. He began at once to plan a European tour, a *Wanderhalbjahr* abroad after he had graduated from divinity school, and to calculate how he might underwrite part of the expense of such a trip with his pen.

Though technically unemployed, both Horatio *père* and *fils* actively pursued careers during the middle months of 1860. In June, the elder Alger commenced to supply the pulpit of the Eliot Church in South Natick, Massachusetts, a few miles east of Marlborough, founded as an Indian mission by John Eliot in 1650.[160] He was invited by the congregation to settle there permanently a few weeks later.[161] Satisfied by his prospects, he accepted the call in July, succeeding the Reverend William Babcock, whose surname Henry James gave to the character of a desiccated Unitarian minister in his novel *The American*. The Reverend Mr. Alger listed his house for sale in early August,[162] resigned from the

Advertisement for the sale of the Marlborough house.

Marlborough school committee in September,[163] and moved his family to South Natick in October.[164]

On his part, Horatio, Jr., was completing his ministerial course and earning a few odd dollars as a platform speaker. On March 14, he delivered a lecture on Corinth in the time of St. Paul before the Young Men's Christian Union of Boston.[165] On June 13, he attended the bicentennial celebration of the incorporation of Marlborough,[166] having composed a valedictory ode for the occasion:

> God bless the old homestead! some linger there still,
>   In the haunts which their childhood has known,
> While others have wandered to places remote,
>   And planted new homes of their own;
> But time cannot weaken the ties Love creates,
>   Nor absence, nor distance, impede
> The filial devotion which thrills all our hearts,
>   As we bid our old mother God-speed.[167]

On July 17, he graduated with five classmates from divinity school and opened the commencement exercises by reading a historical essay about Chrysostom of Antioch and Constantinople entitled "A Popular Preacher in the Fourth Century."[168] Stephen Douglas, on a campaign foray into New England, was present for part of the ceremony, and, twenty years later, Alger would note "a personal remembrance of Mr. Douglas, to whom I was introduced."[169] On August 12, he was on the road, supplying the puplit in Chicopee, Massachusetts.[170] The hard times were past, at least for the moment. He had a profession and money in the bank. His European plans had borne fruit.

On September 5, even before his family left Marlborough for their new home, Horatio Alger, Jr., in company with his college classmate the Reverend Charles Vinal of North Andover and his nineteen-year-old cousin, Cyrus Alger Sears, embarked from the port of Boston per the Cunard steamer *Arabia* bound via Halifax for Liverpool.[171] He anticipated an absence of four to six months, and he had arranged to write a few letters about his grand tour for the *Sun*, under the resurrected "Cantab" psuedonym, to defray part of his expenses. At the age of twenty-eight, he styled himself a foreign correspondent for a major metropolitan daily.[172] He harbored great expectations, and he looked confidently to the future.

2.

Bound to Rise

(1860–1866)

I

*... in 1860–61 ... I went to Europe, visiting the principal
continental countries as well as Great Britain. ... I acted
as foreign correspondent of [the New York* Sun] *during
my first European trip.*

—HORATIO ALGER, JR.,
10 July 1896

The transatlantic crossing, at a top speed of twelve knots, required
ten days.[1] They passed en route the *Adriatic* steaming from Paris to
New York, on board carrying the young Henry James, Jr., home from
his first trip abroad.[2] When they landed in Liverpool on September 15,
Alger, Vinal, and Sears quickly found their bearings and headed for a
whirlwind tour of Wales.[3] Traveling light, they spent a week visiting
such sites as Eton Hall on the River Dee, the palatial country house of
the Marquis of Westminster, and hiking around Mount Snowden. Late
in the month they ferried from Holyhead to Dublin, "a fine looking city,"
as Alger reported a few days later, where "shops make a fine show of
rich goods, and the appearances of poverty are no greater than in most
cities of the size." The three young gentlemen registered at Price's
Hotel on Sackville Street opposite Nelson's Pillar. "It would be difficult
to find a handsomer street," he wrote to readers of the *Sun*, yet lodgings
there were cheap. A traveler might pay as little as eighteen pence per
day, the equivalent of but thirty-seven cents, for a room in a first-class
hotel.

"It is my custom, on arriving in a new city, to make a tour among the shops," Alger continued. "I found the shopmen in Dublin exceedingly civil and obliging." He had already adopted the pose he would maintain throughout the tour: the American gentleman of leisure observing the peculiar manners and customs of foreign peoples. Soon after his arrival in Dublin, moreover, he attended a performance of *Il Trovatore* featuring Giuseppe Mario, the most famous tenor of the century, and his wife, the soprano Giulia Grisi, at the Theatre Royal. Alger and his companions toured Ireland in a rush, visited Belfast, and from there sailed back across the Irish Sea to Glasgow in early October.[4]

In Scotland they maintained their hurried pace. Early one morning, they caught a train from the Bridge Street station in Glasgow for the village Ayr, the home of Robert Burns, forty miles to the southwest. They breakfasted at the Tam O'Shanter Inn, Alger reported, "in the very room where Burns passed so many convivial hours with Tam O'Shanter and Souter Johnny." While they waited to be served their meal, Vinal read aloud the poem of Tam O'Shanter and, during the repast, Sears sat proudly in a chair once reserved for the poet. After eating, they walked to the stone cottage where Burns had been born and whiled away the afternoon by the banks of the Bonnie Doon, "a beautiful little rivulet overshadowed by trees," which the poet had celebrated in song.

From Glasgow they hastened to Edinburgh, where they were detained an entire week when one of Alger's companions fell ill. Alger spent the time "exploring the curious old town, rich with historical associations, in company with a Member of Congress" from his native Massachusetts. One day they visited Holyrood Castle, the one-time home of Mary Queen of Scots; another, they toured Sir Walter Scott's former residence on Castle Street. En route, they fell into conversation with an elderly man "of decent appearance," as Alger later recalled.

> Judging from his age that he might, perhaps, in his early days, have met Sir Walter, I questioned him on this point.
>
> "Yes, sir," he answered; "I knew Sir Walter, well. Mony's the time I've carried him in my sedan chair."
>
> "What can you tell us about him?" I asked, delighted to have found a connecting link between the present and the past. It was something to meet a man who had known the great novelist.
>
> "I mind me," he said, with a shrewd twinkle of the eye; "that when I carried Sir Walter he always gave me half a crown, but Lady Scott never gave me more than a shilling."

When they at last reached the Scott home, Alger and his friend had cause to be disappointed. Compared to the rustic birthplace of Burns,

Alger considered the three-story building undistinguished. Indeed, he thought it appropriate that the rooms were "occupied, at the time of my visit, by lawyers' offices." He was unimpressed until he was ushered into Scott's private chambers: "In the rear part of the house, on the second floor, I believe, is a plain bed-room, where from a bed of pain Scott dictated the magnificent romance of Ivanhoe. It is certainly wonderful that, amid such plain surroundings, he should have been able to imagine and describe the brilliant scenes and characters of his great romance."[5] It was a talent Alger envied.

In mid-October, Alger and his companions headed south, towards England. They normally traveled by third-class rail coach because, as Alger explained in a *Sun* letter, "There is really little or no difference in point of comfort between the second and third class cars, while there is oftentimes a considerable difference in price." In third class, each passenger traveled for an average fare of about three cents per mile. Alger visited Warwick Castle, which he described later as "the best preserved of the old feudal castles of the Middle Ages, and one of the very few now used as a residence." He next stopped with his friends in Stratford-on-Avon to pay homage to William Shakespeare—their trip had become virtually a tour of great British authors' hometowns—and Alger later wrote a brief poem for the *Boston Transcript* about his visit to Holy Trinity Church where the bard was buried:

> One autumn day, when hedges yet were green,
>   And thick-branched trees diffused a leafy gloom,
> Hard by where Avon rolls its silvery tide,
>   I stood in silent thought by Shakspeare's tomb.
>   . . .
>
> Through the stained windows rays of sunshine fall
>   In softened glory on the chancel floor;
> While I, a pilgrim from across the sea,
>   Stand with bare head in reverential awe.

The three tourists visited Oxford ("a dingy place with very little of natural beauty to divert the attention of its students from their scholastic pursuits," which in this respect "compares very unfavorably with our own Cambridge") before reaching London late in the month.

Still, they did not abate their pace. For a day or two, as was his wont, Alger strayed through shops on the Strand, "a business thoroughfare well known to all who have ever visited the great metropolis," and viewed the city's principal attractions. Some of these sites can be identified now only because Alger, an inveterate name-dropper, went to the trouble to mention them later in his novels. "St. James' Palace is a very ugly-looking brick structure," he explained to readers of *Ragged Dick* in 1868. It "appears much more like a factory than like the home of royalty." He punctuated his occasional letters to the *Sun* with other parochial snorts. "Both in England and in Scotland I have inquired vainly for squashes," he once complained. "A vegetarian in England is compelled to make a much greater sacrifice than with us." To be fair, Alger compensated for his fastidiousness about English cuisine by praising the well-oiled English bureaucracy. "London is much better governed than New York," he admitted. "The police are much more efficient, and are invariably courteous and obliging to strangers who may have occasion to question them."[6]

In all, Alger, Vinal, and Sears tarried only a few days in a hotel room near the Strand, remaining in London about as long as would the hero of Alger's later novel *Frank Hunter's Peril*. They planned to stay longer when they returned in the spring. Early in November, they ferried from Dover to Calais to begin their tour of the continent. With Alger, skilled in conversational French and German, sometimes pressed into service as interpreter for the group, they rushed east, through Belgium and Holland, until they struck the Rhine. They embarked on the obligatory cruise up the picturesque river valley dominated by "ruined castles and vine-clad hills," perhaps pausing in Koblenz to climb "the heights of Ehrenbreitstein,"[7] before leaving the boat at Mainz and continuing by rail through southern Germany to Geneva, arriving there in early December. For a few days, they reconnoitered—Alger remembered especially the Musee d' Art et d' Histoire on the Rue Charles-Galland, the cathedral from which John Calvin had directed the Swiss Reformation, and walks along the shore of Lake Geneva.[8] Meanwhile, they planned the next leg of their tour—an excursion to Italy.

"It was not until I reached Geneva," Alger wrote on December 19, "that I decided to undertake a journey which is of course much more formidable in the middle of December than in summer"—that is, a crossing of the Alps. "Desirous of entering Italy in this way rather than via Marseilles," Alger and his companions

> went by rail from Geneva to the little town of St. Jean de Maurienne, near the foot of Mount Cenis. It is a dirty little town, so hemmed in by lofty snow-crowned summits, that it is a mystery how a railroad was ever got there. Arriving late at night, I was obliged to remain there until 2 p.m. the next day—an interval during which I had time to make inquiries respecting the passage.

Assured that the horse-drawn diligence "went regularly in spite of the weather, I booked my name" and, as he later wrote with comic overstatement, "entered the *coupe* with the desperate resolve of facing the peril, fortifying myself by the high examples of Hannibal and Napoleon," two other "illustrious men" who had earlier crossed the Alps in inclement circumstances, and "consoling myself by the thought that I should become the subject of a startling paragraph, which would no doubt be extensively copied," in the event of a fatal accident on the slopes. The travelers spent ten hours and four teams of horses in reaching the crest of the pass over Mount Cenis. "Two hours before attaining the greatest elevation we exchanged the diligence for sledges, the snow having become too deep for wheels," Alger explained. Despite "the cold and the possible danger, we enjoyed the wild and lovely scenery through which we were riding, and did not regret having undertaken the passage." They descended the mountain "in less than half the time required by the ascent, and at 6 a.m. we found ourselves at Lusa, whence after examination of passports and luggage we proceeded to Turin by rail." As Alger reported from the Sardinian capital in mid-December, he and his companions "were now fairly in Italy—a fact which the bright sunshine, forming so vivid a contrast with the weather on the other side, would have sufficiently attested."[9] From Turin they passed on to Florence—"Dante's birthplace, Art's fair home," as Alger pronounced it.[10]

Coincidentally, he toured Italy during an especially tumultuous moment in its national history. During the summer of 1860, Giuseppe Garibaldi, the Italian patriot and revolutionary, had commanded a small army of redshirts which liberated Sicily from French rule. In August, Garibaldi had sailed for the Italian mainland and seized Naples from the Bourbon king Francis II, who withdrew his forces to a fortress at Gaeta on the Mediterranean Sea above the city. Though his army was stopped by Neapolitan soldiers at the Voltumo River north of Naples in October, and though the French would maintain a garrison in Rome to defend the temporal authority of the Pope until 1870, Garibaldi had served mightily the cause of national unification.

Alger was, from his limited perspective, a sympathetic observer of this historic drama as well as, in a small way, an actor in it. With Vinal and Sears, he traveled to Rome in time for Christmas and later reported to the *Sun* readers that the Eternal City "is full of soldiers. Twenty thousand French soldiers are considered necessary . . . to assure the safety of the Holy Father. They appear to enjoy themselves highly, with little to do, and no lack of time to do it in. Many find opportunities to cultivate their taste for art. At all the galleries I meet the French uniform."[11] Because the war had ruptured normal lines of communication between Rome and Naples, Alger was drafted into service as a diplomatic courier. He "had the high honor of bearing dispatches from Rome to Naples in the service of the U.S.A.," he later bragged to his Harvard classmates.[12] En route south, he remembered, "our steamer touched at the famous Gaeta to land a Cardinal despatched from Rome by the Pope, to afford spiritual comfort and consolation" to the Bourbon monarch "in this critical stage of his fortunes." This landing occurred late at night on Alger's twenty-ninth birthday, January 13, 1861, or "rather on the morning of the 14th, about 4 o'clock." Unfortunately, the darkness prevented him from describing the fortress "as I should have liked." A day or two later, upon his arrival in Naples, Alger delivered the diplomatic pouch entrusted to his care to the American consul and registered at a hotel near "the magnificent theatre of San Carlo."[13]

Alger reported his first impressions of the city a week later to readers of the *Sun*. Like Rome, he reported, "Naples is full of soldiers." Indeed, he had heard rumors "that there are nearly double the number here that is officially stated. At any rate they swarm everywhere. At the hotel where I first took up my abode the rooms had been partitioned off, each into several compartments, in order to accommodate as many as possible." To Alger's chagrin, entrepreneurial hostelers were quite willing to exploit the revolution for profit. The soldiers "have so taxed the resources of the city in providing lodgings, that the hotelkeepers, nothing loth, have felt justified in raising their prices to about double the rates usual in other Italian cities." Alger also was compelled to alter his eating habits on account of the military occupation of the city. "I went to the Cafe de l'Europe to breakfast on the first morning of my arrival," he complained, only to find "every seat taken by soldiers." He "was obliged to wait for some time to secure a seat." However, in the cafe, "I found a large subscription book, containing an elaborate drawing of an elegant sword, to be presented to GARIBALDI. On the hilt are these words, in Italian:—'Rome and Venice implore assistance.' The subscription will no doubt be soon completed, for everywhere GARIBALDI's name is held in the highest and most reverential regard." Within months, in fact, Garibaldi would march on Rome.

Ever the reportorial tourist-at-large, Alger wrote a remarkable letter to the *Sun* devoted entirely to his dinner one evening at the Cafe de l'Europe.

> The cafes in Naples are very good places to study the people. Having taken my seat at a table and given my order, I begin to look about me, quite satisfied that I must wait from twenty minutes to half an hour before I shall be attended to. A Frenchman sits at the next table who evidently has no

admiration for Neapolitan restaurants. I hear him grumbling that the poorest cafe in Paris is superior to the best in Naples. A bright-eyed little fellow enters from the street and offers me the daily paper, recently started by Dumas, the French novelist. Out of curiosity I buy a copy, and recognize at once the style of the greatest of egotists. . . . My reading is interrupted by a vendor of eyeglasses, who invites me to purchase. His appeal, which is unavailing, is followed by that of a dry goods dealer who has handkerchiefs and other small articles for sale. Here the waiter arrives with the first installment of dinner, and absorbed in more agreeable employment I neglect utterly the advances of a dealer in books, who is going his rounds. The sound of music arrests my attention, and looking up I perceive that a young woman, quite tastefully and even fashionably dressed, has entered the cafe, and is performing a popular air on a guitar. At the conclusion she goes from table to table, presenting a cup for offerings with the air of a queen exacting tribute. Of course, I cannot resist the appeal. Next enters a merchant on a larger scale. He has blankets for sale, and opening one, displays it in the middle of the room, vaunting its qualities. No one, I believe, is won by his seductive tongue. The tragic succeeds the comic. The next entrance is a poor creature, looking the very embodiment of destitution, who craves not money, but whatever I may have to spare from my dinner. I give her my loaf of bread—the allowance of cash—and with a grateful "Grazia, Signore," she departs, provided with a dinner for this day at least.

And thus succeeds the actors in this real drama. When I rise from the table, I feel that I have accomplished something more than dining—I have been brought face to face with the people.[14]

Of course, he may also have been the victim of a scam or two.

Armed with a copy of Murray's guidebook to the continent, Alger enjoyed ample opportunity to play the interested observer in the region around Naples. There were few other tourists present that season. As he explained, "Rumors of disturbances and midnight assassinations have obtained circulation, so that both at Florence and Rome I met parties who were anxious to visit Naples, but held back, from apprehension of possible danger." However, Alger discounted reports of threats against foreigners, considered the rumors "much exaggerated," and moved about the city and its environs at leisure. On January 17, he visited the buried cities of Pompeii and Herculaneum, returning at dusk to the feast of San Antonio in Naples' great square, the Largo di Castello. A day or two later, he ascended Mount Vesuvius, and on January 20 he left in company with some new friends, including a young Bostonian and military officer named Charles Edward Paine, on a three-day expedition to the picturesque town of Sorrento, about twenty-five miles south of the city. Harriet Beecher Stowe had made the same journey only the previous spring. She would describe in detail the "wonderful path along the high rocky shores of the Mediterranean" in her novel *Agnes of Sorrento*, published the next year. "On one side lies the sea, shimmering in bands of blue, purple, and green to the swaying of gentle winds," she wrote. "The shores rise above the sea in wild, bold precipices." On his part, Alger thought it "the most beautiful bay in the world."

In Sorrento, coincidentally, he and Paine registered at the Hotel de Sireune, where Stowe had stayed only a few months before. They had no trouble finding a room because, Alger explained in a *Sun* letter, as at Naples "there have been but few visitors this season." One evening, he rented a dinghy and visited by moonlight at low tide the Cave of Ulysses and the Temple of Hercules, a natural grotto and subterranean lake in the sea cliff on the Isle of Capri. Mark Twain would visit the same sites on his first trip to Europe seven years later. The most memorable experience Alger had during the excursion to Sorrento, however, was epicurean. Upon payment of a few grani, he and Paine were admitted to an orange grove within the town borders and permitted to pluck and eat fruit from the boughs. "Those which have remained longest upon the trees are the sweetest," he informed Yankee readers unfamiliar with fresh citrus. "I tasted some which had hung fourteen months, which were delicious. They are sometimes allowed to remain two years, and possibly longer." The grand tour often seemed little more than a cook's tour.

Before repairing to Naples, Alger and Paine joined a group of other tourists on a side-excursion to El Deserto, "a convent built on one of the loftiest peaks of the mountains" ringing Sorrento. Ironically, the donkey ride up the steep cliff proved a practical test of Alger's classical education. "Being in advance of the rest of the party," he and Paine "missed the way, turning down a narrow path skirting the edge of a ravine. Retracing our course for nearly a mile we found ourselves still unable to determine the right way." Just as they were about to quirt their donkeys up "another path which would have led us still farther away from our destination," a priest happened by

> to whom I appealed. Unfortunately he did not understand French, and my Italian was exceedingly limited. Happily we could meet upon the common ground of Latinity, and thus the language of Cicero (which I fear he would hardly have recognized in our mouths) served me a practical good turn, which I could hardly have anticipated when toiling as a school-boy over the pages of Andrews & Stoddard's Grammar.

Returning to Naples with Paine on January 22, Alger began to write letters about his recent experiences for papers in the States.[15]

Within a few days, Alger, Vinal, and Sears repacked their bags and returned to Rome. En route, Alger later reported, they witnessed "from the steamer's deck, for perhaps an hour, the bombardment of Gaeta." Garibaldi had tightened the noose around the neck of the Bourbon monarch since they first passed the beleaguered fortress in the dead of night two weeks before. Because "our distance was at least five miles from the scene of hostilities," an "enthusiastic young man" from New York proposed to the other passengers that they "make up a purse for the captain, to induce him to approach nearer. The scheme, however, fell through, and would hardly have found favor with the officers. With some feelings of envy we saw the Neapolitan steamer from Civita Vecchia (our own belonging to the French company) passing us a full mile nearer Gaeta." On February 6, by then safely ensconced in an apartment on the Via Condotti in Rome, Alger reflected on the plight of the doomed garrison. To be sure, he sympathized fully with the freedom fighters of Garibaldi and their cause: "If without French intervention the people of Rome were permitted to act for themselves," he predicted, "the question of the Pope's temporal power would soon be set at rest. There is a strong desire for the rule of VICTOR EMANUEL, who is regarded as the representative of Italian liberty and union." Yet Alger had overheard a rumor to the effect that the beseiged royalists and their king at Gaeta "indulge in dancing and other gayeties" in the face of imminent death. "If such is the case," he concluded, "FRANCIS II is to be admired for his philosophy, if for nothing else." No wizened ascetic he.

They did not pause long in Rome this time, for Alger thought the city now overrun with soldiers as well as priests and beggars. Not only were the streets festooned with uniforms as in Naples, the Roman citizens suffered the peculiar misfortune of ecclesiastical rule. "Every tenth man you meet on the Corso wears the clerical vesture," he complained. A production of *Il Trovatore* at the Apollo Theatre had been interdicted by a local cardinal because audiences each night had greeted with thunderous applause a passage amenable to interpretation as a reference to liberty. Worse yet, the Roman beggars "are as numerous" albeit "less deserving" than those in Naples. "The latter beg from necessity," he explained, but "the former because they like the business." Alger had been gulled by a "little boy who, at about five o'clock each afternoon," made "a 'tour de promenade,' weeping most piteously" down the Via Condotti. "Overcome by compassion, I gave him alms the first day," he wrote. "Since then I have grown more callous." Alger, Vinal, and Sears remained in Rome less than a week on their way north.[16] They hastily left war-torn Italy by ship for France and railed to Paris, their next stop, arriving in time for the beginning of Mardi Gras on February 10.

Alger was underwhelmed by the celebration. He characterized it later as "a grand triumphal procession of fat cattle through the streets of Paris. Antiquity and custom have elevated what would otherwise be a trivial affair," he thought, though once more he played the part of interested observer. For three days, from February 10 to 12, as he reported,

> all Paris is out of doors. Numberless carriages thronged the streets, and crowds of well-dressed people jostled each other on the sidewalks and in the Boulevards. On the third day the crowd was greatest. A grand masked ball was to close the three days' fete, and many who were to participate in it were promenading the streets in the bizarre costume designed for the evening. Some of these dresses exhibited a latitude which would doubtless shock sober Boston and even cosmopolitan New York. Women dressed in male attire jauntily made their way through gazing crowds. I also saw a few of the stronger sex who returned the compliment by arraying themselves in elegant dresses duly set out with crinoline, their heads surmounted by bonnets trimmed with choice lace.

Such was Alger's introduction to the City of Light.

It was reputedly the most licentious city in the world, and Alger only reinforced its reputation for decadence in his letters to the *Sun*. On Sunday, February 24, he took a leisurely jaunt down the Champs Elysées and through the adjacent boulevards, recording impressions of the dandies and *demimondes* of the Second Empire, and afterwards reported with feigned surprise and disdain the sacrilege of the naughty Parisians:

> Could a sober New England deacon of the last century be dropped into the streets of Paris on a Sunday morning, I can imagine the unspeakable horror which the poor man would feel to find a sacred day so disregarded. In truth, there is no Sunday in Paris, or at best a faint resemblance of what the day is in England and America. Some of the shops indeed are closed, but the majority are open. The course of traffic goes on as usual.

Alger also sampled, to his dismay, some of the pastries for sale by street vendors. He warned his readers "not to indulge in any longings for these temptations to the palate," for he had "ventured upon the purchase of a cake, fair in outward seeming," and "I believe the taste is in my mouth yet." Just as he had sat in a cafe in Naples and observed the spectacle about him, he eventually claimed one of the iron chairs which line the Champs Elysées and watched "all Paris sweep by."

Alger, Vinal, and Sears remained in Paris over six weeks, in part because Alger was fluent in the language and could negotiate their treaties. They took an apartment near the Rue Saint Honoré, where they were charged about a dollar in gold per day for room and board. They loitered in the city longer than any other stop on their itinerary. Alger may have pandered to the *Sun* readers by decrying the pleasures of the Parisians, but in truth he thought the city "beyond question the most magnificent capital in Europe," with the program of urban modernization under the direction of Baron Haussmann bearing "it farther and farther beyond the reach of competition" with every passing year. Alger toured the city almost daily—once to the garden and palace of the Tuileries, occupied at the moment by Napoleon III and his Spanish empress, Eugenie, where by chance he caught a glimpse of the five-year-old Prince Impérial; another day to the new baroque Opéra, under construction on the Boulevard des Capucines; other days to the Louvre; and at least once to the Palais Royal.

As he was returning from the Palais Royal to his hotel in the morning of February 22, in fact, he accidentally stumbled upon the funeral of the playwright Eugene Scribe at the ancient church of Saint-Roch. It was the most memorable moment of his entire European tour. "Selecting a favorable point for observation" when he realized the magnitude of the event, Alger watched in silence as the most eminent men in France paid "a last tribute of respect and affection to one who, for nearly half a century, had held possession of the French stage." Alexandre Dumas *père* served as one of the pallbearers. Victor Cousin, "a striking figure, with venerable white hair," represented the Académie Française. The Prefect of the Seine attested by his presence to "the respect in which the deceased had been held as a citizen" of Paris. "Notwithstanding a drizzling rain which fell through the greater part of the day, not less than three thousand persons, embracing those most distinguished by social and literary eminence, took part in the funeral services, and followed the remains of Scribe to their last resting-place in the cemetery of Père la Chaise," Alger later reported.[17]

Unfortunately, the halcyon days in Paris could not last indefinitely. James Buchanan still was President that day in September 1860 when Alger and his companions sailed from Boston harbor. Abraham Lincoln had been elected Buchanan's successor in early November, soon after Alger reached the continent. Lincoln had been inaugurated and civil war had erupted while he was afoot in Paris. With Vinal and Sears in tow, he crossed to England "towards the close of April," unwilling to cut short the trip unless absolutely necessary.[18] Though he long claimed he had returned "to his native land soon after the outbreak of the war," he in fact dallied in Britain.[19] Vinal left in early May[20] to return to his pastoral charge in North Andover, passing somewhere in the North Atlantic a steamer carrying to England the new minister to the Court of St. James, Charles Francis Adams, and his son Henry, embarked upon the most difficult diplomatic mission of the war.[21] On May 13, Great Britain recognized the belligerency of the Confederacy. Still Alger lingered, though he was alert to the escalating conflict. It "aroused his poetic imagination," as he wrote later, and he fired off to the *Boston Transcript* a patriotic tribute to the loyal soldiers who had defended the Stars and Stripes at Fort Sumter.[22] At last, on the first day of June, he and his young cousin sailed from Liverpool, once more aboard the *Arabia*. They landed in Boston at eight in the morning of June 12, the very day Alger's poem appeared in the local press.[23]

> Unfurl the flag, and let it speak
>   A nation's honest pride,
> And reverence for the patriot real
>   Of fathers true and tried.
> The flag that once in triumph waved
>   Along the Southern shore—
> We swear by all we hold most dear
>   Shall float there evermore![24]

It was his first shot in a private war which would exact its toll over the next few years. That morning in June he closed a charming season in his life and began to face less pleasant truths.

II

Now that so large a number of our citizens have been withdrawn from their families and their ordinary business to engage in putting down this Rebellion, it becomes the duty of the boys to take their places as far as they are able to do so. A boy cannot wholly supply the place of a man, but he can do so in part. . . . If he does this voluntarily, and in the right spirit, he is just as patriotic as if he were a soldier in the field.

—HORATIO ALGER, JR.,
Frank's Campaign

The Alger men had bravely hewn the antislavery line. The elder Horatio had signed a petition of protest against the peculiar institution in 1845, soon after opening his ministry in Marlborough, and his work in the parish over the years was marked by aggressive debate of the slavery question. To be sure, he was not a radical abolitionist, any more than was Abraham Lincoln, but he was a strong antislavery man. Moreover, William Alger had delivered a celebrated denunciation of slavery and the Fugitive Slave Law in a speech before the Boston aldermen on the Fourth of July 1857, for which he received letters of appreciation from William Lloyd Garrison, John Greenleaf Whittier, and Theodore Parker, among others. The mere mention of his name at a meeting of the Massachusetts Anti-Slavery Society the next month "was greeted with instant and general cheering," according to a report in the *Liberator*.[25] Horatio, Jr., was plagued not by uncertainty but indecision on the issue. Sympathy for both Union and emancipation was a family trait. But what could he do to serve these causes? Not only was he physically unfit to soldier, but fresh from a tour of Europe he recoiled at the thought of enlisting for the trenches. "As a private you will be mixed up with all sorts of people, and have to mingle with them equally," a mother admonishes her soldier-age son in one of Alger's stories from this period. "You, with your education and refinement, would be thrown away in such a position."[26] Her argument seemed convincing to the writer who put the words in her mouth.

He chose not to enlist. Instead, upon his return to the States, Alger preached regularly, supplying the pulpit in Dover, Massachusetts, a disputatious parish near South Natick composed of Unitarians and Universalists in near-equal proportions.[27] In December 1861, his assignment there completed, he moved to a room in Otis Place in Cambridge to be nearer his friends and to establish himself as a private tutor. During one summer term in Nahant, Massachusetts, he would teach the young Robert Grant, later a popular poet and novelist.[28] Alger had not abandoned his intention to take a church, but he bided his time. In March 1862 he railed west to audition before the Unitarian society in Alton, Illinois, upstream a few miles from St. Louis, where in 1837 the abolitionist editor Elijah P. Lovejoy had been killed by a proslavery mob. The town still swarmed with copperheads. Alger had no wish to be a martyr, so he declined the invitation to settle there permanently and returned to Cambridge.[29]

Only as a writer did Alger find a niche where he might exercise his modest gifts on behalf of the Union. He became a propagandist for the Northern cause. He shared the ambition of Walt Whitman and Herman Melville: to be the great poet of the American War. During the conflict, in fact, he wrote at least eighteen war ballads, with such titles as "A

Copperhead's Creed" and "The Price of Victory," in the styles of Longfellow and James Russell Lowell. Many of these poems first appeared
unsigned—according to editorial policy—in *Harper's Weekly*, a rabidly
pro-North publication with a circulation of about 120,000. Some were
popular enough to warrant republication later in such collections as the
Rebellion Record and *Pen Pictures of the War*. He contributed one
ballad, "Song of the Croaker," to the short-lived *Our Daily Fare*, sponsored by the Philadelphia publisher George W. Childs for the benefit of
the U.S. Sanitary Commission.[30] Meanwhile, he also composed occasional verse, such as a lyric for the consecration of a new cemetery in
South Natick on September 15, 1863.

As in "They Told Me Thou Wert False, Jamie" a decade earlier, Alger
often wrote his Civil War verse from the point of view of a woman,
usually a mother or a sweetheart pining for a young soldier gone to war.

> He has gone, and I have sent him!
>   Could I keep him at my side
> While the brave old ship that bears us
>   Plunges in the perilous tide?
>
> Nay, I blush but at the question,
>   What am I, that I should chill
> All his brave and generous promptings
>   Captive to a woman's will?
>
> He has gone, and I have sent him!
>   I have buckled on his sword,
> I have bidden him strike for Freedom,
>   For his country, for the Lord!
>
> As I marked his lofty bearing,
>   And the flush upon his cheek,
> I have caught my heart rebelling
>   That my woman's arm is weak.

Alger's authorship of this poem can be verified by a manuscript of it in
his hand in the New York Public Library. It originally appeared unsigned in *Harper's Weekly* for November 1, 1862.[31] The date is worth
noting. No later than October 1859, Alger met a sixteen-year-old Bostonian named Joseph F. Dean who lived with his mother and sister over
the shop of a coal dealer at 60 Washington Street. In the fall of 1862, by
then an apprentice apothecary living in Cambridge, Joe Dean enlisted
in the 44th Massachusetts Regiment of Volunteers. He was mustered
into service on September 12 and, on October 22, he was shipped south
with his unit to New Bern, North Carolina. Alger wrote "He Has Gone,

and I Have Sent Him!" when his friend Joe Dean left Boston for the front lines.

During Dean's seven-month tour of duty in North Carolina, moreover, he and Alger corresponded often, according to the letters Dean wrote his mother. On December 1, 1862, for example, he wrote her that he had received "only four of [Alger's six] letters and have written two to him, one of them had a piece of wood in [it from] the whipping post at Plymouth." Only five days later, Dean asked her to "tell Horatio I have written 3 or 4 letters to him." Unfortunately, the letters he and Alger exchanged do not survive, though his letters home resonate with their tenor. At least six of those letters were actually sent in Alger's care and, in turn, Dean occasionally sent through his mother his "regards to Horatio" or "love to Alger." When Dean contracted a mild case of rheumatism from sleeping on the damp ground, Alger appealed directly to the regimental physician, his old Harvard classmate Robert Ware, on his behalf. "Tell Alger," Dean entreated his mother on February 27, 1863, "although I have not been able to write, that he I considerable [sic] as one of the family and I owe Dr. Ware's kind treatment of me to his letter to him." Alger and Dean continued to correspond at least until the following spring. On May 25, 1863, Dean acknowledged receipt of "Algers letter of the 19th." Four days later, he wrote his mother that "Mr. Alger has invited me to his room on the 17th of June," a day or two after he expected to be discharged. He again received a "letter from Mr. Alger" on May 31. At that point, on the eve of Dean's return, the record breaks off.[32]

To be sure, all of this merely proves that Alger and Dean enjoyed an intimate friendship, not a sexual relationship. Still, the circumstantial evidence, sketchy as it is, indicates that Alger's emotional investment in Dean ran high. The extent to which Dean reciprocated is a mystery and is probably destined to remain one.

Though he still hoped to win a reputation as a poet, Alger did not entirely neglect fiction during the war. George William Curtis, a former editor of the original *Putnam's*, joined the staff of *Harper's Weekly* in 1862 and became one of Alger's contacts with the publisher. For over two years, beginning in early 1862, Alger contributed stories often as bombastic as his ballads exclusively to the Harper family of magazines. He even measured his progress as a writer by the compensation he received for this work: "Harper paid me five dollars per column or magazine page, and ten dollars per poem."[33] At those rates he wrote "a large number of poems and stories" for the firm.[34] His seasonal and topical stories in the *Weekly* (e.g., "Farmer Hayden's Thanksgiving-Day" and "Becky Vane's Valentine") appeared alongside political cartoons by Thomas Nast. His stories in the *Monthly* also appeared in good company, with works by such authors as Anthony Trollope, Charles Dickens, and W. D. Howells.

For a few weeks in July 1863, more than purely literary contributions to the war effort seemed to be required of him. The fighting to date has been mostly a disaster for the North. Bull Run, Shiloh, Manassas, Antietam, Fredericksburg, Chancellorsville: The names of these bloody battles made Yankee mothers flinch. The Union ranks had been devastated by death and attrition over the months. On March, 3, 1863, the Congress adopted over the protests of some members the first Conscription Act, an outrageously unfair law which easily allowed the rich to escape military service by either paying three hundred dollars or procuring a substitute. Partly as a result, riots erupted in working-class neighborhoods in New York during the first draft in mid-July. Nor did the law succeed in filling the ranks with soldiers. Over half of all draftees were exempted, most of them for physical unfitness. In all, fewer than 170,000 men, or only about six percent of all recruits, were added to the Northern armies by conscription.

As it happened, Alger was one of the men drafted for service in General George Meade's Army of the Potomac. He apparently was resigned to his fate when his name was drawn in the draft on July 10, 1863—three days before the New York riots and scarcely a week after Meade's army suffered grievous losses in the battle of Gettysburg. Perhaps Alger felt the glare of the public eye: His conscription was sufficiently newsworthy that the next day the *New York Evening Post* reported in its columns that the name of "Horatio Alger, Jr., the well-known poet," had been selected in the draft in Cambridge.[35] He was prepared to go to war, to judge from a story and poem he wrote for *Harper's Weekly* soon after receiving his notice. In the story, a young minister, a "refined and cultivated" gentleman who shepherds the flock "in a small inland village in Massachusetts," heeds his nation's call to arms. The shelves of his study are "crowded with well-chosen books in many departments of literature," leaving only a little space "along the walls for a few choice engravings and photographs" which he had brought back with him "from Europe, where he had passed the two years subsequent to his graduation from the theological school." Yet when his mother brings word to him that his name has been selected in the draft at the "C____" town hall, he resolves to go: "I clearly understand that I shall meet with much that is repugnant to my tastes," he explains to her, "and that I could indulge them better at home. This is a sacrifice which I am ready to make for my country." In the poem he wrote at about the same time, Alger supplied another reason he would serve—to avoid the discredit he would suffer should he fail to meet his obligation. Twenty years hence, he wondered, after the Union has triumphed and "not a single star effaced" from the flag, how would he answer the question posed by the child in his poem?

> "Dear father," now with earnest voice
>   Outspeaks the eager son,
> "My teacher told me yesterday
>   What glorious deeds were done
> In the war that burst upon the land
>   In eighteen sixty-one.
>
> "She told me with what patient hearts
>   Our noble soldier bore
> The toilsome march, the frugal fare,
>   The hardships of the war;
> The greatest—so my teacher says—
>   That History ever saw.
>
> I wish I had been living then,
>   I'd be a soldier too,
> And help defend the noble flag
>   From all the rebel crew;
> I'd be *ashamed* to stay behind;
>   Dear father, wouldn't you?"
>
> Upon the listening father's face
>   A painful flush there came;
> The patriot soldier's meed of praise
>   He could in nowise claim,
> And the question of his little son
>   Smote him with sudden shame.[36]

So Horatio Alger, Jr., an even more unlikely soldier than he was a minister, reported for a preinduction physical examination on July 29. He lied about his age—it would become a habit with him later—for, according to the official records of the day, he claimed he was but twenty-nine. He listed his occupation as "clergyman." His eyes were blue, his hair light, his complexion fair. But he was too nearsighted to pass the eye test ("extreme myopia," the report stated), and at five feet two inches he was too short to meet the minimum height requirement. He was exempted from the army and assigned to the home front for the duration.[37]

Exempt! from what? a knapsack, gun,
    A blanket and a uniform;
Some weary marches in the sun,
    And nights outdoors amid the storm.

That's all:—my boy, I pray you wait
    Before you laugh and say "all right!"
Your papers have not waived your fate,
    You have the battle yet to fight!
    . . .

Exempt! there's no such thing, my boy!
    You're not exempt while war endures;
Think you your pale face can destroy
    Your country's right to you and yours?
Exempt! no more of that poor word—
    Or fill it with a better sense;
So shall your country's voice be heard,
    A calling you to her defence![38]

Alger unexpectedly profited from his exemption. On August 5, a week after he was declared unfit for military service, he was chosen assistant recording secretary of the New England Historic-Genealogical Society, an organization he had joined the previous winter.[39] He was punctual and conscientious. So long as he was still available, he might as well be given a job.

III

I leased my pen to the boys, and the world has been spared much poor poetry and ambitious prose.

               —HORATIO ALGER, JR.,
                   29 November 1875

    Though he had been writing professionally for most of a decade, Alger was still only thirty years old when he became a member, though a virtually anonymous one, of the elite "Harper Bros. corps of writers."[40] As if to signal the end of his literary apprenticeship, in early 1863 he prepared an essay about Eugene Scribe, whose funeral in Paris had so affected him, for the *North American Review*, the stodgy grand dame of American magazines, perhaps the most prestigious journal in the country behind the upstart *Atlantic Monthly*. Under more propitious circumstances, the essay might have represented a real turning point in his otherwise undistinguished career. Unfortunately, Alger would never write for so respectable a journal again. He was forced to reverse his field to Grub Street. With this essay, he reached the pinnacle of his skill as a writer, the high-water mark of his ambition; afterwards, the tide would slowly recede. "The res angusta doni of which Horace speaks compelled me years since to forsake the higher walks of literature," he explained to the poet and editor E. C. Stedman in 1875.[41] "The decision was made when for an article in the North American Review on which I had expended considerable labor I was paid at the rate of a dollar per printed page."[42] Alger received only fourteen dollars for the most ambitious and prestigious piece he ever placed for publication.

When the check arrived upon the appearance of the essay in October 1863, he began to reassess his opportunities. As a contributor "to such periodicals as Harper's Magazine, Harper's Weekly, Putnam's Magazine, and a variety of literary weeklies" he had enjoyed fair success, yet he had to tutor privately to pay his bills. He might continue for years to write for this market with no greater success. He came at last to the grim realization that his best simply was not good enough. He was not fit for a poet's mantle. In "Carving a Name," written a few weeks later for the *New York Evening Post*, he voiced his fear that he was destined never to win more than fleeting literary fame.

> I wrote my name upon the sand,
>   And trusted it would stand for aye;
> But, soon, alas! the refluent sea
>   Had washed my feeble lines away.
>
> I carved my name upon the wood,
>   And, after years, returned again;
> I missed the shadow of the tree
>   That stretched of old upon the plain.
>
> To solid marble next, my name
>   I gave as a perpetual trust;
> An earthquake rent it to the base,
>   And now it lies, o'erlaid with dust.[43]

Early in 1864, Alger published "Marie Bertrand," an adult romance set in Paris, in the old *New York Weekly*.[44] Mark Twain later wrote that this paper only "circulates among stupid people and the *canaille*."[45] Alger sent five stories, three of them under the "Preston" *nom de plume*, to *Frank Leslie's Illustrated Newspaper*, the flagship in the fleet of tabloids published by his old colleague on Gleason's staff.[46] The fiction raised nary a ripple of reader interest. Alger was played out. That summer, he vacationed in the White Mountains of New Hampshire.[47] When he returned to Cambridge, he had concluded to abandon his dream of literary distinction and "devote myself to an humbler department which would pay me better."[48] He would henceforth write for children.

"One day I selected a plot for a two-column sketch for the Harpers," he recalled in 1896.

> Thinking the matter over, it occurred to me that it would be a good plot for a juvenile book. I sat down at once and wrote to A. K. Loring, of Boston, at that time a publisher in only a small way, detailing the plot and asking if he would encourage me to write a juvenile book. He answered: "Go ahead, and if I don't publish it, some other publisher will." In three months I put in his hands the manuscript of "Frank's Campaign."[49]

Alger dedicated the story to Charles Paine, his friend from Naples and Sorrento, with whom he had corresponded after their return to the States. Paine had recently become something of a celebrity: Commissioned a major in the Fourth U. S. Colored Infantry in November 1863, he served with distinction in the Red River campaign in the spring of 1864. That winter, a month after Alger's novel appeared, he died of a fever contracted in the field.[50]

Alger wrote *Frank's Campaign*, as he prefaced the novel, "to show how boys can be of most effectual service in assisting to put down the Rebellion."[51] He promised that if the story found "favor among the class for whom it is written, it will be followed by other volumes devoted to boy-life." The teenaged hero, Frank Frost, volunteers to work the family farm in the absence of his father, who is thus freed to enlist in the Union forces. Young Frank subsequently organizes a drill team composed of youngsters in the village—"all real boys" whom he had known, Alger insisted, "and all, with one exception" still alive in 1890.[52] Moreover, Henry Frost, the hero's father, seems to have been modeled after Joe Dean: Much as Henry is wounded at the battle of Fredericksburg "about the middle of December" 1862, Joe Dean had in fact been wounded during Foster's Raid on Goldsboro in mid-December 1862. Henry writes his wife in the novel that "My injury is only a slight flesh-wound in the arm, which will necessitate my carrying it in a sling for a few days." Joe Dean wrote his mother, and presumably Alger too, on December 21 that he had been "slightly wounded in the right arm below the elbow only a very slight wound." He scribbled the letter with his arm in a sling.[53] Though in the past Alger had written long stories for serialization, *Frank's Campaign* qualifies as his first true novel, a tale premeditatively planned for publication as a book. It was an awkward first effort indeed, perhaps because it was written in haste. Alger even had to pad it with one of his old "Carl Cantab" sketches to fill it out to respectable length.[54]

Aaron K. Loring was delighted with the story, however. A "brisk, business-like man who seemed in earnest," as Louisa May Alcott once described him, Loring had established a circulating library at 319 Washington Street in 1859, and there, presumably, he had first met Alger. On the basis of his library experience, Loring waxed confident he could gauge popular literary taste, and, in 1864, he ventured into juvenile publishing. In a letter written at the time, he outlined the criteria he observed as a publisher: "I judge a book by the impression it makes and leaves in my mind, by the *feelings* solely as I am no scholar.—A story that touches and moves me, I can make others read and believe in. . . . I like a story that starts to teach some lesson of life goes steadily on increasing in interest till it culminates with the closing chapter."[55] Alger's story, however flawed, filled the bill.

For the record, moreover, Loring's instinct for juvenile fiction was fundamentally sound. Over the years he issued popular novels by such writers as Alger, Alcott, and Mrs. A. D. T. Whitney. By Alger's own testimony, *Frank's Campaign* was "well received" upon its publication in November 1864.[56] On November 17, for example, the *Boston Transcript* avowed that the "tone of the book is fresh and vigorous, the incidents natural, and the style clear, simple and pointed, with that due blending of earnestness and sprightliness which is so agreeable to the young. The book is exactly applicable to the time." Both the *New York Evening Post* and the *Christian Inquirer* soon echoed the encomium. Thomas Wentworth Higginson, a prominent Unitarian minister and man of letters, described it—ironically, in the *North American Review*—as "a good story of home life" in time of war, though he wished Alger had not made his black characters speak in a "Babel of dialect."[57] (Alger lamely countered later that "little Pomp" was "intended as a male counterpart to Mrs. Stowe's 'Topsy.'")[58] Sales of the book were brisk, and Loring issued a second edition on December 10.[59] Alger's first experience as a juvenile writer was unexpectedly pleasant. As he would recall, "I soon found reason to believe that I was much more likely to achieve success as a writer for boys than as a writer for adults."[60] In "deference to numerous applications," he concluded to remain in the field where he had "received so cordial a welcome."[61] Though in the course of his career he would occasionally try again to write for adults, Alger mostly confined himself in later years to writing for boys.

IV

*"I don't think Sunday school boys are better than any
other."*
"They ought to be."
"True, but we have to consider facts."
                            —HORATIO ALGER, JR.,
                            Bernard Brooks' Adventures

Alger's success with *Frank's Campaign* occurred too late to dissuade
him from accepting a call to settle over the First Unitarian Church and
Society of Brewster, Massachusetts. Early in 1864, after all, he had
severely discounted his prospects of a literary career. When, in October,
he was invited to audition before the Unitarians in Brewster, he
accepted with alacrity, though the position there was hardly a plum. No
minister had preached regularly in the village for several years. For
several Sundays prior to the publication of his first novel in November,
however, Alger supplied the pulpit and evidently measured up to expectations. The standing parish committee voted on November 13 to
invite Alger to be their minister "provided the terms can be made
satisfactory."

The negotiations were brief. Even before the committee voted
officially on November 26 to engage Alger for one year at a salary of
eight hundred dollars, the minister-designate began to plan his ordination service.[62] Edward Everett Hale, whose patriotic tale, "The Man
Without a Country," had lately appeared in the *Atlantic Monthly* to rave
acclaim, agreed to deliver the charge to Alger and address the congregation. Alger asked his father to deliver the ordaining prayer and Charles
Vinal the concluding prayer. The arrangements completed, he packed
his bags and moved to a room in the village. It was a poignant moment
for him. Cambridge had been, off and on, his residence for ten years. "I
can say with truth," he noted in 1884, "that those ten years were among
the happiest I have spent."[63] He did not plan to return soon. He declined
renomination to his office with the Historic-Genealogical Society.[64]

Though December 8, the day appointed for the service, dawned cold
and wintry, Alger's ordination was a "very pleasant occasion, not soon to
be forgotten by those who were privileged to participate" in it, according
to one observer. The little church had been trimmed by the ladies of the
parish in evergreen and flowers "so that, filled with the intelligent and
animatedly interested congregation that gathered to this service, with
its well-lighted and cheerful aspect, it presented a very beautiful
appearance." Hale, Vinal, and Alger *père* each did his part, and the

Reverend William P. Tilton of Boston delivered a sermon on the text "On this rock I will build my church." In all, reported the *Boston Transcript*, it was an "auspicious commencement of Mr. Alger's ministry, and we doubt if either townspeople or guests will soon forget the pleasant and profitable event."[65] The reporter wrote not well, but true.

For several months, Alger discharged his new duties with aplomb. Even Solomon Freeman admitted later that "he possessed a certain talent" which, at first, pleased and impressed the people.[66] He joined the local chapter of the Cadets for Temperance and soon was elected its president.[67] In the summer of 1865, he began to contribute stories to the *Student and Schoolmate*, a monthly juvenile magazine edited by his old friend William T. Adams and published in Boston by family friend Joseph H. Allen.[68] He wrote a second juvenile novel for Loring, based upon one of his early *Sun* serials, under the working title "Paul Preston's Charge," changed "for business reasons" to *Paul Prescott's Charge*[69] in time for publication early in September 1865.[70] The favorable reviews of this novel only reinforced his conviction that he was ideally suited to the juvenile field. The *Christian Inquirer* thought it "an exciting, almost fascinating tale of adventure." The *Nation* concluded that it "is likely to prove a favorite in spite of occasional 'big words.'"[71] On the strength of his growing reputation as a poet and as a writer for boys, he earned recognition in the *Cyclopedia of American Literature*, prepared for the press in 1865.[72] "I hope in course of time to be more worthy of such mention," he wrote in a letter of thanks to the editor, Evert A. Duyckinck.[73] He had every reason to observe a happy holiday season that year. He was working on a novel for girls entitled *Helen Ford*, scheduled for spring publication, and he had already contracted with Loring to bring out "in the fall a new boy's book, not yet commenced." On December 25—if the evidence of his poem "Lines Written on Christmas Day 1865" is to be accepted—he struck an upbeat note. He reviewed the year in which Lincoln had been assassinated but the Civil War finally concluded.

> The trees are bare, the wind is chill,
>   and skies are dull and gray,
> But hearts are warm, and faces bright,
>   for this is Christmas day.[74]

He could not have known at the time that this would be the last poem he would write for the *Boston Transcript*. Though he had built a respectable record of achievements in 1865, his streak of good fortune had nearly run its course.

Early in the new year 1866 some disquieting rumors about the Reverend Mr. Alger, Jr., began to circulate in the parish. A young boy in the congregation told his aunt that the minister had molested him. The rumors of his "evil deeds" became "more and more aggravating" over the course of a few weeks. "I will name one, the truth of which I have no good reason to doubt," Solomon Freeman later wrote Charles Lowe.

> On the sabbath after services, one of these boys called at his room to leave a book. . . . [Alger] bolted his door and then, and then, committed this unnatural crime, with the boy's poor sister waiting in the carriage, in the cold, [during] this diabolical transaction. From this single circumstance you can readily infer the depth of depravity to which he had descended.[75]

On March 6, unwilling at first to confront the problem directly, the standing committee simply voted not to rehire Alger for the next year. But some members of the church argued that the rumors were too serious to ignore, that unless they investigated and went on record with the results Alger would be free to take another pulpit elsewhere with potentially disastrous consequences. They were obliged to offer a statement, either exonerating or indicting their minister. So at a private meeting on March 14 the congregation empowered a committee of three men—Elisha Bangs, S. H. Gould, and Thomas Crocker—to "investigate Parish affairs" (a charge subsequently amended to read "investigate certain reports in relation to Mr. Alger") and report their findings within five days.[76] Only two months before, on January 23, Alger had officiated at the wedding of Crocker's daughter Sophia.[77] Since then, he had been linked in rumor to Crocker's thirteen-year-old son, Tommy, and a fifteen-year-old friend.

The members of the committee established the truth of the rumor. "We learn from John Clark and Thomas S. Crocker," they reported in open meeting on March 19, "that Horatio Alger Jr. has been practicing on them at different times deeds that are too revolting to relate." The committeemen added that they had "good reason to think" other boys were involved. When they put the charges to Alger privately, "He neither denied or attempted to extenuate" the evidence of his culpability "but received it with the apparent calmness of an old offender." He admitted to the men that he had been "imprudent," considered his connection with the Society dissolved, and "hastily left town on the next train."[78] Solomon Freeman ominously added later that "Had he remained longer an arrest or something worse might have occurred. We should scarcely [have] felt responsible for the consequences in an outraged community, and that outrage committed by a pretended

Christian teacher."[79] The Society, especially one of the parents of the abused boys, considered for a time bringing charges against Alger for child molestation, but cooler heads prevailed.[80] The congregation opted instead for full disclosure of his misconduct to the offices of the American Unitarian Association in Boston. Freeman chaired the committee that filed the report.

> Horatio Alger Jr. who has officiated as our minister for about fifteen months past has recently been charged with gross immorality and a most heinous crime, a crime of no less magnitude than the abominable and revolting crime of unnatural familiarity with *boys*, which is too revolting to think of in the most brutal of our race—the commission of which under any circumstances is to a refined or Christian mind too utterly incomprehensible. . . . No further comment is necessary. You know the penalty attached to such unnatural crime by human as well as divine laws. Please take such action as will prevent his imposing on others and advise us as to what further duties devolve on us as a Christian Society.[81]

Freeman was not easily mollified. The Old Testament book of Leviticus decreed the death penalty for homosexual acts.

While letters, alternately angry and sympathetic, flew between Brewster and Boston, Alger remained at his parents' home in South Natick nursing his wounds and plotting his next career move. What could be salvaged from the debacle in Brewster? He knew he was finished as a minister. He wanted no more of that profession anyway. He had reached a critical crossroads, and the path he chose led straight to New York.

3.

___

Adrift in New York

(1866–1873)

I

How much gayer and more agreeable it would be, he thought, to be in business in a great city like New York than to live in a quiet little country village where nothing was going on.

—HORATIO ALGER, JR.,
Adrift in the City

In the spring of 1866, for the first time in his life, Alger was obliged to earn his living exclusively by writing. As his friend and publisher Frank Munsey decorously noted years later, "Up to this time his revenue from the pen had been inconsiderable."[1] Since attaining his majority, he had worked as an editor, teacher, and minister, always in order to supplement his irregular income from magazines. Suddenly he had neither an editorial nor a ministerial post on which he could fall back, and his prospects as a teacher had dimmed. However, if he could broaden his audience with local-color stories about life in New York, or if he could exploit the good offices of editors in New York, the only American city outside New England to qualify as a literary center, his move there might yet prove the Brewster disaster a mixed blessing.

"I send you a poem—Friar Anselmo's Sin—in response to your invitation to contributors," Alger wrote on April 20 to William Conant Church, editor of the *Galaxy*, a magazine recently launched in the city. He had rented a room in a cheap hotel on East Fourth Street and begun the task of rebuilding his life. "I have established myself in New York with the intention of devoting myself solely to literary pursuits and increasing my acquaintance with publishers," he added. "I inclose a stamp for the return of the M.S. if it is not adapted to your purposes. Should it be, I should be tempted to offer you something else ere long."[2] Unconsciously, he echoed a speech of Bayard Taylor's John Godfrey: "I have come to New York to make literature my profession, and should therefore expect to be paid for my articles."[3]

At first, Church confused him with his cousin William. Horatio tactfully corrected him in his next letter. "My name may not be familiar to you," he observed. "I have contributed to the North American Review, Putnam's Magazine in its last days, Harper's Weekly and Magazine, etc. A. K. Loring of Boston is my publisher," for whom he was at present "engaged in writing juveniles and other books." Evert Duyckinck had included "a brief sketch of me in his recent edition of the 'Cyclopedia of Am. Literature.'"[4] The diplomacy was wasted on Church. Though he subsequently hung in the *Galaxy's* firmament several essays by William Alger, Church rejected Horatio's manuscript. "Write a sonnet on a railroad accident, or something else that everybody will read," an editor had once admonished John Godfrey, "and then I'll talk to you. You can't expect me to pay, while there's a young and rising genius on every bush, and to be had for the picking."[5] In fact, "Friar Anselmo" would not reach print for over six years.

Still, the hackneyed poem silhouettes Alger's turbulent state of mind in the wake of his departure from Brewster. Moored in the *bathos* of his recent experience, the ballad both betrays the extent to which he was tormented by guilt during late March and April 1866 and suggests how he finally allayed his fears. Friar Anselmo, like the late pastor, "Committed one sad day a deadly sin" and

> drew back, self-abhorred,
> From the rebuking presence of the Lord,
> And, kneeling down, besought, with bitter cry,
> Since life was worthless grown, that he might die.

He is roused from his death-reverie when,

> looking down from the convent window high,
> He saw a wounded traveller gasping lie
> Just underneath, who, bruised and stricken sore,
> Had crawled for aid unto the convent door.

Like the Good Samaritan, Friar Anselmo bathed the wounds of the stranger and thus inaugurated "A blessed ministry of noble deeds." The stranger slowly recuperates his strength until, suddenly transformed into an angel, he commissions the pious friar:

> "Courage, Anselmo, though thy sin be great,
> God grants thee life that thou may'st expiate.
> "Thy guilty stains shall be washed white again,
> By noble service done thy fellow-man."

Then followed a couplet Alger in later years would often send young readers who solicited his autograph:

> "His soul draws nearest unto God above,
> Who to his brother ministers in love."[6]

Anselmo dedicated the rest of his life to "his heaven-appointed mission" to do good just as, in April 1866, Alger resolved to expiate his own sin through a literary ministry. His move to New York to promote his writing career went hand in glove with his desire to write didactic juvenile fiction. Thirty years later, in one of the last pieces he prepared for print, he reflected obliquely on his decision that spring to transfer his ministry from pulpit to pen: "It seems to me that no writer should undertake to write for boys who does not feel that he has been called to that particular work."[7] Alger took care not to repeat his error, moreover. Friar Horatio may have remained celibate the rest of his life.

The Brewster trauma healed, but left a scar. In the spring of 1870, four years after the event, Alger discussed the incident with William James, son of the eminent philosopher Henry James, brother of the novelist Henry, Jr., and a distinguished psychologist in his own right. Alger had been afflicted with lingering guilt so intense that the elder Henry James likened it to dementia in a letter to his namesake: "Alger talks freely about his own late insanity—which he in fact appears to enjoy as a subject of conversation and in which I believe he has somewhat interested William."[8] There is no evidence Alger ever discussed the matter again with anyone. Perhaps he was embarrassed by his frank revelations to Williams James. At any rate, he afterwards renewed his vow of silence and went to his grave with his reputation intact.

However anxiety-ridden he may have been, Alger faced a more pressing problem upon his arrival in New York in April 1866: finding remunerative employment. He not only had been disgraced, he had lost the salary he enjoyed in Brewster. If, as "Friar Anselmo" suggests, he had decided to live, he now had to earn his living. He had to satisfy the needs of the body before he could redress the sins of the soul. He had interrupted work on *Helen Ford*, his novel for girls, and Loring had postponed its appearance until the fall. So many of his tales were backlogged for publication in *Gleason's Literary Companion* that contributions signed by the "Rev. Horatio Alger, Jr." were printed regularly in the magazine until December 1867. But at the rate of two dollars per column the author could hardly pay his rent with these stories. His old colleague John Trowbridge had accepted his tale "How Johnny Bought a Sewing Machine" for *Our Young Folks*, a new juvenile monthly launched by the Boston firm of Ticknor & Fields and billed as an *Atlantic Monthly* for children.[9] He also had placed several pieces with the *Student and Schoolmate*, including the dialogue "Seeking His Fortune," the tale of a country Jonathan who abandons his rustic home in "Beanville" in the vain hope of improving his station in the city. Ironically, it appeared in the issues for March and April 1866, even as the author was fleeing Brewster and settling in New York. The moral of the story—the city is both demoralizing and expensive—threatened to come home to roost in Alger's thinning hair if he failed to increase his own income substantially and soon.[10]

He struck upon a simple, albeit temporary solution. He resurrected two of his old serials, originally written for adults, from the morgue of the *New York Sun*.[11] First he rewrote and abridged "The Cooper's Ward; or, The Waif of the New Year," a Dickensian tale of the hardships and heartaches suffered by a working-class family during the depression winter of 1836–37. Loring published it on August 7 under the even more awkward title *Timothy Crump's Ward; or, The New Years Loan, And What Came of It.*[12] Alger rewrote from old clippings so quickly that he failed at one point—on page 27 of the published novel—to change the name of "Mr. Cooper" to "Mr. Crump." Next he revised for a juvenile audience "Manson the Miser; or Life and Its Vicissitudes," the sensational tale of a Fagin-type cursed with terminal gold fever. Loring issued it late in 1866 under the title *Charlie Codman's Cruise*, the final novel in Alger's three-volume "Campaign series" for boys. Alger again rewrote from old clippings so quickly that he failed at one point—on page 206 of the published novel—to change the name of a young girl from Ida, as it had originally appeared, to Bertha, as she is called in *Charlie*. Young readers, if they noticed, did not seem to mind.

Unfortunately, neither novel made Alger much money, though both garnered favorable reviews. The *Sun*, with a kind of vested interest in its success, praised *Charlie* as a "very pleasant story for boys, containing many wonderful adventures on land and water," and the *Boston Transcript* identified its author as "that prince of story-tellers, Horatio Alger,

Jr." Similarly, the *Springfield Republican* indicated that readers would find in *Timothy* "amusement, if not instruction, for a lazy hour," and the *Christian Inquirer*, the weekly paper of New York Unitarianism, commended it in its August 30 issue as

> a pleasant, entertaining story, with so little that is objectionable and so much that is interesting in it that we gladly give it a place in our library. Though its author's name is not given, we more than suspect that it is from the same pen which has written three or four charming juveniles, and is in a fair way to make a deep and lasting mark in our literature. We mean that of H. A., Jr.[13]

This was lavish praise indeed, especially for a lapsed Unitarian.

Or so it seemed to Solomon Freeman. Back in Brewster, the frustrated elder deacon read this review and reached for his own pen. After months of silence on the subject, he angrily wrote Charles Lowe on September 1 to demand more definite censure of his late pastor. "You will recollect a communication addressed to you from a committee of our society," he began, "in March last in relation to certain unnatural and revolting criminality of H. Alger Jr., who had officiated as our pastor, and who on being detected had left without taking leave. The details of this criminality as afterwards disclosed were too revolting to describe." The committee had solicited "your advice & direction" and "taken no further notice of the matter, supposing the offices of the association would see that, so far as our denomination was concerned, he was permitted to sink into that insignificance which his criminality indictated." However, in June a woman

> whose son was one of his victims of criminality and a subscriber to the "Student & Schoolmate," called my attention to an article published over his name. . . . I anxiously wrote the publisher, referring him to record in your office, and stating the pernicious influence it would have . . . if he was still permitted to contribute to the respectable periodicals, particularly those intended for boys to read.

All of the boys "in this and neighboring towns" who "knew of his criminality," he explained, would "be led to suppose that such criminality was at most trifling." However,

> the next issue contained another article from his pen, . . . and now in looking over my Aug. 30th Christian Inquirer, under the head "Literary" I see a recommendation in very high terms of a new book supposed to be from the pen of H. A., Jr. . . . I would ask you, is this right or proper, should a man branded by such infamous crime, and who it is self-evident is an old offender in such criminality, and who is consequently secretly known to many in every neighborhood his presence has cursed since he arrived at

years of puberty should he be still allowed to contribute to our literature[?] . . . One would have naturally supposed that an educated man . . . who had so grossly disgraced his profession as a minister, after exposure, would have sunk into such an obscurity that his name should never have appeared in any production before the public, at least any production sanctioned by his own denomination. . . .[14]

A month after Alger's abrupt resignation, the Unitarians in Brewster had raised twelve hundred dollars through the rental of pews, more than enough to entice another minister to settle over them.[15] Freeman feared the vitality of his church was threatened by the apparent indifference of the national officers to the crimes of young Mr. Alger and by their willingness to ignore praise of his work appearing in Unitarian journals. As he concluded, "We have reason to fear that his influence for evil will be felt here in its secret operations for a long time."

In his reply on September 7, Lowe sympathized with Freeman, if only to disarm the complainant, even as he protested his utter impotence to exact revenge on behalf of the association. He allowed that he was as "sorry as you at the readiness to come forward into public so soon, on the part of Mr. Alger." He regretted "that his name has been, as you say, though I have not seen it, connected in our papers with moral teachings to youth when it is so freshly associated with such moral perverseness of life. But I do not know how we as an Association have anything to do with the matter." Lowe assured Freeman that he had removed Alger's name "from our Lists" and had received his father's solemn promise "that he will never again seek to act as belonging to the ministerial profession. We also made known to the editors of our papers—Register and Inquirer—the facts of the case, that they might—without public notice of them—be guided in future reference to him." Beyond that he could do nothing. "We have no more control over any paper or other periodical—except the Monthly Journal—than you have. If I should hear that Mr. Alger was exercising ministerial functions, I should feel bound by a sense of duty to the denomination to interfere in some way, but as it is I do not see how anthing can be done here."[16] So far as Lowe was concerned, the Brewster case was closed.

A month later, in early October, Loring finally issued *Helen Ford*, so that three Alger novels—one each for adults, boys, and young women—were offered for sale during the holiday season of 1866. Like her companions *Timothy* and *Charlie*, *Helen* was well-received by reviewers, though sales were disappointing. The *New York Evening Post*, in one of the first notices of the story, declared that "some of the passages are lively." The *Boston Transcript* found the narrative "interesting, and

the spirit of the writer thoroughly kindly and benevolent." More importantly, Lowe had failed to discourage favorable notice of Alger's work in
Unitarian papers. The *Christian Inquirer* for October 25 commended
Helen for "good thoughts, pure feeling, and well-developed Christian
lessons" and favorably compared the novel "with almost any of Trollope's productions." A week later, the *Christian Register* echoed the
compliment, describing *Helen* as an "ambitious" story which "contains
beautiful lessons of self-sacrifice and trust" and praising Alger by name
as a writer with "talent of a peculiar and high order."[17] Despite Freeman's complaints and Lowe's confidential letters to the editors, references to Alger were not expunged from these journals.

The reason? The scheme, such as it was, to ostracize Alger from
Unitarian circles failed largely because of the efforts of one man—
Joseph H. Allen. Graduated with honors from Harvard College in 1840
and ordained to the Unitarian ministry in 1843, Allen met young Horatio no later than January 1845, scarcely a week after his thirteenth
birthday, when he helped to supervise the elder Alger's installation in
Marlborough.[18] Between 1863 and 1865, Allen and William Alger co-
edited the *Christian Examiner*, a leading Unitarian journal. (A story
later circulated that, after one of William's prolix pieces appeared in the
magazine, a reader asked Allen why he had not pruned it. "Oh!" he
replied, "I was in Europe; you got the pure Algerine.")[19] Both Horatio *fils*
and his sister Augusta occasionally wrote for Allen's juvenile monthly
Student and Schoolmate. Allen thought the younger Horatio might
prove in time a worthy successor to his own uncle, Henry Ware, Jr., one
of the first Unitarians to write for children. As family adviser and
influential publisher, Allen played an instrumental role in Alger's career
when, in 1866, he urged him to continue writing for juveniles despite
the animadversions stemming from Brewster.

In short, after Alger left the ministry in disgrace, Allen became his
patron as well as his publisher. Not only did he turn a deaf ear to
Freeman's ardent protests that Alger was morally unfit to write for boys,
he showed his good faith by occasionally suggesting story ideas to him.
As a general agent of the *Christian Inquirer*, later retitled the *Liberal
Christian*, Allen also arranged for that magazine to reprint several of
Alger's juvenile tales, most of them from the *Schoolmate*, and to print
two of his original pieces. It is hardly surprising that the editors of the
Inquirer and *Register*, unwilling to offend Allen, continued to review
Alger's books. With Allen as his ally, Alger was a writer worthy of notice,
too important at least to be ignored.

Unfortunately, even with Allen's patronage, Alger could not rely for long upon recycled serials for his livelihood. In fact, Loring developed a strong prejudice against *Timothy* despite its critical success, as Alger recalled in 1877, "& I allowed it to pass out of print" even though "I had a considerably better opinion of it" than he did.[20] Today *Timothy Crump's Ward*, in either of its two editions, is the Alger novel most coveted by book collectors.

For several months after settling in New York, Alger was compelled by financial necessity to write hastily, if not carelessly. His manuscripts sometimes were rejected, though he enjoyed one signal success during his first summer in the city. One Sunday, he later reminisced, "I attended an afternoon service at the Five Points mission" and heard a speaker recount the tale of John Maynard, a courageous if mythical sailor on a Lake Erie steamer who steers his burning ship and its passengers to shore and safety just before he is consumed by the flames. Alger was so impressed by the sailor's sacrifice that after the service he asked the speaker "where I could find the particulars of the incident. He referred me to a weekly religious paper of recent date." The next day, Alger went to the reading room of the local YMCA, found the story, actually an inspirational lecture by the popular speaker John B. Gough, and copied it. He returned to his room in St. Mark's Place and, that evening, in a single sitting, composed his most famous poem, a familiar ballad simply entitled "John Maynard."[21] It was a faithful adaptation of the Gough lecture. "Only the name of the vessel I furnished," he added later. "I called it 'Ocean Queen,' not a very fitting name for a lake steamer, but I had no idea when I wrote the ballad that it would become so popular or I would have tried to find a better one."[22] In fact, Alger borrowed the name of a real steamship which at the time plied a route between New York and California via Cape Horn.[23]

The poem was written, as Alger explained, under incommodious circumstances. "The evening was very hot, and I was forced to lay aside my coat, vest, and collar, but I became so much interested that I could not make up my mind to retire till the poem of nearly one hundred lines was finished." Like a hybrid of Whitman's "O Captain! My Captain!" and Mrs. Hemans's "The Boy Stood on the Burning Deck," the ballad concluded with two stanzas which may illustrate Alger at his best as a versifier:

> One moment yet! One moment yet!
>   Brave heart, thy task is o'er,
> The pebbles grate beneath the keel,

> The steamer touches shore.
> Three hundred grateful voices rise
>   In praise to God that he
> Hath saved them from the fearful fire,
>   And from the engulphing sea.
>
> But where is he, that helmsman bold?
>   The captain saw him reel,—
> His nerveless hands released their task.
>   He sank beneath the wheel.
> The waves received his lifeless corpse,
>   Blackened with smoke and fire.
> God rest him! Never hero had
>   A nobler funeral pyre![24]

The next day, Alger mailed the poem to Allen, who printed it with an illustration in the *Schoolmate* for January 1868. Alger dryly noted thirty years later that he had been paid "the munificent sum of three dollars" for it. Desperate as he was for ready cash that summer, however, he had been pleased with that payment at the time. "I never expected to hear from it again," he admitted, "but soon it began to be copied." It was reprinted in the March 1871 number of *Merry's Museum*, one of Allen's competitors recently edited by Louisa May Alcott, and it became a popular declamation piece for schoolchildren. By Alger's own count it was anthologized at least a dozen times before the end of the century.[25]

Though fraught with risks, his move to New York had begun to yield modest dividends. To date, however, Alger had exploited neither the offices of local publishers nor the local color of the city. He had earned little more than a subsistence. But a marked change in his fortunes was about to occur, one perhaps best signaled by an innocuous paragraph in the *New York Sun* for January 9, 1867: The *Student and Schoolmate*, it announced, "commences the new year and a new volume with a story from the pen of Horatio Alger, Jr., (who will be remembered by some of the readers of THE SUN as a contributor to its columns many years ago), bearing the title of 'Ragged Dick; or, Street Life in New York.'"[26]

II

The Lodging House, though it cannot supply the place of a private home, steps between hundreds of boys and complete vagabondage, into which, but for its existence, they would quickly lapse. Probably no money is more wisely expended than that which enables the Children's Aid Soci-

*ety of New York to maintain this and kindred institu-
tions.*

—HORATIO ALGER, JR.,
Ben the Luggage Boy

Soon after his arrival in New York in the spring of 1866, Alger began to study the habits and to visit the habitats of the so-called "street Arabs," homeless and/or indigent children who roamed the city. "The first street boy with whom I became acquainted in New York," he later recalled, "was Johnny Nolan, a young boot-black, who made daily calls at the office of one of my friends" at the corner of Nassau and Spruce streets. "My conversations with him gave me my first knowledge of street-boys and their mode of life," he added. "My interest was excited, and led me a few months later to undertake the story of 'Ragged Dick,' in which Johnny figures."[27] Alger began to haunt the docks and other sites where "the friendless urchins could be found."[28] In the spirit of the philanthropic Friar Anselmo, he sometimes treated the children to candy or gave them small sums of money.

These crude attempts at ingratiation succeeded. Alger's room, first in St. Mark's Place and after 1875 in various boarding houses around the city, became a veritable salon for street boys. As his sister Augusta reflected, "Nothing delighted him more than to get a lot of boys between the ages of 12 and 16 years in the room with him, and while they were cutting up and playing about he would sit down and write letters or a paragraph of a story."[29] A generation after he settled in New York, Alger remained a kind and popular benefactor of the street Arabs. After speaking with some of his young friends in 1885, a reporter concluded that Alger's "pleasant ways, his open-handed charity, and his thorough sympathy with the unfortunates rendered him a favorite wherever he went." One of these lads claimed that "Mr. Alger could raise a regiment of boys in New York alone, who would fight to the death for him."[30] Alger himself observed in 1890 that over the years he had "made friends with hundreds of urchins."[31] He doubtless deserved their esteem.

During the summer of 1866, Alger also began to frequent charitable institutions around the city, including the Five Points mission, the YMCA, and especially the Newsboys' Lodging House on the southwest corner of Fulton and Nassau streets. In January 1853, Charles Loring Brace, an urban reformer and Unitarian minister, founded the Children's Aid Society, a local agency which at first sponsored a few industrial schools and placed orphans with families in the West. During the winter of 1853, however, Brace and other members of the society laid plans to help vagrant newsboys and bootblacks in the city by establishing a so-called "street boys' hotel." The editor of the *New York Sun*, Moses Beach, agreed to let a loft atop the *Sun* building for this purpose, and, on March 18, 1854, the Newsboys' Lodging House opened its doors. There, for a few pennies a day, a boy might obtain a warm meal and a clean bed. The residents soon found that the lodge provided basic necessities at a cheap price while "leaving them free" to "go or stay as [they] pleased." The experiment proved so successful that within a few years the lodge expanded to another floor of the building, and a Girls' Lodging House and several other newsboys' lodges were opened in other parts of the city. The idea subsequently spread to other major cities. In 1866, Alger's first year in New York, the original lodge at 128 Fulton Street sheltered 8,192 different boys. A total of about fifty thousand lodgings and thirty-four thousand meals were furnished to three thousand orphans and four thousand half-orphans.[32]

Alger had been familiar with the charitable work of the Children's Aid Society a decade before he migrated to the city. In 1855, when he was barely twenty-three, in a prefatory note to his poem "The Child of the Streets" in the *Boston Transcript*, he had praised the efforts of the society to ameliorate the suffering "of the large number of homeless and friendless children who wander about the streets" of New York "by day, and at night sleep in old wagons, or wherever else they can find a corner to shelter them."[33] During the late 1850s, when the *Sun* serialized several of his stories, Alger also had occasion to inspect the work of the lodge at first hand.

Moreover, in the spring of 1867, within a year of his move to New York, Alger appealed for public support of the society on behalf of the street Arabs he had befriended. He described a recent visit to the Newsboys' Lodging House in a sketch for the *Liberal Christian*. "One evening I climbed the narrow winding staircase" to the sixth floor of the *Sun* building where "I found myself at the door of the school-room" of the lodge. He entered and found a space about fifty by thirty feet occupied by about a hundred and fifty newsboys and bootblacks sitting on benches and

listening with every appearance of attention to an exposition of Scripture. This was the Sunday evening exercise. On other evenings instruction is given in the ordinary English branches.

The boys differed largely in personal appearance. Some were apparently seventeen or eighteen; others not more than six or seven. Their faces were not all clean, nor, as may be imagined, was the toilet irreproachable. The garments of many presented a curious mosaic of many-colored patching. Some were clad merely in shirts and pants, with the addition of a fragmentary vest, while in other cases the shirt was wanting. A few were quite decently dressed. But generally speaking, they were ill and insufficiently clad.

In spite of their wretched clothing, Alger was favorably impressed by their appearance. Precociously street-wise,

> the boys looked bright and intelligent; their faces were marked by a certain sharpness produced by the circumstances of their condition. Thrown upon the world almost in infancy, compelled to depend upon their own energy for a living, there was about them an air of self-reliance and calculation which usually comes much later. But this advantage had been gained at the expense of exposure to temptations of various kinds.

After the exercises, "the obliging superintendent" Charles O'Connor guided Alger on a tour of the dormitory, three rooms connected by folding doors on the fifth floor of the building.

> Here are one hundred and forty neat beds, which must seem luxurious to the weary newsboy, who not unfrequently finds a less comfortable bed in an empty box or old wagon, or on the hard pavement in some arched passage. . . . For a night's lodging the charge is but five cents, and the same for a plain meal of coffee and bread, sometimes with soup. . . . The charges, of course, are much below what would be required if it was the design to make the institution self-supporting.

The cheapest commercial lodging in the city charged boys twenty-five cents per night. The Newsboys' Lodging House offered cleaner sheets and better ventilation at less cost.

The lodge also encouraged its residents to form productive habits and to become upright citizens. For example, Alger explained, "There is a newsboys' savings-bank in the school-room, or a table with over a hundred closed boxes appropriated to different boys; through slits in the top they drop such sums as they can spare. In the course of a month this amounts in the aggregate to several hundred dollars." Another room in the loft had been "fitted up with a few simple appliances, and used as a gymnasium." Unfortunately, though many of the boys liked to read, the lodge contained "no library to speak of." Mrs. John Jacob Astor once had donated a dozen volumes of the *Illustrated London News*, and another gentleman had donated some *Patent Office Reports*, O'Connor noted, "but beside these we have little or nothing. Good boys' books they would gladly receive, and read eagerly." Alger urged his readers "to make up a parcel of books" they no longer needed and send it to the lodge, where it might "do more good than they imagined."

He also appealed for contributions of money to underwrite the work. "The expense of this institution for the last year was $11,000," he noted.

"This year it will probably be more, as the rent has been raised from $1500 to $5300." Eventually, too, the lodge would require even larger quarters, for "the present accommodations are insufficient" to satisfy demand for services. "Sometimes two hundred boys are crowded into the hundred and forty single beds," Alger reported, "and oftentimes even more are provided for somehow." Considering the temptations of the streets, he commended such herculean efforts to help as many boys as possible. In "low gambling-houses on Baxter street," the youngsters might wager and lose their money or even imbibe "a villainous mixture of gin which is sold at these places at two cents a glass. One evening a descent was made upon one of these establishments by the police, and over a hundred boys were arrested. That these friendless boys, left very much to their own guidance, should yield to such temptation is not strange."

Like Brace, Alger feared no greater threat to stable society than a class of ignorant and vagabond children grown to adulthood.

> But for the instruction and advice received at the lodging-house more would doubtless go astray and be ruined. We do not wonder that lodging-houses and similar institutions do not save all, but that with their present means they save and help so many. How cheap is virtue; how costly is crime. For one a little money and care discreetly bestowed at the outset; for the other untold suffering, and losses, and expenses for courts and jails, and a ruined man at the end.

Through "the instrumentality of the newsboys' home and the society that maintains it," Alger concluded, many street Arabs "will grow up intelligent and useful citizens"—that is, responsible voters—"instead of outcasts and criminals."[34]

In the Newsboys' Lodging House, in short, Alger found at once an opportunity to practice what he called "practical beneficence," as well as a setting filled with characters he would recreate in his fictional world. Quite apart from his occasional contributions in cash to the support of the Lodge,[35] he wrote such novels as *Ragged Dick, Mark the Match Boy, Ben the Luggage Boy*, and *Rough and Ready* to advertise its work.

III

> *. . . it was not until I removed to New York and wrote 'Ragged Dick' that I scored a decided success.*
>
> —Horatio Alger, Jr.,
> "Writing Stories for Boys"

In October 1866, the Boston firm of Lee & Shepard issued a new novel by the Reverend Henry Morgan entitled *Ned Nevins, the Newsboy; or, Street Life in Boston.*[36] Morgan purported to depict realistically the juvenile pariahs of that city. At the suggestion of Joseph Allen, to whom he eventually dedicated the work "with friendly regard," Alger soon began to write a similar story for boys. The result was *Ragged Dick; or, Street Life in New York,* a brief tale serialized in monthly installments in Allen's magazine *Student and Schoolmate.* "The necessary information has been gathered mainly from personal observation and conversations with the boys," the author later averred, though Charles O'Connor had provided "some facts of which [I was] able to make use."[37] Despite his profession of a documentary strategy, Alger obviously sentimentalized his portrayal of street life. He did not stir the placid waters of his narrative stream with references either to violence or sex, the real poles of the street Arabs' planet.

On his part, Allen hardly acted the part of disinterested altruist. In October, the same month *Ned Nevins* appeared, William T. Adams had resigned from *Student and Schoolmate* to launch a competitor for Lee & Shepard.[38] Allen was grooming Alger partly to compensate for his loss. Thus his recommendation that Alger model a juvenile story after *Ned Nevins* was a strategic stroke: Lee & Shepard had raided his office for an editor. He retaliated by raiding their fall catalog for a plot.

Alger's story opened prosaically enough in the January 1867 issue of the magazine.[39] Decked out in a tattered coat and torn pants he claims were first worn by George Washington and Louis Napoleon, Dick arrives one morning at his boot-blacking station on Spruce Street. He has spent the night in a nearby alley. To be sure, Alger advised his readers, Dick "wasn't a model boy in all respects," but his grimy hero "was above doing anything mean or dishonorable. He would not steal, or cheat, or impose upon younger boys." He was a natural aristocrat whose innate nobility could not be hidden by dirt. "I hope my young readers will like him as I do," the author added. "Perhaps, although he was only a bootblack, they may find something in him to imitate."

In this first installment, Alger contrasted Dick with Johnny Nolan, the bootblack he had met at his friend's office a few months before. The author later claimed to have portrayed Johnny "as he was—a good natured but lazy boy, without enterprise or ambition."[40] At any rate, the contrast served as the springboard to a short sermon:

> Now, in the boot-blacking business, as well as in higher avocations, the same rule prevails, that energy and industry are rewarded, and indolence suffers. Dick was energetic and on the alert for business, but Johnny was

the reverse. The consequence was that Dick earned probably three times as much as the other.

The real Johnny Nolan seems not to have minded his role as foil to Our Hero. When the story was published, Alger "gave Johnny a copy" of it, "and he was quite proud of figuring in print."[41]

By chance, Dick is hired by a merchant to guide his nephew Frank Whitney around the city in exchange for a better suit of clothes. The next several chapters, like a Baedeker guidebook, highlight historical and other sites in New York, among them the Newsboys' Lodging House.

> "You told me," said Frank, "that there was a place where you could get lodging for five cents. Where's that?"
> "It's the Newsboys' Lodgin' House, on Fulton Street," said Dick, "up over the 'Sun' office. It's a good place. I don't know what us boys would do without it."

In the course of the day with Frank, Dick is exposed to refined habits for the first time, and he soon resolves "to turn over a new leaf, and try to grow up 'spectable," and receive at least a rudimentary education so that he can get a job "in an office or counting room." Frank's uncle reinforces his resolution: "I hope, my lad," he adjures Dick, "you will prosper and rise in the world. You know in this free country poverty in early life is no bar to a man's advancement. . . . Save your money, my lad, buy books, and determine to be somebody, and you may yet fill an honorable position." The next day, Dick takes a room on Mott Street, a move he considers his "first step towards respectability," and he decides to open a savings account.

He soon is accused by other street Arabs, in particular an Irish tough from the Five Points named Micky Maguire, of "putting on airs." Like the lazy Johnny Nolan, this bully also was modeled upon a real boy. As Alger later explained, "The original of 'Micky Maguire' was Paddy Shea, a tough character who lived not far from the City Hall, and generally passed the summer at 'the island.'"[42] In the story, Micky is a Tammany politician in training who would have "been prominent at ward meetings, and a terror to respectable voters on election day" were he but fifteen years older. He "not infrequently served" a term at the prison on Blackwell's Island as punishment for his "acts of ruffianism."

Slowly but surely, Dick rises from his low station. He invites a recent orphan, Henry Fosdick, to share his flat and tutor him. The two boys begin to frequent the home of one of Dick's old customers, a Mr. Greyson, who in turn recommends Fosdick for a position as clerk in a hat store, a job coveted by the snobbish Roswell Crawford, a conde-scending "son of a gentleman." Nine months later, Dick's period of gestation is complete. He has learned to read and write and has ac-quired the rudiments of arithmetic and geography. When he receives a letter from Frank Whitney, he is able both to read it and to compose a reply. While crossing Brooklyn Ferry in the penultimate chapter, Dick rescues a child who has fallen overboard. The child's father, James Rockwell, rewards him with another suit of clothes and a job in his counting house at a salary of ten dollars per week. The money is of small account, however, for Dick admits he would have accepted such a respectable white-collar position even if it paid him less than he had received as a bootblack. Alger concluded that

> It was indeed a bright prospect for a boy who, only a year before, could neither read nor write, and depended for a night's lodging upon the chance hospitality of an alley-way or old wagon. Dick's great ambition to "grow up 'spectable" seemed likely to be accomplished after all.

In his final incarnation, he is named Richard Hunter, Esq., "a young gentleman on the way to fame and fortune."

However coarse, it is one of the best yarns Alger ever spun. He introduced in it the major contrivances of his juvenile formula—a disadvantaged hero who rises from rags to respectability, a status only partly defined in economic terms; his receipt of a new suit of clothes, a symbolic rite of passage; and his patronage by benevolent adults. This latter device was by far the most significant structural innovation. Unlike the stories in Alger's early "Campaign series," the juvenile fiction he began to write in late 1866 contained a stock adult character, the Patron, whose role paralleled the part Alger had begun to assume among the street children of the city. He literally projected himself into the stories, which may in part explain his popularity among young readers. "A writer for boys should have abundant sympathy with them," he once declared. "He should be able to enter into their plans, hopes, and aspirations. He should learn to look upon life as they do. . . . A boy's heart opens to the man or writer who understands him."[43]

Alger's expectations for the serial, modest at best, were not dis-appointed, if only because publisher Allen orchestrated a crescendo of fanfare for it. As early as November 1866, two months before the first episode appeared, Allen puffed *Ragged Dick* in the magazine. "This story is drawn from life as it actually exists in the great metropolis," he asserted, "and will be sketched with that fidelity which actual observa-tion on the spot affords." In the February 1867 number, he reported that the first installment "had created no little excitement among our numerous readers, as we supposed it would. Everybody is delighted."[44] Though Alger originally planned a seven-part serial, he soon realized that he needed more space to do justice to the subject. When he asked if he might extend the story, Allen replied, as Alger remembered, "Yes; go ahead; make it as long as you like."[45] The serial eventually ran to twelve parts. Reader response to it was so favorable that in the spring Allen opened negotiations with Alger to insure his stories would remain a fixture in the magazine. On April 13, 1867, he announced the agreement he had reached with his new star contributor: "Horatio Alger, Jr., one of the best juvenile writers in the country, is exclusively engaged" to write for the *Student and Schoolmate*.[46] In truth, Allen had contracted for first magazine rights only. He would serialize a new Alger juvenile every year for the next six years, actually less than half of Alger's total work during this period. Though the exact terms of the agreement are unknown, Alger probably received about $350 per serial, or about thirty dollars per installment, about half what his ministerial salary had been. Allen lost few opportunities to plug Alger's work in editorial asides over the next several months. On one occasion he crowed that "Probably no magazine story has ever excited so much attention" as *Ragged Dick*. Not only did young people enjoy it, "but because of its naturalness and vigor it has equally interested their parents and adult friends. It cannot fail to place Mr. Alger at the head of successful writers for the young." This was no small praise for one whom Solomon Freeman had condemned only a few months before as morally unfit to write at all, especially for boys.

At the time Alger began to plan *Ragged Dick*, he "never dreamed" of issuing it later in book form.[47] However, in late 1867, in the final months of its run in the *Schoolmate*, he passed through Boston en route to South Natick and there visited his publisher A. K. Loring at his bookstore on Washington Street.[48] Loring congratulated him heartily on the story and reported that a number of people had recommended it to him, including a minister. Never reticent to capitalize on an opportunity, Loring asked to take a flyer on *Ragged Dick*, to bring it out as a book. He made what Alger considered a "liberal offer"—probably the standard royalty of ten percent, or twelve and a half cents for every copy sold at the retail price of $1.25—to revise and enlarge the serial and publish it as the first in a series of six juveniles mined from the same vein. Allen blessed the arrangement, apparently hoping more publicity for Alger's fiction would lift his own magazine sales. During the holidays he could offer a bound volume of *Student and Schoolmate* containing an entire Alger serial plus other works and a photographic likeness of the author for only a few cents more than Loring charged for the novel alone.[49] At first, Alger's fortunes were materially improved by the agreements he reached with Allen and Loring. Though he would hardly grow rich under their terms, he had entered upon a respectable profession at a reasonable salary much like Richard Hunter, Esq. A few months before, he had left Brewster disgraced and unemployed. Now he was a minor literary celebrity and, better yet, self-supporting. If ever there was an *annus mirablilis* in Alger's life, it was the year 1867.

With the story of Ragged Dick, in brief, Alger struck paydirt. In the course of its serialization, as he explained in the preface to the Loring edition, the tale had been "received with so many evidences of favor" by

Carte de visite of Alger about 1868, a bonus to subscribers to *Student and Schoolmate*.
Courtesy of the Harvard University Archives.

so many readers that he had agreed to write a "Ragged Dick series" depicting "the life and experiences of the friendless and vagrant children who are now numbered by thousands in New York and other cities." Though he hoped that the novels might "prove interesting as stories," he prayed they would have the larger "effect of enlisting the sympathies" of readers "in behalf of the unfortunate children whose life is described, and of leading them to co-operate with the praiseworthy efforts" of such organizations as the Children's Aid Society "to ameliorate their condition."[50] At Loring's suggestion, he padded the original story with elaborate descriptions of confidence games and five new chapters of local color.

The book-length *Ragged Dick* enjoyed immediate popularity. The first edition of several thousand copies was sold out within a few weeks of its publication on May 5, 1868,[51] and a second edition appeared in August.[52] It was the most popular story Alger ever wrote, technically his only best seller, and it remained continuously in print for at least forty years.[53] Booth Tarkington, who read it as a Hoosier schoolboy in the 1880s, later listed it among the ten books that had made the greatest impression on his life.[54] After it finally lapsed from print, its reputation only improved. In 1947, the Grolier Club of New York selected it as one of the hundred most influential American books published before 1900.[55]

Upon its publication, it was also received warmly, though not so effusively, by reviewers. It was hardly recognized instantly as a classic. The *Providence Evening Press* praised it as "simply charming" and cited Alger as "a sweet writer" with "a good heart behind his pen" who "will win the love of the lads and lasses." A few days later, on May 16, the *Boston Transcript* enthusiastically endorsed the story in terms Alger doubtless appreciated: By portraying "the courage, the ambition, the struggling nobility" of the street Arabs, the author had become "something more than a mere writer of juvenile books. He becomes the philanthropist, he touches the poet's sphere in thus opening up the secret beauty of human souls." The reviewer concluded that *Ragged Dick* "is Mr. Alger's best production so far." Allen lauded the novel in the *Student and Schoolmate*, and the reliable *Christian Register* plugged it as an "excellent story. . . . Mr. Alger has a clear insight into boy-nature, and knows how to touch their hearts and awaken the aspiration for good in them; he need not desire a nobler sphere than thus to plant good seed in the minds of the future man." In July, Rufus Ellis, an old friend of Alger *père*, described the novel in the *Monthly Religious Magazine* as "a spirited and inspiring book for children" and *Putnam's* touted it as "a much more valuable addition to the Sunday-school library than the tales of inebriates, and treatises on the nature of sin, that so often find place there."[56] In his preface to *Fame and Fortune*, the sequel published the following December, Alger acknowledged the "generous commendations" accorded *Ragged Dick* "by the Press."[57] He could not have guessed that, at the modest age of thirty-five, he had written his best book, and that he would try in vain the remainder of his life to surpass it by writing dozens of stories according to the same stale formula.

IV

As to . . . my own books there is undoubtedly a family resemblance . . . but I find this does not seem an objection to readers.

—Horatio Alger, Jr.,
23 December 1896

In the wake of his success with *Ragged Dick*, Alger was more prolific than ever. Between 1867 and mid-1873, when he took a brief respite from authorship, he wrote eighteen juvenile novels—an average of almost three per year—as well as occasional short stories, poems, and other pieces. He cranked out five more books in the "Ragged Dick series" on schedule—one every six months or so until, by Christmas 1870, he had fulfilled the terms of his original contract with Loring.

Unfortunately, compared with the other books in the series, *Ragged Dick* seems inspired. Like most sequels, *Fame and Fortune* was dull stuff.[58] Alger followed his formula to the letter, in effect merely rewriting the first story without the saving grace of its wit. He seemed wedded to the same plot and characters, unwilling or unable to break new ground. Perhaps he had begun to believe his notices. Dick still spends his evenings in study, engaged in a program of self-culture so ambitious it would have shamed Chautauquans. Having mastered the rudiments of arithmetic and geography, he adds French to the curriculum. Johnny Nolan still is poor and lazy. Micky Maguire and Roswell Crawford still are thug and snob, respectively, though near the close of the story Micky is converted "from a vagabond to a useful member of society"— that is, a responsible voter—through the agency of Our Hero. On his part, Dick succeeds to the position of bookkeeper in Mr. Rockwell's firm at the age of seventeen, is admitted to junior partnership at twenty-one, and marries Ida Greyson, the genteel daughter of his old patron, at twenty-four. In the *dénouement* Alger voiced his own fond fantasy:

"The past with its trials is over; the future expands before him, a bright vista of merited success." He dedicated the novel to his father, "from whom I have never failed to receive literary sympathy and encouragement."[59] The adjective seems a crucial qualifier.

Allen serialized the story during 1868 in the *Schoolmate*, and Loring issued it in book form on December 2, in time for Christmas sales. Alger wrote at least one of the ads for it which Loring placed in the *Boston Transcript*, and he plugged the book at the Newsboys' Lodging House.[60] His publicity campaign may have spurred sales of the book but had negligible effect on its critical reception. Reviews were polite but restrained. Though predicting it would win "the largest sale of any book for the holidays," for example, a reviewer for the *Boston Transcript* seemed more impressed by the decorations in Loring's bookstore.[61] Allen refused to puff the new book in the *Schoolmate* for the simple reason that he had set up to compete with Loring.[62] In his office at 203 Washington Street, a block from Loring's store, he offered for sale the "handsome illustrated octavo" volume of the magazine for 1868 containing the whole of *Fame and Fortune* plus "a number of other stories, essays, poems, declamations, and dialogues,—four pieces of music,— and the immense variety of agreeable things which go to make up a magazine for the young." All this for two dollars—only seventy-five cents more than Loring charged for the novel alone! Unfortunately, the juvenile market could not long sustain two separate editions of the same mediocre story. Allen's sales served largely to depress Loring's sales and, in turn, reduce Alger's royalties.

Under the circumstances, the author was prompted to write even more rapidly in an attempt to exploit his popularity. Loring issued *Mark the Match Boy*, the third volume in the series, on April 10, 1869.[63] In it, Alger reintroduced Dick and Fosdick as ancillary characters. The story focuses on an abandoned waif who, with their help, is reunited with his rich grandfather and finds "a comfortable and even luxurious home."[64] Alger clipped and saved the review of this novel which appeared on the front page of the *New York Evening Post* for April 22: "The author of the 'Ragged Dick series' of stories has been even more successful in New York than Greenwood in London, in depicting the street life of the great city," it read. "His sketches of the little Arabs of our streets are very life-like and effective, and there is a pathos in some of his descriptions that goes directly to the heart." Three years later, Alger quoted this notice verbatim in a brief autobiographical sketch he prepared at the request of new editors. By then, the comments were even less accurate than they had been in 1869.[65]

Alger wrote the final three stories in the series according to the same tired and tested formula. His titles seem but exercises in alliteration. He invented new names for his characters, but no new characters. The hero of *Rough and Ready*—serialized by Allen during 1869 and issued by Loring in December—is a newsboy with an alcoholic stepfather, otherwise indistinguishable from Ragged Dick. Johnny Nolan again serves as a convenient foil to Our Hero. On the whole, the tale reads like a temperance tract draped over a flimsy story line. In *Ben the Luggage Boy*—issued by Loring in 1870—Alger recounted the ostensibly "true history" of a young runaway from the rural districts, a friend of Rough and Ready, who earns his living in the city by "smashing" or carrying baggage.[66] He dedicated this novel to his invalid sister, Annie, who died unmarried, aged twenty-nine, at their parents' home in South Natick on April 7, two days after he completed the manuscript. In *Rufus and Rose*—serialized by Allen during 1870 and issued by Loring in November—Alger continued the flagging saga of Rufus Rushton, alias Rough and Ready, who closes the sequel, like Richard Hunter in *Fame and Fortune*, a junior partner in his patron's firm.

Reviewers greeted these later issues in the series with indifference, if not outright hostility. The simple charms and moral admonitions of *Ragged Dick* had dissolved in a rush of heavy-handed didacticism. As early as December 1869, in a review of *Rough and Ready*, the *Nation* warned that Alger seemed bent upon self-parody and excoriated him for portraying newsboys as paragons of virtue. Alger had no excuse "for doing as he has done," the reviewer complained. "The newsboy is not a Christian of the first two centuries." Rather, "he smokes ends of cigars which he picks up in the streets. . . . The newsboys who read 'Rough and Ready,' however they may approve it as a work of fiction, will say 'my eye' when asked to lay it to heart and make it a practical guide." Similarly, a reader for Henry Ward Beecher's *Christian Union* protested that *Ben the Luggage Boy* had "far too many words in proportion to the matter." The *Boston Transcript* damned *Rufus and Rose* with faint praise, merely allowing that the tale "will not disappoint those who are eagerly looking for it."[67] Disinterested readers, apparently, should beware.

Despite their literary demerits, the six stories in the "Ragged Dick series" generally sold well because they were an acceptable alternative to the more sensational fare of dime novels and more interesting than conventional Sunday-school literature. In 1872, Alger estimated total sales of all six titles at 60,000; in 1888, his estimate was 150,000; and in 1890, it was 180,000.[68] His expectations for the books were more than realized. "Hundreds of Sunday-school libraries bought them," he bragged, "and they were read in every State and Territory in the Union."[69]

The popularity of the series had a predictable, though not entirely welcome, side-effect: Alger became something of a celebrity. He was willing to submit to publicity so long as it served to boost his sales. He began to receive requests for his autograph as soon as *Ragged Dick* appeared, and he always obliged. While visiting his family in Massachusetts over the Christmas holidays in 1869, he helped to promote *Student and Schoolmate* by meeting young subscribers in Allen's office on Washington Street in Boston.[70] With Alger as his star contributor, Allen later noted, "It is no wonder that our bound volumes for the last two years have been so much in demand." In the first bloom of his slender fame, Alger even complied with a request from a playing card company in Worcester, Massachusetts, to provide a portrait suitable for reproduction in a game of "Authors."[71] (He sent one of the photos Allen

Alger in 1872 at the twenty-year reunion of the Harvard College Class of 1852.

gave gratis to subscribers, and he subsequently appeared in the "Moral and Religious" suit along with Henry Ward Beecher, Edward Everett Hale, and T. S. Arthur, author of the temperance tract *Ten Nights in a Barroom and What I Saw There.*) Throughout his years in the public eye, however, Alger carefully concealed the circumstances of his dismissal from the pulpit in Brewster. He sometimes implied that he had never in fact been ordained. Even though he had claimed the title of "Reverend" immediately upon completing his ministerial course in 1860, even though he signed dozens of stories "Rev. Horatio Alger, Jr." during the mid-1860s, he asked a correspondent in 1869 to "Be kind enough in addressing me to omit the 'Rev' as I wish my name identified only with the literary profession."[72] Charles Lowe would have approved. In 1891, Alger responded to an inquiry from the secretary of his Harvard class, who was planning the forty-year reunion, with a blunt declaration: "My life has been strictly literary."[73] The less said about his nonliterary life the better. As late as 1896, he wrote a close friend that "I studied theology chiefly as a branch of literary culture and without any intention of devoting myself to it as a profession."[74] Under the circumstances, perhaps such deceit was warranted. His *fin de siècle* reputation as a gentleman and as a "moral and religious" author could not have long survived scrutiny under the limelight.

Though he harbored larger literary ambitions, Alger acceded to popular and publishers' demands for more juvenile stories. Even before he completed the "Ragged Dick series," he contracted with Loring to write a comparable six-volume series about poor country boys who struggle against adversity and rise to respectability. He designed each novel in this "Luck and Pluck series" to illustrate the idea "that a manly spirit is better than the gifts of fortune. Early trial and struggle, as the history of the majority of our successful men abundantly attests, tend to strengthen and invigorate the character."[75] In the title volume (1869), the hero, temporarily denied his birthright by an evil stepmother, at length obtains both his inheritance and a classical education. A reviewer for *Peterson's* described it as "a well-written story" with an "excellent moral"—standard fare.[76]

Alger varied the recipe but little in the next five novels in the series— *Sink or Swim* (1870), *Strong and Steady* (1871), *Strive and Succeed* (1871), *Try and Trust* (1871), and *Bound to Rise* (1873). Even the notices of these novels sound alike. A reviewer of *Strong and Steady*, which Alger modeled in part upon Taylor's *John Godfrey's Fortunes*, noted that "Mr. Alger has not lost the charm of his fascinating pen in painting boy-life." The Boston *Literary World* suggested that *Strive and Succeed* "manifests a remarkably correct knowledge of boy-nature," and *Youth's Companion* commended it as "a very admirable specimen of the right kind of story-telling for boys." According to the *Boston Transcript*, Alger was "a favorite storyteller with the boys," and *Try and Trust* would but "add to his popularity."[77] Years later, Clarence Day would recall reading several "Luck and Pluck" stories as a boy, adding that "they seemed to be right on my level, or not too much above it."[78] However predictable the formula by which the stories were written, in early 1873 Loring ordered two more "Luck and Pluck" tales and raised the price of each book in the series to $1.50. They were not best sellers, but they made money.

Though these stories were no less didactic than those in the "Ragged Dick series," Alger soft-pedaled in them his appeals on behalf of the Children's Aid Society and other charities. Perhaps for this reason Allen chose not to claim serialization rights to them. In fact, Allen had nearly decided to suspend publication of the *Schoolmate*, which was badly beaten in the subscription wars. By the middle of 1871, the magazine was a poor fourth and fast fading behind *Our Young Folks, Oliver Optic's Magazine,* and *Merry's Museum* among juvenile monthlies published in Boston. Allen had lost the edge on the competition because he no longer could publish more than a small fraction of the works the prolific Alger produced. His star contributor had found other buyers for his stories, often placing them with Allen's out-of-town competitors. Three of the first six "Luck and Pluck" tales appeared serially in *Young Israel,* two appeared in *Ballou's,* and the other in the *New York Weekly.*

Meanwhile, Alger had contracted to begin another cycle of books. As the *Boston Transcript* reported on April 22, 1871, "The success of 'The Ragged Dick Series' has led to the commencement, by A. K. Loring, of 'The Tattered Tom Series' from the story-telling pen of Horatio Alger."[79] He had been persuaded to continue the earlier series with six more novels about "other phases of street life" and "other classes of street Arabs," though cut from the same bolt of fabric according to the same simple pattern. In the title volume (1871), as if to betray his own sexual insecurity, Alger allowed that "It was not quite easy to determine" whether his protagonist "was a boy or a girl."[80] As it happens, "Tom" is a petticoated streetsweeper named Jane Lindsay who eventually blossoms into a genteel young lady. Though granting that Alger had "evidently studied his subject with care, and drawn his portrait from life," Lyman Abbott thought "the first part of his story, which contains the street Arab," by far "the best part of the book."[81]

Because the "Tattered Tom" stories were lineal descendants from

Ragged Dick, Allen exercised his option to two of them. In *Paul the Peddler*, serialized in the *Schoolmate* during 1871, Alger depicted the early struggles of an enterprising young merchant who, by novel's end, owns a necktie stand from which he nets ten to fifteen dollars a week. The author dedicated the book, which Loring issued in October, to his "dear friend" Charles Davies Scudder, a physician who specialized in the prevention and treatment of venereal disease.[82] The sequel, *Slow and Sure*, in which Paul rises "from the humble position of a street merchant to be the proprietor of a shop," was the last Alger story Allen printed even in part.[83] In October 1872, before the serial had closed, he folded *Student and Schoolmate*. Allen went on to lecture in ecclesiastical history at Harvard and to edit the *Unitarian Review*. Alger took the chance to negotiate serial rights to his stories with new publishers.

He quickly struck a bargain. Alger had contributed his story "Marie Bertrand" to the *New York Weekly* in 1864, and he had placed *Try and Trust*, one of the overflow from the *Schoolmate*, with the *Weekly* in the spring of 1871 under the serial title "Abner Holden's Bound Boy." The publishers, Francis S. Street and Francis S. Smith, were so pleased by reader response to this story that, when Allen's monthly collapsed and Alger was contractually free, they deemed "the gifted author an attractive card" and "therefore induced him to become a regular contributor" to their magazine.[84] In 1869, they had agreed to pay Edward Z. C. Judson ("Ned Buntline") about twenty thousand dollars a year to write sensational Westerns, particularly about the adventures of Buffalo Bill.[85] Though Alger earned much less money, he received more than Allen had paid him—the *Weekly* claimed a circulation of 300,000—and he was assured a steady market for his work.[86] Though sales of his individual titles had declined, he still earned about $3500 annually from his writing—the equivalent of about $35,000 in inflated modern currency.[87]

Thus in the spring of 1873 Alger politely declined an invitation to write for *St. Nicholas*, a juvenile monthly planned by Scribner's. "Horatio Alger, Jr., finds that his contract with another periodical will not allow him to write for us," assistant editor Frank Stockton—later the author of "The Lady or the Tiger?"—explained in a memo to the publisher.[88] Alger apparently did not lament his missed opportunity to write for a prestigious juvenile magazine. Over the years, in fact, he grew quite fond of his new publishers. Francis Street, the senior partner, had gone to work at the age of twelve, later worked as a printer, and bought the *Weekly* for forty thousand dollars in 1857. He would die a millionaire in 1883.[89] Street occasionally suggested story titles to Alger, and, on his part, the writer dedicated his novel *Jack's Ward* to him in 1875. Alger wrote Street in 1879 that "In all my stories and books I have labored to induce boys to rise in the world by precisely the same means, which have helped you to rise. The example of individuals is of more value than the appeals of writers, and you may unconsciously by your success have led to the success of many others."[90] Similarly, Alger often met Francis Smith, the junior partner, socially during the 1870s. "His cordial and genial manners and warmth of heart impressed me," Alger recalled upon Smith's death in 1887. "It was always a pleasure to me to return his warm and kindly greeting."[91]

At the behest of his new publishers, Alger began at once to write more sensational and violent fiction. If he had spoon-fed Allen's audience a diet so bland that many had lost appetite, then he would add a dash of spice to his stories for the *Weekly*. He alluded casually to such titillating topics as murder, suicide, insanity, and vast wealth. Whereas Allen had refused "Friar Anselmo," apparently because he thought it a too-free treatment of a death wish, the *Weekly* editors snapped it up.[92] It appeared in the same issue, dated August 5, 1872, as the first installment of Alger's serial *Brave and Bold*, the title story in his new "Brave and Bold series" of sensational juveniles.[93] The hero of this horrifying tale at one point defends an old man by shooting a ruffian in the shoulder. This villain later is stabbed in the heart and killed. Another character commits suicide by drowning. The hero ends the story "in easy circumstances" and "promises in time to become a prominent and wealthy merchant." Alger's "The Western Boy," serialized in the *Weekly* in mid-1873, entertained its readers with similar escapades. A brute is tempted at one point to spring upon the hero "and pound him to a jelly." The hero eventually reclaims his inheritance of $150,000 from the villain who had defrauded him. This was a far cry indeed from the insipid stories Allen had serialized. Alger tailored his formula to a new audience, retaining the basic plot outline and stock characters but sensationalizing details, and he seemed pleased with the result. "The Western Boy" was later translated into Norwegian,[94] and, as Alger wrote Robert Bonner of the *New York Ledger*, in 1879, "The publisher of the London Reader told me [*Brave and Bold*] was the only juvenile serial which the Reader had ever copied." Reprinted in England in the fall of 1872, the story was as successful there as in America, he bragged. It was "the sort of story that I should like to write for the Ledger." Given the chance, "I should look to its favorable reception with a good deal of confidence."[95] Bonner declined the offer.

Though as a boy Theodore Dreiser read *Brave and Bold* behind a barn in Indiana,[96] and though as boys both Carl Sandburg and William Shirer read "The Western Boy" under its later and more popular reprint title *Tom the Bootblack*,[97] reviewers almost unanimously replied to Alger's mild blood-and-thunder with crossed knives. In *St. Nicholas*—the very magazine that had invited Alger to contribute to its pages only a few months before—a reader complained that *Brave and Bold* "is of the 'sensational' order, while the characters are such as we do not meet in real life—and we are very glad we don't meet them." It "appears more hurriedly composed than some of the author's other works."[98] It was the last review of an Alger novel the magazine printed, and presaged a literary controversy over sensationalism in juvenile fiction which smouldered for over a decade.

The suspension of the *Schoolmate* also allowed Alger to mend fences with the publishers Lee & Shepard. In May 1872, with the collapse of the magazine imminent, he recommended to them the work of Charles A. Fosdick ("Harry Castlemon"), author of the "Gunboat series" of books published in Cincinnati. Fosdick wished "to make arrangements with some Eastern publisher for the publication of a new series of books, of an adventurous character," Alger explained. "Loring, I know, does not want to take any additional juvenile authors, and I know of no house which I could more conscientiously recommend to a juvenile author than yours."[99] Lee & Shepard had no room for Castlemon either—he subsequently signed with Henry T. Coates & Co. of Philadelphia—but Alger had made an overture of friendship after years of cutthroat competition. When, the following November, Lee & Shepard suffered a loss of over fifty thousand dollars in the Great Boston Fire, Alger was even more conciliatory.[100] All the publishers on Washington Street near the Old South Church had been threatened with devastating losses of both inventories and plates, and some sixty acres of warehouses had been consumed. Fearing the worst, Alger had rushed to Boston "and learned that Loring had had a narrow escape. But for my brief stay," he wrote Lee & Shepard, he would have stepped down the street and "called on you also. In these days authors and publishers are naturally interested in each others' welfare and prosperity. There is not that natural antagonism which was once supposed to exist."[101] Let the dead bury the dead. Alger had learned well the lesson of Brewster.

V

If the story of "Phil the Fiddler," in revealing for the first time to the American public the hardships and ill-

> *treatment of these wandering musicians, shall excite an*
> *active sympathy in their behalf, the author will feel abun-*
> *dantly repaid for his labors.*
>
> —HORATIO ALGER, JR.,
> preface to *Phil the Fiddler*

The assertion in his preface notwithstanding, the horrors of the
padrone system were discussed in the New York press as early as March
1868.[102] Thousands of native Italian children had been legally inden-
tured to *padroni* or overseers, carried to American port cities, and there
forced to beg or steal for a living. To his credit, Alger was so troubled by
this flagrant exploitation that he decided in the winter of 1871 to
investigate it. "I found, at the outset, unusual difficulty on account of
the inadequate information" available about the children, he later
admitted, so he tried without much success to interview them in
Italian.[103] He eventually sought out A. E. Cerqua, superintendent of the
Italian school at the Five Points, a "thoroughly vicious district" in lower
Manhattan[104] which had not appreciably changed in the thirty years
since Dickens described it in his *American Notes* as "reeking everywhere with dirt and filth."[105] Through Cerqua, Alger met G. F. Secchi de
Casale, editor of the weekly newspaper *Eco d' Italia*, from whom he
"obtained full and trustworthy information."[106] He presumed to write a
social novel in the tradition of Dickens and Stowe, and he even insisted
when he finished the manuscript that an Italian street musician sit for
the frontispiece to the book.[107] In *Phil the Fiddler*, Alger again appealed
to his readers to help abused children. He struck once more the humanitarian notes he had sounded in his earliest tales of street life in New
York.

However, in *Phil* more than in any other novel Alger wrote, his
altruistic impulses were at war with his formula. Like Stowe, he tried to
raise an issue and galvanize public opinion by writing a popular novel,
which obliged him in turn to observe the conventions of sentimental
fiction. His dilemma may be simply summarized: His angry story had to
end happily. Stowe had succeeded despite the conventional param-
eters, and Alger envied her achievement. He once wrote that "all the
efforts of all the anti-slavery orators sink into insignificance compared
with the work of this plain and unassuming woman."[108] In *Phil the
Fiddler* he imitated Stowe's story to the point of parody.[109] His opening
chapters detail abuses to human dignity permitted by a peculiar institution. Alger's hero Filippo and his young friend Giacomo, the Neapolitan
incarnations of Dick and Fosdick, are flogged. Like Uncle Tom, Giacomo dies and, like Eliza, Phil escapes from bondage across an icy river

(though in this case to New Jersey). There he is rescued from a snow drift by a kind doctor and his wife, who nurse him to health and adopt him.

> So our little hero had drifted into a snug harbor. His toils and privations were over. And for the doctor and his wife it was a glad day also. On Christmas day four years before they had lost a child. On this Christmas, God had sent them another to fill the void in their hearts.

Insofar as Alger detailed the plight of these Italian children, he risked losing a juvenile audience inured to dime-novel westerns. Insofar as he adopted the conventions of melodrama, he blunted the point of his protest.

Predictably, the novel neither sold especially well nor appreciably influenced the reform movement upon its publication by Loring in April 1872. Alger could not serve two masters. To be sure, the Boston *Literary World* commended the author for his graphic depiction of the suffering children, and the *Boston Transcript* concluded that "No one can follow [Phil's] fortunes without a strong desire that such inhuman slavery should be made to cease by the strong arm of the law." But the novel was ignored completely by the major New York dailies.[110] Incredibly, Alger would claim in 1885 that within six months of publication the padrone system "was effectually broken up, not only in New York but in all the large cities of America."[111] He reiterated the assertion a decade later, declaring in an interview that *Phil* "was largely instrumental in breaking up the tyrannical padrone system by which poor Italian boys were brought to this country and made to work long hours on starvation wages."[112] There is no evidence to corroborate this claim. Apart from Alger's own statements, no contemporary source credited *Phil the Fiddler* with a significant role in reforming the system. Indeed, in April 1873, a year after its publication, over three hundred *padroni* children, all under fourteen and most under eight years of age, landed at the port of New York.[113] The system was not rooted out and broken up for years.

VI

. . . one's education is never complete, and those who attain eminence in any branch confess themselves perpetual learners.

—HORATIO ALGER, JR.,
Strive and Succeed

He was both a man of letters and an author of juvenile stories, a classical scholar whose compromised ambitions permitted him to write for boys, a Phi Beta Kappan who alluded in pulp fiction to Shakespeare and Milton, Raphael and Jenny Lind, the "Essay on Man" and *Il Trovatore*. Though a defrocked minister, he was an experienced and accomplished teacher. Not long after moving to New York he was offered another chance to teach. He made the most of it.

Joseph Seligman, one of the richest men in America and founder of the international banking house of J. & W. Seligman Co., required a tutor for his five sons. He wished to hire someone who might double as a guardian during the frequent and prolonged illnesses of his wife, Babet. That Alger was qualified for the post is indisputable; how he came to be a candidate for it, however, is open to speculation. Perhaps his charitable work among the street Arabs brought him to the attention of Seligman, a patron of the German Hebrew Orphan Asylum. Perhaps he applied for the job through the office of George W. Childs, for whose short-lived paper *Our Daily Fare* Alger had written during the Civil War. Childs was a neighbor of the Seligmans in the resort town of Long Branch, on the New Jersey coast. In any case, Alger was hired by banker Seligman much as Ragged Dick had been hired by banker Rockwell. By the first of January 1869, he was firmly ensconced in an upper room of the brownstone mansion at 26 West 34th Street, which Joseph Seligman leased from John Jacob Astor III and which years later would be razed to make way for the Empire State Building.[114]

Alger lived in the house and tutored the sons—David Joseph, Isaac Newton, George Washington, Edwin Robert Anderson, and Alfred Lincoln—for the next several years.[115] Occasionally he ran errands for the family, or escorted the boys on out-of-town holidays. He took the job, it seems, to supplement his income. He kept it, clearly enough, out of affection for the Seligmans. He was a regular Sunday dinner guest in their home long after the close of his formal tenure there. Joseph Seligman had reason to be pleased by the quality of instruction his sons received. "Mr. Alger was in the office Saturday and said that he thought Ike, George, and Eddie passed their examinations in good shape," he wrote Babet in June 1872. "George excelled in Latin, Eddie in mathematics, and Ike should also rank high."[116] Alger prepared the four youngest boys—Isaac, George, Edwin, and Alfred—for admission to Columbia College. All earned their degrees. Isaac graduated *cum laude* in 1876. Edwin later completed a Ph.D. and studied at the universities of Berlin, Heidelberg, Geneva, and Paris. "Until the age of eleven I was tutored at home and had the pleasure to have Horatio Alger, Jr., as my teacher," E. R. A. Seligman recalled in his autobiography. "I am indebted to him for a sense of good literature and a solid grounding in the classical languages."[117]

Unfortunately, Alger was both a lax disciplinarian and more diminutive than his charges. As a result, he was often the butt of their boyish pranks.[118] According to George Hellman, a nephew of the Seligman sons who as a child knew Alger from his visits to the mansion, "the little, unassertive tutor" tolerated "a great deal from the lads who greatly liked him, but could not refrain from taking occasional advantage of his lack of authority." Sometimes they tried to drop hot wax from a burning candle onto his balding pate. Once, according to family tradition, several Seligman sons and cousins were wrestling in the schoolroom in the garret of the brownstone. Rosie Seligman, wife of Joseph's brother James, climbed the stairs to ask Alger to identify the culprits. "Her sons and nephews knew from experience that the angry woman would be able to wring the facts from their easily dominated tutor, and that subsequent punishment would be severe," as Hellman told the story. The only escape "was through the temporary disappearance of Mr. Alger. So the boys opened a large trunk and hurriedly placed the little fellow in it" with instructions "to keep perfectly quiet. After their Aunt Rosie, baffled, had departed, they helped their tutor out, with many thanks for having uttered no syllable. He, as was his usual custom, forgave them. He loved the boys—always forgave them. He loved all boys."

Even as adults, the Seligman sons delighted in teasing their old teacher during his regular Sunday visits. Their pranks became the stuff of family legend. One of them would routinely place Alger's arm around Helene, their ugly-duckling sister, in a "warm embrace," whereupon Helene's husband, "affecting furious jealousy would rush at Horatio with a carving knife." After dinner, Alger

> always had a game of billiards with one of his former charges, usually Isaac or George. He was very nearsighted—very nearsighted indeed. So nearsighted that when, in the course of the game, George replaced one of the red balls with an equally red apple, Mr. Alger never distinguished the fruit from the ivory. Bang went his cue, and smash went the apple. Sunday after Sunday the little comedy was repeated.

Hellman admitted that "all this sounds rather silly but, in a manner of speaking, it was ritual and had to be observed."

During the period of his employment in the Seligman home, Alger continued to write, of course, often snatching moments between lessons to pen a few words. Apparently at the elder Seligman's suggestion, he began in 1871 to contribute a serial each year to *Young Israel*, a practice he continued until 1878. He dedicated the Loring editions of many of these and other novels to the Seligman children and their friends. All was not sweetness and games in the mansion, however. On June 25, 1872, for example, three days after reporting to his employer the favorable progress of his pupils, Alger asked for a raise from fifty to a hundred dollars a month and that the increase be made retroactive to April 1. He also asked for an extended vacation the next summer so that he might go to Europe. He was able to earn more money by writing than by teaching, he explained, and required additional compensation for the time he devoted to the boys' lessons. As Joseph wrote Babet Seligman the next day,

> I told Alger yesterday evening that I would first check with you before I responded to his crude request for a salary increase from 600 to 1200 dollars, in addition to three months vacation from July until October 1873 and, the best yet, double salary for the past three months. Yet he admitted that he saved $3000 from writing his books in the last year. I am willing to defer to your opinion, but I am prepared this time to hire another tutor who is more energetic.[119]

The disagreement was eventually resolved. Alger was granted the extended vacation, for he traveled to Europe the next year; and he apparently received a raise, though perhaps not as much as he requested, for he continued to live in the home and would tutor the Seligman sons until 1877. Over the years, in fact, Alger reached an accommodation with Joseph Seligman. The two men often spent the evening together in the library. "He closed a day engrossed by business cares," Alger reflected upon Seligman's death in 1880, "in the delightful companionship of the master spirits in the domain of literature and science."[120]

Such testimony ought not be discounted as the tribute of an ignorant hack. Alger did not live in an intellectual vacuum, however banal his fiction. He occasionally socialized during his New York years with old Harvard classmates, notably the jurists Joseph Choate and Addison Brown.[121] In 1869, he joined the Harvard Club of New York, and, on February 23, he attended the third annual dinner of the club at Delmonico's, the fashionable restaurant on Broadway.[122] Henry Bellows, a local Unitarian minister and a founding member, declared in his opening remarks that "all the wisest and best men of Boston society were educated at Harvard," a claim unchallenged by this audience. The company toasted the memory of the late Jared Sparks and then sang the ode composed for the occasion "by Horatio Alger, of Boston" to the tune of "Fair Harvard."

> Though dimmed are our hopes, and our visions are fled,
>   Our dreams were but dreams, it is true;
> Dust-stained from the contest we gather to-night,
>   The sweet dreams of youth to renew.
> Enough for to-morrow the cares it shall bring,
>   We are boys, we are brothers, to-night;
> And our hearts, warm with love, Alma Mater, to thee,
>   Shall in loyal devotion unite.[123]

It was not great poetry. It was no more than a brief item on an overlong program. It was first published on a menu. But it was well received. Graduates of Harvard, eminent men in their professions, sang lyrics he had written. He must have been thrilled. A few moments later William Cullen Bryant rose and declared that "some of the most renowned" American literati—"the majority, perhaps, of our most famous poets— are nurselings of Harvard." The officers of the club may have construed Bryant's remark as praise for Alger, among others. At their invitation, at any rate, he composed the ode sung at each of the next four dinners of the Club.

The dinner held on the evening of February 11, 1870, was another memorable fête.[124] On the dais were Charles Eliot, the new president of Harvard; O. B. Frothingham, one of the founders and first president of the Free Religious Association; George Putnam, publisher of the magazine that bore his name; and E. L. Godkin, editor of the *Nation*. After an address by Eliot, the hundred men in attendance sang "in chorus to fine effect" Alger's latest ode, according to the *New York Times*. The lyrics again struck a nostalgic note.

> As we meet in thy name, Alma Mater, to-night,
>   All our hearts and our hopes are as one,
> And love for the mother that nurtured his youth
>   Beats high in the breast of each son.
> The sweet chords of memory bridge o'er the past,
>   The years fade away like a dream,
> By the banks of Cephissus, beneath the green trees,
>   We tread thy fair walks, Academe.[125]

Frothingham next delivered a long toast to the reverend clergy in which he declared that there was "less rowdyism, less violence, more gentlemanlyness" among modern Harvard students despite the curricular

reforms which deemphasized the study of religion. Ironically, the conclusion of his remarks was "greeted with prolonged cheers." The party
lasted until after midnight.

The scene was reenacted with minor variations in each of the next
three years. On February 22, 1871, Edward Everett Hale and Bryant
offered toasts.[126] On February 1, 1872, Alger's classmate William
Choate presided.[127] Despite inclement weather, the dinner on February
21, 1873, was attended by James Freeman Clarke, another founding
member of the old Transcendentalist Club; Parke Godwin, one of the
editors of the original *Putnam's*; and Frederick Law Olmsted, the
landscape architect who had designed Central Park.[128] Always the
assembly sang together a crude but serviceable three-stanza paean to
Fair Harvard composed for the occasion by Horatio Alger, Jr.[129]

He had rebuilt his life during the years since he had arrived in New
York adrift and destitute of career. "The last seven years have been busy
ones with me," he confided to a friend in February 1873, a week after
the Harvard Club dinner that year. "I have now in press my twenty-
second book (18 juveniles) besides which I have contributed considerable matter to magazines & papers which has not yet been issued in
book form."[130] Though he admitted his claims to literary respectability
were "but slender," his rehabilitation was complete. His family had
remained loyal to him through the years. In appreciation, he invited his
parents, his brother Frank, and his sister Augusta and her husband
Amos Cheney to join him on a grand tour of Europe at his expense. Like
one of his heroes, he had been industrious and frugal. On Saturday,
June 7, in the crisp morning air, the six of them boarded the steamship
Greece bound from New York harbor for Liverpool.[131] Solomon Freeman
had thought Alger would soon sink into the lake of fire. Instead, he had
learned, if not to swim, at least to stay afloat.

4.

Facing the World

(1873–1887)

I

He could not help wishing that he were the possessor of the magic carpet mentioned in the Arabian tale, upon which the person seated had only to wish himself to be transported anywhere, and he was carried there in the twinkling of an eye.

—HORATIO ALGER, JR.,
Joe's Luck

Alger was a cub among the literary lions who sailed to Europe in 1873. James Russell Lowell and Edward Everett Hale were prominent among the Boston Brahmins on the continent that summer, and the upstart westerner Mark Twain returned to England in May to plan a sequel to his *Innocents Abroad*—a project he eventually abandoned. Those visits were well publicized. In contrast, Alger and his family traveled in virtual anonymity.

Unlike his first trip to Europe in 1860–61, moreover, Alger's grand tour in 1873 was desultory. For several weeks after they docked in Liverpool, the family toured the British Isles. Among their stops was the elaborate Gothic mansion at Abbotsford, on the Tweed River south of Edinburgh, which Sir Walter Scott had built with the proceeds from the Waverley romances.[1] Sometime in July the Algers and Cheneys reached London. While in the city, Horatio, Jr., took the liberty to look up the editor of the London *Reader*, which had serialized *Brave and Bold* the year before.[2] The party took a "leisurely course from London, staying three weeks in Paris, visiting the interior of France, and spending some weeks in Switzerland and northern Italy."[3] During his residence at a hotel in the Bernese Alps, Alger completed the last chapters of *Bound to Rise*, another book in the "Tattered Tom series."[4] When the summer heat began to wane, the family slipped south to Italy—first to Milan, then to Verona, finally to Venice.

Alger later reminisced in detail about his visit to the city on the Adriatic. "Venice justifies all that has been said or imagined about her," he declared. He had been reading Howells's *Venetian Life*. From the moment of his arrival, Alger felt as though he had reached a special spot on the globe. The Algers and Cheneys traveled by gondola from the train depot to their hotel, the San Marco, which faced the famous square of the same name. Horatio, Jr., was evidently pinching lire, for the hotel was first cousin to a fleabag, "a favorite resort for mosquitoes" which were "unremitting in their attentions" despite its location. Soon after registering, the Alger brothers crossed the piazza to St. Mark's Cathedral and the Palace of the Doges. Later, they climbed the adjacent bell tower to gaze upon the city and the sea. With the rest of his family, Horatio *fils* toured the catacombs and crossed the Bridge of Sighs. In all, Venice impressed him during his brief stay as perhaps "a third-rate port" but "a most wonderful city."[5]

From Italy, the travelers swept north and east to the Vienna Exhibition, an early type of world's fair. Like one of his characters, Alger wandered among the displays "surrounded by triumphs of art and skill gathered from all parts of the world."[6] By late September they had passed through Germany and returned to England. On October 1 they left per the steamer *Italy* for New York, landing eleven days later.[7] En route, Alger befriended Charles Pratt, a boy from Rahway, New Jersey, to whom he subsequently dedicated a novel.[8] Ironically, his trip abroad had again coincided with domestic disaster. During his first European tour the Civil War had erupted. During his second European tour a panic on Wall Street sparked the longest and most severe economic depression Americans had yet known. Though barely forty years old, Alger never returned to Europe. Perhaps he felt he ought to spare the nation another absence.

To protect his sensitive lungs from the soot and smells of New York, Alger usually escaped the city during the summer months, most often to New England.[9] So regular were his visits to his parents' home in South Natick that, in 1874, he joined the Natick Historical Society, over which his father presided. Later, he became a member of the Natick

Woman's Suffrage League, which his sister Augusta founded.[10] The parsonage of the Eliot Church of South Natick was declared a National Historic Landmark in 1972, even though Alger, Jr., never claimed it as his permanent residence.[11] Occasionally he selected other retreats. For example, in 1875, toward the end of his vacation from books and boys, he headed west from South Natick, his first extended trip in that direction since he declined the call to Alton a dozen years before. On August 12 he reigstered at the Sherman House in Chicago, "one of the noted buildings in the lake city" he later declared, located at the corner of Clark and Randolph streets. The visit was mostly recreational—a hiatus from deadlines and other obligations. A week later, he checked out and returned east.[12] Back in New York, he was soon busy packing and moving from the Seligman mansion—only Alfred, the youngest son, remained to be tutored at home—to a flat at 133 East 46th Street. His summer vacation left little impression on him. For the next decade, Alger alluded to Chicago infrequently in his stories. But before long he would travel west with literary purpose.

II

An author's compensation consists less in the checks he receives from his publishers than in the evidences of appreciation [he receives from his readers]. Few adopt the literary profession as a means of gaining a livelihood. The true author finds the greatest pleasure in his work.

—HORATIO ALGER, JR.,
16 March 1894

By the mid-1870s, Alger confronted an imposing array of problems. He had overworked to the point of exhaustion the plot of a boot-black/newsboy/baggage smasher who rises from the alley way to Broad-way. "My sales of books have of course fallen off with the times," he admitted in the summer of 1877.[13] Even as his sales dipped, reviewers harped on the contrived incidents and unrealistic characters that were his staple. Yet Alger continued to manufacture juvenile novels during these years. No less than twelve different, albeit not exactly new stories appeared from his pen between mid-1873 and the end of 1877.

He tested a number of alternatives to his stale formula. At first, he timidly improvised on his standard theme by depicting country boys who struggle against adversity in the city. In such tales as *Only an Irish Boy* (1874), *The Young Outlaw* (1875), and its sequel *Sam's Chance*

(1876), he tried to negotiate a middle course between the Scylla of blood-and-thunder dime novels and the Charybdis of bloodlessly banal Sunday-school primers. He was not entirely successful. W. D. Howells later satirized *The Young Outlaw* and *Sam's Chance* in his novel *The Minister's Charge*.[14] Alger also rewrote his old adult novel *Timothy Crump's Ward*, a revision of his still earlier *New York Sun* serial "The Cooper's Ward," for a juvenile audience and published it in 1875 under the title *Jack's Ward*. His experiment failed. A reviewer for the *Independent*, for example, averred that while some of Alger's stories were "breezy and entertaining," this one savored of pap.[15] Alger increasingly borrowed incidents and characters from more respected works in a desperate effort to find suitable material for his own fiction. He modeled parts of *Bound to Rise* (1873) and its sequel *Risen from the Ranks* (1874) upon Benjamin Franklin's memoirs, recently published in an authorized American edition. He depicted a hunter in *Try and Trust* (1873) who was little more than a caricature of Cooper's Leatherstocking. He studded his stories of the 1870s and 1880s with characters and incidents borrowed from Dickens, Melville, and Mark Twain.[16] Among the stars in the American literary firmament, Alger was a moon dimly reflecting others' brilliance.

He stubbornly tried yet another tack. Despite his reputation as a writer for boys, he had not abandoned all hope of winning renown as a serious artist. He never entirely renounced his early ambition to write for adults. As early as the summer of 1869, barely a year after the appearance of *Ragged Dick* in bookstores, he contributed an adult serial, "Ralph Raymond's Heir," to *Gleason's Literary Companion*.[17] Because he had assigned Joseph Allen first rights to serials published under his name, he signed the pen name "Arthur Hamilton" to this forgettable tale of a failing merchant who tries to defraud his ward of his inheritance. Early in this century the story was issued indiscriminately in a series of cheap Alger reprints, and, in 1911, it was read in this format by teen-aged F. Scott Fitzgerald.[18] Between 1872 and 1878, moreover, over two dozen of Alger's old short stories for adults were reprinted in *Gleason's*.

Alger's irrespressible ambition to write for adults also prompted him to collaborate with his cousin William on the official biography of the American actor Edwin Forrest.[19] In the wake of his notorious feud with William Macready and a scandalous divorce, Forrest had been branded a disreputable roué in the press, and he well understood that his authorized biographer faced a difficult task in public relations. Throughout the early months of 1869, he conducted a careful search for

a qualified biographer with a distinguished name, at last commission-
ing cousin William. Forrest's choice was especially fortuitious, for with
one appointment he obtained the services of an apologetic biographer
and the signature of a distinguished author—though he probably did
not realize the apologist and the signator were different men. William
Rounseville Alger, whose health was failing, probably wrote little of the
biography, though the completed work would bear his name. Instead,
he wrote interchapters of theatre history and apparently assigned the
job of researching and writing the biographical chapters to his enterprising and ambitious cousin Horatio.

In the spring of 1870, in his first flush of enthusiasm for the project,
Horatio interviewed the elder Henry James, who had once been "a
particular friend of Forrest," at his home in Cambridge.[20] James described his early morning visits to the actor years before. He recalled
that Forrest displayed prodigious strength during his gymnastic exercises and admitted that on "his own part he never could bring himself to
do anything of the kind." Later, Horatio worked James's reminiscences
into a chapter about Forrest's young manhood entitled, characteristically, "Breaking the Way to Fame and Fortune." He described James,
though not by name, as "one of the most distinguished philosophical
writers of our country." Over a decade later, he again cited him, this
time by name, in his biography of James A. Garfield.[21]

In the course of the interview, Horatio professed admiration for
James's work, especially *The Secret of Swedenborg*, published the previous year, and he discussed with him the progress of the Forrest
biography. The philosopher harbored private misgivings. He feared that
the author of *Ragged Dick* would simply pen another tale of low life. As
he wrote his son Henry, "Horatio Alger is writing a Life of Edwin
Forrest, and I am afraid will give him a Bowery appreciation. He reports
his hero as a very 'fine' talker—in which light I myself don't so much
recall him."[22] James's fear was well founded. The hand of a juvenile
novelist is plainly and painfully evident in the finished work. The
chapter about Forrest's early manhood, for example, opens with a
contrived incident wrenched from Alger's juvenile formula and developed in his stilted style:

> One morning, early in August, 1825, a young man of fine figure and
> stately bearing, with bright dark-brown eyes, raven hair, and a clear, firm
> complexion like veined marble, approached the door of a modest house in
> Cedar Street, Philadelphia. Without knocking, he entered quickly.
> "Mother! Henrietta!" he cried, springing towards them with open arms.
> "Gracious heaven, Edwin!" they exclaimed, "is it possible that this is you,

changed so much and grown so tall?" "Yes, mother," he said, "Heaven has indeed been gracious to me; and here I am once more with you, after three years of strolling and struggling among strangers. Here I am, with a light pocket but a stout heart. I shall be something yet, mother; and then the first thing I am resolved to do is to make you and the girls independent, so far as the goods of this world go."[23]

Reviewing the work upon its publication, Brander Matthews criticized it for treating two distinct subjects—the life of an actor and the history of the theatre.[24] Had Matthews or another reviewer also noted that each subject was treated in a distinctive style—the biographical chapters in the short, declarative sentences of a juvenile novelist and the abstruse interchapters in the florid prose of a metaphysician—he would have been forced to conclude that the work was the disjointed product of different pens.

Not only was theirs a flawed collaboration, it was grievously protracted. In 1874, W. R. Alger accepted a call to the Church of the Messiah in New York, at least in part for logistical reasons. He wished to minimize the distance separating the coauthors. "I shall at once secure a sitting [in the church], and enroll myself among your parishioners," Horatio wrote William on December 7. "I look forward with satisfaction to seeing more of you, and of your family, when you have fairly entered upon your charge."[25] As in Boston nearly twenty years before, the cousins occasionally socialized when they resided in the same city. On the first Tuesday in November 1876, for example, they discussed politics until late in the evening. It seemed as though the Democratic candidate Samuel P. Tilden had been elected President of the United States that day, defeating the Republican Rutherford B. Hayes. William was depressed by the prospect of a Tilden administration. "He insisted that we were overwhelmingly defeated," Horatio wrote Edwin Seligman on November 9, "and laughed at me for expressing confidence that Hayes would be elected after all."[26] Horatio was either a lucky guesser or an astute political forecaster: The party regulars eventually cut a deal to end Reconstruction in the South and Hayes, though he received fewer popular votes than Tilden, was elected President in the Electoral College. Despite their opportunities to meet and work together, however, the cousins did not complete the two-volume *Life of Edwin Forrest* until 1877, three years behind schedule and five years after Forrest died. They received a total of three thousand dollars for the work.[27] The next year, William Alger resigned his pulpit in New York and moved to Denver.

Meanwhile, in the fall of 1875, Horatio made a stab at literary respectability in his own name by publishing *Grand'ther Baldwin's Thanksgiving*, a selection of his best verse. The volume contained thirty-two poems harvested from ephemeral sources, as if the juvenile novelist wished to prove he once had aspired to nobler literary purpose. Ironically, he had written virtually no new poetry in a decade. By all indications, the reception accorded *Grand'ther Baldwin* was one of the highlights of Alger's dismal career. He broadcast dozens of copies among friends and family—almost every copy known today contains his signature—and he reaped letters of appreciation from, among others, his old editor at *Yankee Blade*, William Mathews, who now taught rhetoric and literature at the University of Chicago, and the humorist B. P. Shillaber ("Mrs. Partington").[28] Through a mutual friend he sent a copy to E. C. Stedman, who received it with kind words. "I am afraid you do me too much honor in calling me a fellow craftsman," Alger replied, "but I am glad to accept the pleasant title."[29] He also received a kind letter from Longfellow, his old instructor, commending the collection. "It is hardly necessary for me to say how much I am gratified by your words of approval," Alger gushed in his reply.[30] For the record, he also sent a copy of the collection to John Greenleaf Whittier, who apparently ignored it.[31]

Reviewers greeted the thin anthology with a chorus of polite praise. "While there is nothing remarkably striking about any of these poems," the *Boston Transcript* reported on November 27, "some of them, and especially the one from which the volume takes its name, are very agreeable reading, impressing the reader with the idea that the author has felt what he has not, perhaps, altogether perfectly expressed." The Boston *Literary World* seconded this opinion a few days later: The collection "contains some very agreeable poems." To be sure, "Mr. Alger is not a professional poet and his work is not faultless artistically," but "he writes with genuine feeling, and often with felicity and force." The *Nation* added that Alger "writes in an unpretending style." His war ballads, especially, "are simple and direct in sentiment and expression, and may well have gained some popularity. His volume, altogether, is one which many people will like to read, though it will not secure him a high place on the roll of poets."[32]

On the whole, Alger was encouraged, if not elated by this response. Still hoping to win a reputation as a serious author, he decided to strike while the iron was hot. On vacation with his parents in Saratoga and in Wolfeboro, New Hampshire, in August 1877, he began to work on an adult nouvelle entitled *The New Schoolma'am, or A Summer in North*

Sparta. He borrowed the premise from "The Disguised Schoolmaster," a sketch he had published twenty years before in *True Flag.* In the nouvelle, a wealthy debutante who has wearied of her life among the *haut monde* in Saratoga and other fashionable watering places repudiates her class privilege and comes incognito to a New Hampshire village to teach school. "It is an experiment," Alger confided to a friend. "If successful, I shall probably write one novel a year."[33] Loring issued it, unsigned at the author's request, in paperback format in early October. Just as his genteel heroine changes her name so that she may prove her mettle, Alger wanted his story to be judged on its merits, not on his reputation. "Will my experiment end in failure?" his heroine asks rhetorically in the first chapter.[34] The question was Alger's own.

Again, he had reason to be encouraged. The London *Academy* for December 15 praised *The New Schoolma'am* as "a sparkling American tale, full of humor."[35] "I am quite ready to believe, as Loring tells me, that there is no higher critical authority in England than the Academy," Alger bragged to Edwin Seligman after he read the review.[36] Early in the new year, the *Nation* also commended the anonymous author's "little hits at the country people and the city people who spend the summer in the country." Loring issued a second edition in the summer of 1879.[37] Overall, however, the book was a weak seller. Only three copies of the first edition are known to exist, all of them in institutional libraries, and no copies of the second edition have ever been located.

Undaunted, Alger grabbed for the brass ring and missed once more before the end of the decade. On July 15, 1878, he reported to young Seligman that he had "completed a new novel, nearly half as long again as 'New Schoolma'am.'" However, he added, "I am not sure that it will be published this year. The book trade is dull, and I prefer to delay it, rather than have it a comparative failure."[38] It apparently was laid aside and forgotten. The original, 203-page manuscript of "Mabel Parker, or The Hidden Treasure. A Tale of the Frontier Settlements," is deposited today in the Street and Smith collection of the Arents Research Library at Syracuse University. It has never been published in its original form. Alger would never realize his fond ambition to be known as a writer for adults.

III

All day he thought of the Golden State of the Pacific Coast, and all night he dreamed of it. For him it had the greatest fascination. The idea of wandering across the

*continent to this wonderful new land became strength-
ened.*

—HORATIO ALGER, JR.,
Digging for Gold

Throughout the 1850s and 1860s, the favorite subject of dime novel-ists had been the American Revolution. In the 1870s, however, the pulp writers, to broaden their appeal by reducing the quality of their fiction to its lowest denominator, turned with a vengeance to the Wild West for setting, incidents, and character types. Writers such as Edward S. Ellis began to describe lurid adventures of such heroes as "Ralph Rockwood, the Reckless Ranger," "Deadwood Dick," and "Calamity Jane." Even so staid a Massachusetts patrician as William T. Adams was infected with sagebrush virus and promptly revised his fiction formula. Adams pub-lished a juvenile novel entitled *Going West* in 1875 and a sequel, *Out West*, in 1877. The revised formula enjoyed tremendous popular suc-cess. By 1881, according to one historian of the genre, "dime novels had attained their majority. Business was good." Ironically, much of the new market was in the West.[39]

Alger was swept along by the undertow, obliged to adjust the style of his juvenile fiction to keep abreast of his competitors. As early as 1874, in *Julius, or The Street Boy Out West*, one of the last stories in the "Tattered Tom series," he had detailed the experience of an orphaned street Arab who is resettled on the frontier under the auspices of the Children's Aid Society. By the end of the novel, the hero has become a prosperous farmer. He returns to New York to visit his old haunts and exhorts the boys at the Lodging House "to leave the city streets, and go out West" if they wish to rise in the world.[40] Alger, who had not yet traveled west of the Mississippi, followed his own advice a few months later. On February 1, 1877, he left New York for California, partly for reasons of health, partly for the purpose of collecting local color for a projected "Pacific series" of juvenile westerns he hoped would stem the decline in his sales.[41]

Though a journey by rail across the continent in 1877 required but six and a half days, Alger took sixteen "owing to my stops."[42] His trip carried him first to Philadelphia, then to Pittsburgh and Chicago. On February 9, he reached Omaha, "one of the most important [cities] on the transcontinental route," where he admired "the new high-school building, built on the site of the old capitol, with its spire rising nearly two hundred feet above the street, the elegant private dwellings on the hill," as well as "the huge railroad bridge that spans the Missouri

River."[43] Alger spent a few days, "a most agreeable time," as a guest in the home near Omaha of U. S. Senator Phineas W. Hitchcock of Nebraska, a man he later acclaimed "the architect of his own fortunes."[44] He subsequently dedicated one of the novels in the "Pacific series" to the Hitchcock children, Grace and Gilbert.[45] He left Omaha at noon on February 12, soon passed through Cheyenne, which seemed to him to have "sprung up as if by magic on the prairies,"[46] and reached Salt Lake City, on a spur of the Union Pacific, in the evening of February 14. He registered at the Townsend House and, the next day, he was escorted around the Mormon mecca by the proprietor of the hotel, one of the original pilgrims to Utah. Townsend took him to Temple Block, where Elder C. J. Thomas guided him through the Tabernacle. Townsend also showed Alger the house where Brigham Young lived with his wives, "the Zion Cooperative store, and would have introduced me to the prophet but the latter is visiting a village 50 miles distant." In all, Alger found the city "quite lively" the day he visited.[47]

On the evening of February 15, he started on the final leg of his trip westward. The next day, he passed Carlin, Nevada, and on Saturday evening, February 17, he reached San Francisco. In the cars, he struck up an acquaintance with Mrs. H. W. Pennell of Philadelphia and her children, Hill and Tillie, to whom he later dedicated another one of the novels in the "Pacific series." Alger was met a few miles outside the city by an old friend, Henry Seligman, Joseph's nephew. He dined with Henry the evening of his arrival and lunched with him at the German Club the next day.[48]

Alger quickly concluded that California in 1877 was no rustic outpost from civilization. "To-day a man may journey across the continent and find the same comfort, luxury and magnificence in San Francisco which he left behind him in New York," he reported.[49] The western city would serve as the hub for his excursions up and down the coast over the ensuing months. He registered at the Palace Hotel, a first-class establishment erected two years before at the corner of Market and New Montgomery streets. Each of the seven floors contained a parlor adorned with bronze statuary, sofas, and a piano, bathed in gaslight and multiplied in cut-glass mirrors. Alger was delighted by the accommodations. "I am charmed with San Francisco & find the Palace Hotel unsurpassed," he wrote Edwin Seligman. "I pay only ordinary rates— $4 per day gold—but I have a room 20 feet square, with bath room, &c., adjoining. The building covers 2¼ acres, & is 165 feet high." Alger rode the elevator to the roof garden and "scanned with delighted eyes a handsome and substantial city apparently the growth of a century, and including within its broad limits a population of three hundred thousand souls. It will not be many years before it reaches half a million, and may fairly be ranked among the great cities of the world."[50]

On February 20, he was introduced to H. H. Bancroft, a noted historian and the author of *The Native Races of America*, which Alger considered "a most valuable contribution to ethnology." At the time, Bancroft was preparing an early history of California. For over a year he had employed a dozen clerks who rummaged among the Spanish and Mexican archives of the state and transcribed extracts germane to his work. Later, Alger caricatured Bancroft in his novel *Silas Snobden's Office Boy* as an aged historian who is writing a History of the Saracens. Bancroft told Alger that on one recent day he had written "for fourteen hours steadily." Alger in turn confessed that "Such persistent labor would soon use me up."[51] On February 23, Alger visited a local school where the students were "curious to see the historian of Ragged Dick, whose wonderful story," he was delighted to discover, "is included in the Public School Libraries."[52] He attended a meeting of a literary society of young men and, a few days later, he took an excursion to the Geysers, transferring his bags upon his return in early March to the Grand Hotel, a less expensive and less luxurious hotel across the street from the Palace.[53]

On March 3, in his room at the Grand, Alger began to write *Joe's Luck*, the first of his western tales.[54] "I hope to complete my California story out here," he wrote on March 13. However, he explained, "I have made a good many acquaintances, and am only afraid of making so many as to involve me in engagements which will interfere with my work."[55] Only the day before he had visited Henry Seligman and his father Jesse, who was in San Francisco to supervise the operation of the west coast branch of J. & W. Seligman Co. Moreover, Alger was

> invited to go Saturday to Pescadero, to visit a ranch of 3500 acres, by the son of the proprietor, & may go if I find I can get back in time to meet a dinner engagement on Sunday. Pescadero is about 50 miles away. Last Sunday I had three dinner invitations. I have one on Thursday, and an invitation to a small evening party on Friday.

Alger also received unexpected and uninvited visitors at his hotel room. "Two boys knocked at my door the other day & asked if I would teach them to fight," he reported to Edwin Seligman. "I declined. I don't give free lessons in fighting any longer." The tutor had been punched once too often.

Thirteen years later, on the eve of his second trip to the Pacific coast,

Alger remembered the people of San Francisco as "warm-hearted and cordial."[56] At the time, however, he wanted the time to work. "If I go out too much I can't write during the day," he complained. "On the other hand, I find the climate stimulating so that I can do 50 percent more work in a week [here] than in New York." Despite his hectic social schedule, Alger was able to complete *Joe's Luck* in California, though it would not be serialized in the *New York Weekly* until the following year. A gold mine in South Africa was later named after the story, and a picture of this mine appeared in the *Illustrated London News* in 1887, only a few weeks after the story was issued in book form.[57] Almost a half-century later, at the nadir of the Great Depression, Nathanael West copied whole pages of *Joe's Luck* virtually word-for-word into his Alger parody *A Cool Million.*[58]

On March 26, Alger left San Francisco for southern California, going first to Santa Barbara, where he met friends who had preceded him there, and continuing on to Los Angeles.[59] The day he departed, both the *Daily Examiner* and the *Daily Morning Call* announced in their social columns that "Horatio Alger is sojourning in California, with a view of gathering information for stories descriptive of California life."[60] On his trip, he would meet several of the old Forty-Niners and hear their "graphic accounts" of the overland journey and the gold rush.[61] But he did not much rely on these oral histories in his western stories, preferring the information he later gleaned from such records as the *Pacific Coast Mining Review* for 1878–79, Barry and Patten's *Men and Memories of San Francisco in the Spring of 1850*, and Mark Twain's *Roughing It.*[62] After a fortnight in southern California, Alger returned to San Francisco and to the manuscript of *Joe's Luck.*

Three weeks later, he once more laid the story aside. In the morning of April 29, he sailed through the Golden Gate for Portland, Oregon, aboard the steamer *George W. Elder.*[63] He reached the bar of the Columbia River three days later, "there being a steady head wind, which retarded our progress," and made most of the passengers seasick, Alger included. At Astoria, twenty miles above the bar, he met old friends who insisted that he dine with them and then guided him through "their salmon canning establishment which is on a large scale." Alger at length reached Portland on the *Elder* early in the morning of May 3 and registered at the Clarendon Hotel near the waterfront.[64]

"I find Portland a handsome city of 15,000 inhabitants," he reported from the city a few days later. "I have been very cordially received and find myself, rather to my surprise, well known here."[65] In the morning of May 3, after sleeping a few hours, he visited the offices of the *Portland*

Oregonian, whose editor described him in the paper the next day as "a cultivated and affable gentleman" of "very considerable literary reputation."[66] He embarked the same morning on a two-day excursion to The Dalles, a small fishing town a hundred miles up the mighty Columbia. "The scenery is far beyond any river scenery I ever witnessed," he reported to young Seligman. "Imagine the scenery of Lake George on a grander scale—extending for a hundred miles, & that will give you some idea of it." On May 8 he headed south from Portland through the Willamette Valley to Salem, the state capital, and on May 12 he started north from Portland for Washington Territory and Vancouver Island.[67]

On board a small steamer on Puget Sound a few days later, Alger engaged a young man about twenty years old in a memorable conversation he later summarized in one of his books. Accompanied by his wife and their two children, the young farmer had left the Old Northwest to start anew in the Pacific Northwest. "My new acquaintance told me with perfect cheerfulness that when he arrived at Seattle, he would have just ten dollars left, to keep himself and his family till he could secure work," Alger recalled with unbridled admiration. "'How should I feel,' I could not help asking myself, 'if I were placed in similar circumstances, though I had only myself to provide for?'" Alger's self-doubt crept into the question. He was not at all sanguine about his ability to start over from scratch, yet his new friend "appeared quite undisturbed. He had faith in himself, and in Providence, and borrowed no trouble. I have no doubt he found something to do before his money gave out."[68] The land was young and full of opportunities, Alger thought, though he was not equal to them. He spent a week admiring the beauty of the region. At midnight on May 21, he boarded the steamer *Dakota* in Victoria, British Columbia, and three days later he again landed in San Francisco.[69]

Two weeks later, Alger left the Bay City for a final excursion, virtually an afterthought, to the abandoned mining settlement of Murphy's, two hundred miles to the east near Angel's Camp in Calaveras County. He registered at a hotel there on June 7, although he found little to see or do. "The surface diggings are exhausted," he later reported, so that the decaying boom town "is best known to-day by its vicinity to the famous Calaveras grove of big trees."[70] He left California a few days later, railing east on the Union Pacific. He spent several days at the Hitchcock home near Omaha in late June[71] and was vacationing with his parents in New England by the middle of July.[72]

Alger had so enjoyed his venture to the West Coast in 1877 that he took a similar trip the following year. He left New York on March 13, barely a week after *Joe's Luck* began to appear serially in the *Weekly*, and he stopped to visit friends in Philadelphia, Washington, Cincinnati, and St. Louis. After registering at the Gibson Hotel in Cincinnati on March 21, he dined with the editor of the *Daily Gazette*, who noted in his social column the next day that Alger was in the city "on his way to the Pacific Coast." In St. Louis four days later, he registered at the Planters' Hotel and "attended a little party, besides spending another evening out." He also passed through Topeka, Kansas, and Pueblo, Colorado, before reaching Denver on March 30.[73]

"I am charmed with Denver," Alger wrote a friend on April 1. Lamentably, he had arrived "rather too early" in the spring to hike around the mountains safely. Still, he thought, "I shall be able to see enough to repay me for coming. . . . Imagine a city of 30,000 inhabitants, with all the luxuries of a larger city, set down in the heart of the Rocky Mountains, in a state which does not average one person to a square mile. It is like an oasis in the desert." From his balcony at the Grand Central Hotel he could "see to the north & west long lines of snowy mountains, appearing in the clear air about five miles away. Really they are distant from 50 to 75." Though he was a thousand miles west of the Mississippi, "in this fine hotel I do not realize it. Twenty years ago, on the site of Denver, there was not one house standing—to-day a city. The change is wonderful." A few days later he traveled fifty miles northwest to Georgetown, nestled "just at the foot of mountains." He planned to remain in the area about two weeks, partly because it had been recommended to him "as a good health resort for all who are troubled with lung complaints," before continuing west.[74]

Unfortunately, he was forced to abandon the trip. By April 15, he had reversed his direction. His brother Frank had unexpectedly fallen ill, and he had been summoned back to Natick. On April 17, however, before Horatio could reach his side, Frank died. "I last saw him alive," Horatio wrote from South Natick on April 22, at the store in Boston where he had worked as a salesman. "The transition to death was so abrupt, that I have not yet succeeded in realizing he is indeed gone." To be sure, "the tie of brotherhood is sometimes loosened by circumstances." He had not been close to his brother James for years. But he had enjoyed intimate relations with Frank, whose "genial qualities had made him many friends."[75] Three lodges of Odd Fellows were represented at the funeral.

Horatio remained in South Natick a week, largely on his mother's account. He spent a bittersweet summer with her in the parsonage on

Pleasant Street, accompanied sometimes by his sister Augusta and her husband, Amos, a local florist and librarian.[76] The old woman was in failing health, her condition complicated by the sudden death of her youngest child. As the summer wore on, the unusually intense heat sapped her strength.[77] She was not the only member of the family suffering the effects. Augusta began to wear her hair cropped short in the belief that improved ventilation of the skull would help to prevent sunstroke.[78] Horatio spent most of his time that summer completing "Mabel Parker" and "reading in a desultory way." He wrote Edwin Seligman on August 19 that "My mother is within a day or two weaker, being very weak before."[79] The end of her anguish was near. She died two weeks later.

After the funeral, Alger returned to New York to mourn. He had written almost nothing for months except the final chapters of an unpublished adult novel, and he had to get back in harness. He resumed a career that had increasingly come under fire in the interim.

IV

Ben doubted whether such stories as "The Ragpicker's Curse" would be likely to win enduring fame for the author, but out of consideration for the feelings of Mr. Snodgrass he kept silent on this point.

"I hear that Howells makes a good deal of money by his novels," he said.

"Howells!" repeated Mr. Snodgrass scornfully. "He couldn't write a story for the Weekly Bugle. *There isn't excitement enough in his productions."*

— HORATIO ALGER, JR.,
Ben Bruce

One of the least remembered tempests which has raged in the teapot of American criticism occurred during the late 1870s and 1880s over the question of sensationalism in popular juvenile fiction. In 1874, during a much-publicized murder trial in Boston, the prosecution alleged that the defendant, Jesse Pomeroy, had been inspired by dime-novel westerns to commit his crime. The charge confirmed the worst suspicions of some parents, librarians, and ministers, zealous and self-appointed "custodians of culture" who warned that dime novels and stories of their ilk demoralized impressionable young readers. Just as poison should be kept out of the reach of young children, they argued, the circulation of these books should be proscribed. Louisa May Alcott fired one of the first shots across the bow of pulp fiction when, in her novel *Eight Cousins* (1875), she derisively punned on William T. Adams' pen name, referring to the stories produced by writers of his school as "optical delusions."[80] By 1878, the same year Alger published his first two juveniles about the west, no less a luminary than William Graham Sumner, professor of sociology at Yale, had entered the fray. Sumner specifically decried boys' books about "hunting, Indian warfare, California desperado life" which were "spiced to the highest degree with sensation."[81] The controversy grew so intense that, in 1885, Mark Twain's *The Adventures of Huckleberry Finn* was censured in the Boston press and banned from the shelves of the Free Library of Concord on the grounds that it was "no better in tone than the dime novels which flood the blood-and-thunder reading population."[82]

Though Adams usually bore the brunt of these attacks, his name was often linked with Alger's. As a historian of the controversy has explained, "most of the criticisms aimed at Adams were equally applicable to Alger's books."[83] Both men worked at the fringe of middle-class respectability. On December 5, 1877, at the opening of a branch of the Boston Public Library, James Freeman Clarke delivered a stinging denunciation of the "endless reams" of "drivel poured forth by Horatio Alger, Jr., and Oliver Optic."[84] In oblique reply, Alger would give the villain of his story "Mabel Parker" the surname Clarke a few months later. Clarke's opinion, however, was widely shared. Soon no respectable periodical deigned to notice Alger's stories except to vilify them. The *Boston Herald*, for example, editorialized that boys who are "raw at reading" and who want, "fighting, killing, and thrilling adventures" often "go for 'Oliver Optic' and Horatio Alger's books."[85] In 1879, the Fletcher Free Library in Burlington, Vermont, became the first public library in the nation to remove books by Alger, "Optic," and "Harry Castlemon" from its shelves.[86]

In a word, Alger's problems were complicated, not corrected, when he tried to broaden his audience with stories set on the frontier. His western strategy backfired. Not only had he worn out the popularity he had enjoyed as the creator of the "Ragged Dick series," but his books were increasingly more condemned than approved. As another historian of the controversy has recently remarked, "From the 1870's until the 1920's, public librarians embarked upon an anti-Alger crusade. This kind of pressure inevitably had its effect. When the Sunday schools, which had once ordered Alger books by the thousands, stopped their buying, the librarians became confident that they had made their point."[87] Under the circumstances, Alger welcomed any signal, no matter how trivial—such as an invitation to join the Chester Literary Union of New York—that indicated he had not fallen into utter disrepute.[88]

So controversial was the question of sensationalism that the American Library Association hosted a conference in Boston in the summer of 1879 to discuss the threat to young readers posed by the pulps.[89] At this conference, some librarians protested "the freedom which most of our public librarians afford for the daily supply and exchange of this class of books among school children." On the other hand, S. S. Green, head of the Worcester, Massachusetts, Public Library, advanced the lesser-evil argument in defense of Alger and Adams in particular. Green readily admitted that their stories were banal. "Poor as they are, however," he argued, "they have a work to do in the world. Many persons need them"—for example, the children of recent immigrants. "I heard a year or two ago," he explained,

> of the formation of a club among some boys to buy dime novels, copies of the *Police Gazette*, and other books and periodicals, from a railroad stall or news-room. Now, I felt very sure that if these boys had not been considered too young to take books from the public library, but had been allowed to read the stories of Messrs. Alger and Adams, that they would not have been contented with these books, and not have sought worse reading.

Ideally, of course, such readers' tastes gradually improve: "A boy begins by reading Alger's books. He goes to school. His mind matures. He outgrows the books that pleased him as a boy." In any event, Green concluded, the motives of writers such as Alger and Adams were above dispute: "Mr. Alger is a son of a clergyman, and himself a graduate of Harvard College and the Divinity School at Cambridge." That he had been forced to abandon his ministry in Brewster mercifully was never mentioned.

A few months later, Alger meekly echoed Green's argument in his own defense. Invited by the editors of the *Christian Union* to express his opinion on the issue of sensationalism, he contended that children should be allowed wide latitude in their selection of literature. "If the young reader thirsts for tales of gore, rapine, and crime gilded with heroism," he wrote, "then his taste should not be arbitrarily repressed by those who consider the 'Memoir of Harriet Newell,' or the 'Guide to the Thoughtful' superior to all other publications intended for the young." Of course, he added, "a young man ought not to be satisfied with the same class of books which he enjoyed when a boy."[90]

The lesser-evil argument did not carry many rounds. In 1894, of a hundred and forty-five libraries surveyed by the A.L.A., thirty-four did not carry Alger novels, and eighteen more were pursuing a policy of removal by attrition, allowing the stories to wear out without replacement. Other libraries reported that they issued Alger books only to adults, presumably parents who closely monitored the reading of their children.[91] The removal of Alger novels from the shelves of the Carnegie Free Library in Allegheny, Pennsylvania, in 1896 was editorially hailed in the pages of the *Nation*.[92] Books by Alger and Adams were finally removed from the shelves of Green's old library in Worcester in 1907.[93] Even Alger, in one of the last pieces he prepared for publication, seemed to side with his critics, at least publicly, on the question of blood-and-thunder. "Sensational stories, such as are found in the dime and half-dime libraries, do much harm, and are very objectionable," he opined in 1896. "Many a boy has been tempted to crime by them. Such stories as 'The Boy Highwayman,' 'The Boy Pirate,' and books of that class, do incalculable mischief. Better that a boy's life should be humdrum than filled with such dangerous excitement."[94] By then, his career on the wane, the author was more concerned with his legacy than his sales.

However inconsequential the skirmish over sensationalism may seem in retrospect, it littered the field with victims. Among the casualties was the firm of A. K. Loring.[95] As early as 1875, Loring tried to compensate for the dull book trade and Alger's slipping popularity by opening a coffee shop at 1 Bromfield Street in Boston. He staved off bankruptcy for over five years by serving cheap lunches and coffee at five cents a cup. He issued a few new books during this period, including Alger's *The Young Explorer*, the third novel in the "Pacific series," in the autumn of 1880. It would be the last Alger story issued under his imprint, however. In early June 1881, with Loring's collapse imminent, Alger went to Philadelphia to meet with Henry T. Coates, junior partner in the publishing firm of Porter & Coates.[96] On June 15, Loring declared bankruptcy. At a meeting of his creditors on June 28, his liabilities were placed at over $28,500 and his assets at less than $20,000. His stereotype plates were appraised at over $10,000, though they were subsequently sold for a total of only $1118.80. Porter & Coates purchased the copyrights and plates of Loring's thirty-seven Alger books for perhaps $600, an average of less than twenty dollars per book. In late October, the firm advertised it would begin to issue new editions of the stories "in new and beautiful bindings" as soon as possible. Both Joseph H. Allen and Aaron K. Loring—the two men who banked on Alger early and long—lost their gambles and went broke. In 1881, Porter & Coates bid short for the rights to issue his books. No one, it seems, was getting rich off Alger, least of all his publishers.

After the bankruptcy, Alger tested another alternative to sensational stories. If he was mostly a failure as a writer for adults and if he was attacked for rattling windows with his juvenile fiction, then he would try his hand at juvenile nonfiction. Opportunity knocked barely two weeks after Loring suspended operations. On July 2, 1881, President James Garfield was shot by a disgruntled office seeker, an infamous act which recalled to Alger's mind the day sixteen years before when, during his ministry in Brewster, "Abraham Lincoln was treacherously killed by an assassin."[97] Though Garfield lingered through the summer, his wounds were mortal. He died on September 19. At the suggestion of a New York publisher, John R. Anderson, Alger began to write a boys' biography of the martyred President on September 24, soon after his return to the city from a summer divided between South Natick and Hampton Beach, New Hampshire. Unlike the Forrest biography, Alger would neither research primary sources nor collaborate with another writer. He "wrote it against time in 14 days," as he later admitted, gleaning his data from other biographies and recent newspaper articles and completing the manuscript on October 8.[98] "Even as I write," Alger noted near the end of the book, "the insignia of grief are still to be seen in the tenement-house districts of the East Side of New York."[99] His biography, *From Canal Boy to President*, was the first account of Garfield's life and death on the juvenile market, and it sold exceptionally well during the first weeks of national mourning. In Oakland, the young Jack London read it.[100] In all, twenty thousand copies of the book were sold within a few months, and, as Alger later acknowledged, as a result "I was quite handsomely paid" for it.[101]

By assuming the mantle of biographer, moreover, he outmaneuvered his critics. He was immune to complaint when paying homage to a fallen leader. No one could accuse him of sensationalizing this story. Predictably, reviewers ignored the controversy over the merits of his fiction to commend his patriotism. The *Journal of Education* congratulated Alger in November for presenting the story of Garfield's life "in a most attractive style. . . . Every school and home library should have this record of a life, ripe in experience and noble in character." The *Ohio Educational Monthly* agreed the next month that the "book is written in a style that would at once attract the attention of boys, even of those whom we see with dime novels protruding from their pockets."[102] That, it seems, was Alger's plan.

The large sales and favorable reviews of *From Canal Boy to President* prompted Alger to undertake a series of "readable lives of the greatest and best men in our history."[103] Over the next two years, he wrote two more boys' lives of illustrious Americans—Abraham Lincoln and Daniel Webster—both based on the works of earlier biographers. He broke no new ground, but simplified the legends which had accreted around his subjects. Though not as popular as the panegyric to Garfield, Alger's *Abraham Lincoln, the Backwoods Boy* and *From Farm Boy to Senator* served as firebreaks around his reputation, dampening the storm of protests about his work in general. Alger abandoned the field of juvenile biography only when it became too time-consuming. In *From Farm Boy to Senator*, as he later explained, "I wished to revive the memory of Webster and make the young people of to-day acquainted with him." But the biography had been extremely "difficult to write."[104] During the political campaign in the fall of 1884, Alger was invited by John R. Anderson "to write a boys' life of the President, as soon as the matter is settled" between James Blaine and Grover Cleveland. However, by early August he had "about decided to decline" the offer. Referring obliquely to his earlier troubles with the Forrest biography, he explained that "It would be a most delicate matter . . . to write the life of a living man, and I should be likely to incur criticism. I think I will stick to stories."[105] As late as 1898, a juvenile magazine invited him to write three biographical serials "like my Garfield & Lincoln books" each year. "I shall decline," he quickly added, "as it would involve much more labor than ordinary serials."[106]

Though an effective rear-guard action, Alger's experiments with nonfiction were not entirely successful. Despite good sales and favorable reviews, he had no future as a biographer. Moreover, he was so controversial a writer of fiction that, with the expiration in 1880 of the contract which bound him exclusively to the *New York Weekly*, he was compelled to place some of his stories in such marginal or untested magazines as *Golden Days for Boys and Girls* and *Golden Argosy* and such decidedly *déclassé* periodicals as the *Boston Weekly Globe* newspaper. The editors of the *Globe*, Alger advised an ambitious young writer in 1897, "like an exciting story, with frequent crises."[107] He maintained standards, to be sure, but they were woefully low ones: "I have never received less for a serial I wrote than $250," he once bragged.[108] He finally completed the four-volume "Pacific series" in 1882, five years after he traveled to California, and he began a similar "Atlantic series" of "stories of life and adventure" the following year.[109] He would write no more juveniles with philanthropic purpose, to advertise the work of the Newsboys' Lodging House or to solicit contributions to the Children's

Aid Society. At fifty, Alger already had entered the twilight of a low-trajectory career.

V

"How kind you are, Mrs. Vernon," ejaculated Mrs. Mordaunt.

"No, I am selfish. I have plenty of money, and no one to care for, or to care for me. I have taken a fancy to you all, and I am quite sure that we can all live happily together."

—Horatio Alger, Jr.,
Dan the Newsboy

Alger lived in a succession of boarding houses after he moved from the Seligman home in 1875 until he left New York permanently in 1896.[110] Though he continued to socialize with the Seligmans, even visiting them occasionally at their summer home in Long Branch,[111] and though he remained an active member of the Harvard Club of New York,[112] he suffered bouts of loneliness and depression. He tried to fill

Etching of Alger.
From *Golden Argosy*, October 17, 1885.

the void in his life, so far as possible, with children, usually boys whom he tutored or adopted or accompanied on short trips. "I hope to spend a couple of hours daily in teaching during the coming year," he wrote Edwin Seligman in 1879. That summer, Alger and Edwin's brother Alfred had traveled together through New England, visiting Boston, Natick, and Cambridge, and touring Maine, "going by steamer to Bangor"[113] and returning by rail through Portland. "I never travel alone if I can help it," he later noted.[114] Alger spent Thanksgiving that year with friends in Philadelphia.[115] Try as he might, however, he could not always exorcise the solitude.

His family offered little comfort. Cousin William had moved west. His mother, sister Annie, and brother Frank were all dead. His brother James, an optician, had been largely estranged from the rest of the family for years.[116] In 1859, he had moved to San Francisco to seek his fortune, but he never found it. He eventually abandoned a wife and two daughters there. In 1869, he traveled to Peru on business, returned to Boston, and at the age of thirty-four, soon married Harriet Bacon Locke, who was seventeen and pregnant. They were divorced shortly after the birth of a daughter, and James eventually wed a woman from Natick. A ne'er-do-well with a case of acute wanderlust, he pulled up stakes again to move to Denver in 1878 where, as Horatio diplomatically explained, "he hopes to find inducement to remain."[117]

In his dotage, the elder Horatio Alger was more a distress than a companion.[118] His health failing, Alger *père* had retired from the ministry in April 1874, a few months after the family returned from Europe, following a term of nearly fourteen years at the helm of the Unitarian Church in South Natick. In 1878, the elder Alger publicly thanked the members of the congregation there for "doing what they could for my support" in exchange for "my poor labors in their service." Upon his retirement, "not knowing where else I could find so pleasant a home in my loneliness," he had remained in the town. He died there on his seventy-fifth birthday in 1881. His disconsolate son afterwards offered a simple epitaph to his life: "My father was kept in the background by his own modesty."[119]

Alger tried desperately to compensate for his losses by assuming most of the expenses of his niece Annie, James's daughter by his second wife,[120] and by informally adopting three New York street boys. One of these boys, Charlie Davis, had actually run away from home to join a circus. Alger based his juvenile novel *The Young Circus Rider* (1883), the first story in the "Atlantic series," partly upon young Davis's experiences. The lad worked for a circus until August 1885, when Alger set him up in business in Biddeford, Maine, five miles from Old Orchard Beach, a resort town where he sometimes vacationed. Later, according to Annie Alger Richardson, Davis proved "much of a disappointment."[121] A second ward, John Downie, a newsboy whom Alger met on the streets of the Bowery, had been orphaned at the age of twelve. "He was left to struggle alone and unaided till at 15 I began to care for him," Alger wrote later. He cast young Downie, "a blond young man who looked honest and reliable," as a character in two of his novels, *Mark Manning's Mission* (1886) and *Chester Rand* (1892). The boy moved into Alger's flat at 52 West 26th Street in May 1883, spent several months at Brooklyn Business College at Alger's expense, was apprenticed to a photographer in Biddeford in August 1885, and again lived with Alger as late as May 1888.[122] The writer assumed charge of a third boy, fourteen-year-old Edward J. (Tommy) Downie, younger brother of John, in the spring of 1894. However, he used him as a character as early as 1889 in *The Odds Against Him*.[123]

No natural father, it was said, could have been more faithful and self-sacrificing than Alger.[124] Yet his self-sacrifice seems to have had distinct ethnic overtones. He was proud of the Anglo-Saxon descent of all the boys he adopted.[125] He bragged that Charlie Davis's parents were French Canadian and that the Downie brothers were second-generation Scotch. In his fiction, too, Alger began about this time to characterize by ethnic shorthand.[126] He described a Scottish character in *The Young Adventurer* (1878) as "rather sedate, but entirely trustworthy." A similar character in *Chester Rand* (1892) declares that "The Scotch are careful and conservative." A character "of Scotch ancestry on his mother's side" in *Lester's Luck* (1893) was "inclined to be cautious." Worse yet, Alger also introduced in his stories a caricatured Shylock-type whom he variously named Joshua Starr in *Forging Ahead* (1881), Job Green in *Frank Hunter's Peril* (1885), and Aaron Wolverton in *Bob Burton* (1886). After years of tutoring in the home of Joseph Seligman and contributing to *Young Israel*, Alger should have known better than to portray Jewish characters as usurious moneylenders and pawnbrokers. Significantly, he began to employ anti-Semitic stereotypes in his fiction only after the elder Seligman's death, as if to comment upon the parsimony of the employer who had sometimes refused his demands for more money.

The Jewish stereotype in his late fiction is all the more disturbing in light of Alger's continued employment in the homes of prominent Jewish families. In 1883, he was hired by Albert Cardozo, a former New York State Supreme Court justice and a summer neighbor of the

Seligmans, to tutor his children Benjamin and Elizabeth, especially to prepare the boy for admission to college.[127] A half-century later, Benjamin Cardozo noted with tongue in cheek that Alger "did not do as successful a job for me as he did with the careers of his newsboy heroes." He had been admitted to Columbia College at the age of only fifteen. With Alger as her teacher and patron, moreover, Elizabeth Cardozo began to write poetry. Her verse subsequently appeared in such magazines as *Scribner's, Cosmopolitan,* and the *Century.* In July 1885, his assignment in the Cardozo home completed, Alger was hired by David Einstein, a prominent New York businessman and another friend of the Seligman family, to tutor his eight-year-old son, Lewis.[128]

For both reasons of health—he found the sea breezes invigorating—and in order to stay in touch with his wards in Biddeford, Alger throughout the mid-1880s divided his summers between his sister's home in Natick and the elegant seafront hotels at Old Orchard Beach.[129] He spent a few days in July 1886 at the Fiske Hotel there in company with two young friends, W. S. Scott of Boston and Adin Gould of South Natick, and he returned the next month for another week of fresh air accompanied by a third boy, Mort Bean. "The air is delightfully cool" at the beach, he reported to yet another friend from his hotel on August 19, "and as the beach is full of people there is no lack of recreation. I passed last evening at the home of 'the young circus rider' in Biddeford." Alger so devoted his life to children during these years that he had little time for extended trips. In the summer of 1887, however, he once more traveled west with literary purpose. Charlie Davis and John Downie were in business in Maine, and Tommy Downie had not yet come to live with him. In August he headed for Chicago to research a new serial for the *Golden Argosy.*[130] The story would be set in "that young but mighty Western city" and entitled *Luke Walton, or The Chicago Newsboy,* as the editors of the magazine announced. It was one of the last of Alger's juveniles worthy of note.

5.

Cast upon the Breakers

(1887–1899)

> *Rupert did not envy his father's old partner. "I would*
> *rather be poor and honest," he reflected, "than live in a*
> *fine house, surrounded by luxury, gained by grinding the*
> *faces of the poor."*
>
> —HORATIO ALGER, JR.,
> *Rupert's Ambition*

Alger was a mugwump, a liberal Republican committed to principles of fair prices and decent wages, a critic of sharp business practices and cutthroat competition. He was neither an apologist for the wealthy class nor a stalking horse for industrial capitalism. Rather, his appeal was fundamentally nostalgic. He often set his tales in idealized villages modeled upon preindustrial Marlborough. His heroes never worked in mechanized factories, and in his later stories they were more often sons of poor farmers than indigent street Arabs. Whereas Alger wrote his early juvenile fiction to publicize the work of the Children's Aid Society and kindred institutions, many of the stories he wrote in the 1880s and 1890s were thinly-disguised critiques of the corrupt captains of industry.

Alger was dismayed by the rebate scandal, for example. Soon after government investigators first revealed, in 1879, that railroads often granted special rate concessions or "midnight tariffs" to oil companies, especially the Standard, he joined his voice to the chorus protesting the practice. He later described it by analogy in his novel *Number 91* (1886): A corrupt housekeeper, like a robber baron, levies tribute from every merchant whom she patronizes "as a compensation for turning the trade in his direction." As a result, the consumer, "without being aware of it, paid a larger price than any one else for what articles she purchased, the storekeeper and others compensating themselves in this way for the percentage they had to pay the housekeeper."[1] A simple enough scheme, however unfair.

Alger also indicted in his stories the unscrupulous investors who profited by manipulating stock values to personal advantage. The most notorious case of market plunder also occurred in 1879, when Jay Gould, James R. Keene, and their confederates circulated exuberant reports of the profitability of the Union Pacific railroad and the dividends to be realized from prudent investment in Union Pacific stock. According to contemporary accounts, "widows and orphans and lady stockholders rushed to buy the stock," whereupon Gould quietly sold most of his shares on the bull market and reaped a windfall profit of about ten million dollars.[2] Later the artificially inflated stock crashed, of course, though Gould stoutly fended off charges of malfeasance by maintaining he still owned stock in the railroad and thus shared in the loss. He neglected to add that it was a paper loss only. In Alger's *The Store Boy* (1883), a character who has lost money speculating in the stocks complains that "Keene or Jay Gould or some of those fellows" had upset the market.[3] Alger alluded to the scheme again in *Luke Walton*. He transferred the scene to Chicago and substituted the "Excelsior Mine" for the Union Pacific railroad, but otherwise the story remained the same. A "mock philanthropist" named Thomas Browning explains how, like Gould, he profited by a stock swindle with a modest initial investment:

> "I hired an office, printed circulars, distributed glowing accounts of imaginary wealth, etc. It cost considerable for advertising, but I sold seventy thousand shares, and when I had gathered in the money I let the bottom fall out. There was a great fuss, of course, but I figured as the largest loser, being the owner of thirty thousand shares (for which I hadn't paid a cent), and so shared the sympathy extended to losers. It was a nice scheme, and after deducting all expenses, I made a clean seventy-five thousand dollars out of it."

A widow, the mother of two children who has lost all her money in this confidence game, comes to Browning to plead her case.

> "One of your circulars fell into my hands. The shares were two dollars each, and it was stated that they would probably yield fifty per cent.

dividends. That would support me handsomely. . . . You endorsed all that the circular contained. You said that within a year you thought the shares would rise to at least ten dollars. So I invested all the money I had. You know what followed. In six months the shares went down to nothing, and I found myself penniless. . . . But you seem to be a rich man."[4]

Alger's opinion of the profiteer is obvious: "He has done more harm than he can ever repair."

His modern reputation as a capitalist ideologue notwithstanding, Alger was a doctrinaire advocate of neither wage- nor price-competition. As early as 1871, in *Paul the Peddler*, he explained to his young readers that when too many workers compete for jobs in the marketplace, the entire labor force suffers from depressed wages and economic hardship.[5] Later, the mother of Luke Walton, who works as a seamstress in a glutted market, estimates that she earns only about three cents an hour sewing shirts.[6] On the other hand, her newsboy son enjoys the "advantage of diminished competition" when two other newsies quit the business. Alger often invoked in his fiction the biblical injunction "the laborer is worthy of his hire," arguing that employers should pay a living wage, not the lowest wage the market would bear. He even advocated organization or unionization of the working class in such novels as *Ben the Luggage Boy* and *Slow and Sure*.

He also recognized the advantages of economic cooperation, at least on a modest scale, in fixing fair prices. Though he was no socialist, he was interested in cooperative experiments as early as 1877, when he visited the Zion Cooperative Store in Salt Lake City. In 1885, he sent Edwin Seligman, by then an economist investigating the merits of socialism, a circular about a cooperative store recently opened in Natick. In an accompanying letter, the supposed champion of free enterprise opined that the store

> has been a remarkable success, and paid extraordinary dividends. Yet I do not know that there has been anything exceptionally favorable in the circumstances attending its formation and history. The secret of its success has been good management, and where coöperation fails, I suspect that failure is due to poor management.[7]

Alger sometimes went so far in his late fiction as to criticize the profit motive. In *Tom Tracy* (1886), he complained that some haberdashers aim "to get their clothing made for the lowest market prices, and to make the best possible bargain with the customers." In *Luke Walton*, he endorsed usury laws which would limit the interest charged on loans.[8]

Despite his mugwumpish inclinations, Alger carefully hewed the

Republican party line on election days.[9] His correspondence reveals that he proudly voted for Rutherford Hayes in 1876, William Henry Harrison in 1888, and William McKinley in 1896. "With the election of McKinley," he accurately predicted in September 1896, two months before the vote, "an era of confidence and prosperity will be ushered in." He wrote the same friend in December, after the election, that "All eyes are now turned to Washington. I have great hopes of the success of the coming administration."[10] He supported anti-Tammany candidates in New York municipal elections and advocated civil service reforms. He believed that tariffs were necessary to protect the business interests of the nation, and he opposed the campaigns to inflate American currency with greenbacks and Free Silver.[11] To their everlasting credit, as he reported in his juvenile biographies, Garfield and Webster had battled for "sound" or "hard" money. On the other hand, as he observed in June 1896. "The Democrats seem to be all at sea with the silverites predominating."[12] At least the Gold Democrats had "nominated a good ticket," which was more than he could say of the populist supporters of William Jennings Bryan.[13]

He reserved his strongest endorsements for two politicians with whom he enjoyed some personal acquaintance. He was first attracted to Russell A. Alger by reports that the former governor of Michigan, a

Left to right: Amos Parker Cheney (husband of Alger's sister Olive Augusta), of Natick, Massachusetts; Louis Schick, of New York; and Horatio Alger, Jr. August 7, 1889.
Courtesy of the Harvard University Archives.

distant cousin, had generously contributed money to help a thousand poor boys in Detroit. General Alger was a candidate for the Republican nomination for President in 1888, and Horatio wrote to assure him that spring that he "should be glad of an opportunity to vote" for him and that he would "be glad to meet one who has made our family name so honorably conspicuous." A few weeks later, Horatio lurked in the lobby of the Fifth Avenue Hotel in New York and sent up his card to General Alger's room, though his kinsman was not receiving visitors. On June 30, after the Republican national convention, the defeated candidate wrote Horatio to ask his support of the party in the fall. Horrified by the prospect of Grover Cleveland's reelection, Horatio was amenable to the appeal. "I think you would have been a stronger candidate than Harrison," he replied on July 4. "However, the strongest feeling with me as with you is the hope that our party may win against an Administration which is unAmerican." A decade later, Secretary of War Russell Alger became the target of intense criticism when spoiled meats and other substandard supplies were shipped to American troops fighting the Spanish in Cuba. Horatio again wrote his cousin to express both his displeasure "at the senseless and unreasonable criticisms on your official course" and his confidence that "the public will do you justice in the end."[14] This prediction fell far short of the mark. On July 19, 1899, the day after Horatio died, Russell Alger resigned under fire from McKinley's cabinet.

Horatio was also favorably impressed by young Theodore Roosevelt, a patrician New Yorker and graduate of Harvard, whose father had helped Charles Loring Brace found the Children's Aid Society. Alger was acquainted with the foppish Roosevelt through the Harvard Club as early as 1881 and watched his star rise over the next eighteen years. Late in 1895, John Downie passed a civil service exam, one of Roosevelt's innovations while the New York City police commissioner, and became "one of Roosevelt's reform police," as the proud foster father bragged. A few weeks later, Alger went to Railroad Hall on Madison Avenue to hear Roosevelt speak, and, when the commissioner failed to appear, he was called to the podium as a stopgap. Late in 1896, Alger was disturbed to learn that Roosevelt was shopping "for a position in Washington" in the McKinley administration, for he "will be a loss to New York."[15] Roosevelt was subsequently appointed to the post of Assistant Secretary of the Navy and, less than two years later, elected governor of New York. Unfortunately, Alger did not live long enough to learn he would be elected Vice-President in 1900 and assume the presidency upon McKinley's assassination the next year.

II

I am content to share in the successes of my young friends, and feel satisfied with the little I have myself achieved. My work has been chiefly satisfactory because it has brought me so many friends whom I value.

—HORATIO ALGER, JR.,
7 October 1894

For a decade before he retired in 1896, Alger was so prolific that he had to invent a new pseudonym to prevent confusion. In all, he wrote thirty-nine serials during the decade, in large part because Frank Munsey, the entrepreneur who launched *Golden Argosy* on a string in 1882, had succeeded beyond all expectations. Munsey had built the circulation of the weekly simply by pricing it below the competition. Each issue cost but a nickel, an annual subscription but a dollar and a half. Alger contributed so much pulp fiction to it that in 1886, even as its circulation peaked at 115,000, his serials began to overlap. Some numbers contained both the closing chapters of one of his stories and the opening installment of another. Between the spring of 1886 and the summer of 1894, Alger published a total of thirty serials in the *Golden Argosy*, eleven of them under the penname "Arthur Lee Putnam." Meanwhile, circulation dipped to about nine thousand. The more Alger wrote for the magazine, the fewer copies it sold.[16]

Natick, Massachusetts, about 1890.

The fault was not entirely Alger's, to be sure. Munsey increasingly aimed the paper at semi-literate adults rather than at juveniles, and he raised the subscription price about the time the national economy turned sour in 1893. But Alger was one more albatross around the masthead. As his career sputtered, he abandoned all pretense of writing stories in thematically-organized series. He wrote hurriedly, haphazardly, without pride, for the cash. Publicly, he continued to assert that "If a writer finds his own interest in the story he is writing failing, he may be sure that the same effect will be produced on the mind of the reader."[17] Privately, he wished he "could enjoy work as I used to" and allowed, for example, that he "did not care much" for his story *Adrift in the City*.[18] Most of the juveniles he wrote during these years, including most of the serials "Putnam" wrote for *Golden Argosy*, appeared in book format only after his death.

Partly to collect more material for stories in the style of the "Pacific series," partly to escape the harsh New York winter, Alger returned to the West Coast in the fall of 1890. He left New York, "stopped at Niagara Falls, but only for a few hours, and spent a day in Chicago," where he visited Jackson Park, soon to be the site of the Columbian Exhibition. He headed on to St. Paul and Minneapolis, where he boarded the cars of the Northern Pacific for the trip "over the broad plains of North Dakota and through the mountains of Montana." He reached Helena on Saturday, October 25, where he passed the weekend with Albert Seligman, another of Joseph's nephews, and his wife. He left Helena two days later and passed Arlee, Montana, on October 28, reached Portland a day or two later, and arrived in San Francisco on November 2.[19] A week later, the *Morning Call* reported in a feature article that Alger had "a host of warm personal friends" in the city whom he had come to visit.[20] He wintered in California and returned east the next spring. As late as June 1896 he considered another trip to California, one via the Canadian Pacific road.[21]

Unfortunately, the western stories Alger researched in 1890–91 were neither popular nor critically well received. His novel *Digging for Gold*, for example, was panned in the *Dial*: Alger "attempts to mine the wealth that lies hidden in the early history of California, but he brings back little to enrich us." In fact, reviewers usually reviled Alger's late stories. The *Bookman* concluded that *Adrift in the City* evinced "mediocre ability," and the *Literary World* damned it with faint praise as "written in the most polished Oliver Optic style." Some reviewers reiterated the old charge of sensationalism. The *Literary World* in December 1893 asserted that Alger "might do something better than pour forth this unceasing stream of sensational, impossible literature." Other readers found fault with his weak characterizations: He "could not possibly be more puerile in the selection of characters or more clumsy in their delineation," the *Literary World* concluded. Still others lamented the predictability of his plots: The *Critic* complained in 1895 that Alger always finds an audience of boys

> no matter how bad his rhetoric, how unreal his situations, or how crude his workmanship. His latest book, "Victor Vane, the Young Secretary," tells, as usual, of the impossible virtues, triumphs and successes of a boy of seventeen, who becomes private secretary and confidential adviser and friend to a Western Congressman, and transacts a large amount of important business in the most experienced fashion. Such stories as this call for little comment.

Alger in 1890.
Courtesy of the Harvard University Archives.

Similarly, according to the *Dial*, in *The Young Salesman* Alger "tells how a poor young English orphan, landing in New York with a small sum of money, becomes, without apparent effort, an earl's friend, a merchant prince, and a general philanthropist to small boys." The *Critic* averred that "there is nothing new" about *The Five Hundred Dollar Check* "except the cover and the paper and possibly the pictures. . . . It is such an obvious, worn-out theme for a story that we wonder any author with the instinct of literary self-preservation should employ it." Still other reviewers chided Alger for his overreliance on coincidence as a plot contrivance: In *Rupert's Ambition*, according to the *Dial*, "everything happens at precisely the right moment, in precisely the manner in which everything fails to happen in real life."[22] Reviewers rarely rallied to Alger's defense. Yet some young readers thought well of these late, limp stories. To judge from his autobiographical novel *Look Homeward, Angel*, Thomas Wolfe read dozens of Alger's books, including *Jed the Poorhouse Boy* (1892). In 1890, two of Alger's stories were even translated into Russian and published in a juvenile magazine issued in St. Petersburg.[23]

Alger readily admitted whenever asked that he wrote his stories without outlining their plots in advance. Instead, he chose an opening incident and began to write without regard to subsequent chapters, with no preconceptions about pace or direction.[24] He built each novel at the rate of a chapter or so per day, usually writing only in the afternoons amid the noise and bustle of a group of boys in his room.[25] Quiet confused him, he said. His rationale for this strategy echoed, if on a lower frequency, Henry James's argument in "The Art of Fiction" that a story should grow organically from its original conception like a plant from a seed. "I never fully understand a character, to begin with," Alger explained, "but gradually become acquainted with it as I go on. The characters, once introduced, gradually develop and in turn shape the story."[26] As in the cases of Johnny Nolan and Micky Maguire, he tried to model characters upon real boys whom he met, whenever it was "possible for me to find a character" suited to his tale. "I have always made a close study of boys in order that my characters might seem to be drawn from life," he added.[27] "I have a natural liking for boys, which has made it easy for me to win their confidence and become intimately acquainted with them."[28] Once a week, usually on Friday evening, he invited boys to his room, where he sat at his writing desk and asked questions. As George Steele Seymour, a minor poet who as a boy once attended the circle, recalled years later, "I did not see him take any notes," but "it was understood that he was gathering material—that boys' personalities were somehow in process of filtering through to the printed page."[29] Alger identified some of these boys by name in the stories, such as Arthur Burks, John Schickling, Eugene Sweetland, and Tommy Keegan.[30]

Even in old age he centered his routine both in New York and in Natick around boys. "What gratifies me most," he wrote privately in 1897, "is that boys, though strangers, seem to regard me as a personal friend."[31] He went so far as to claim that in his experience boys were "natural" and girls "artificial."[32] James Montgomery Flagg, later a popular artist, as a boy in the 1890s often visited Alger, that "dear little pink old gentleman from Natick." In his autobiography, Flagg recalled

Alger in 1892.
Courtesy of the Marlborough Public Library.

attending "some of his parties for Ragged Dicks and other Alger characters. He fed them ice cream and told them stories and they loved him."[33]
Like Flagg, Seymour later supplied one of the few eyewitness descriptions of Alger's appearance in his declining years. He was a "short,
almost bald man wearing nose glasses, with a protruding lower lip and
an upward tilt of the head." He thought there was "a New England air
about Mr. Alger, and something birdlike too."[34] Arthur Burks's brother
Ernest also remembered Alger fondly years later. "He was very stout
and short," he recalled, with a fair complexion. He was "very near
sighted" and "almost completely bald" but for a few tufts of white hair.[35]

Fortunately, a few letters Alger wrote to his young friends during
these years have survived. Most are filled with banal amenities and
gossip. In some of them, however, Alger told of his disappointment
when one of his boys was arrested. His moral maxims were no fail-safe
deterrent to crime. In 1892, Oren Trott, a boy he knew from his summer
vacations at Peak's Island, Maine, near Portland, was persuaded by a
young thief to fence a few watches. "The sum realized was only a dollar
and a quarter, but the fact that Oren sold them makes him an accom-
plice in the eyes of the law," Alger explained to Ernest Burks.

> If Oren knew that the watches were stolen he was very weak and foolish to
> consent to sell them, and he realizes this now. I hope his previous good
> character will help him. . . . Of course I shall stand by him whatever
> happens. I always do stand by a friend in time of trouble.[36]

Similarly, Alger later wrote his friend Irving Blake that

> one of the boys who used to frequent my room—not to my satisfaction—is
> now at Sing Sing prison, confined for burglary. I exerted myself to obtain a
> mitigation of his sentence, and was very successful. . . . I don't think he
> realized what he was doing. I have sent him an autoharp to fill up his time
> as the prisoners are not now employed.[37]

Occasionally, Alger lost patience with boys who demanded his favors,
and he changed apartments every three or four years to shake hang-
ers-on. "I gave up my room on 34th St. because I had too many young
callers who were unwelcome," he explained to Blake in March 1896.
"For this reason please don't mention where I am."[38]

Over the years he increasingly indulged his taste for popular theater
and classical music. In New York during the 1870s and 1880s, he
frequented the Grand Opera House, Niblo's Theatre, and Lester Wal-
lack's playhouse on the Great White Way, where he struck up
friendships with members of the stock companies.[39] He praised in his
books and letters such period actors as James Lewis, Sir Henry Irving,

Edwin Booth in the role of Cardinal Richelieu, Richard Mansfield as Jekyll/Hyde, Joseph Jefferson as Rip Van Winkle and, of course, Edwin Forrest.[40] While in New England for Christmas in 1877, he commuted from Natick to Boston to attend "two or three amusements including 'Pippin,' the new American Opera bouffe."[41] He saw Mark Twain perform on stage on three occasions ("peculiar lectures, but interesting"),[42] and, in 1890, he befriended little Elsie Leslie, child star of "The Prince and the Pauper" stage adaptation.[43] During the winter of 1896–97, after his retirement to Natick, Alger regularly attended Boston theaters. "I go with young friends and consult their tastes as to the plays," he explained.[44] On December 3, 1896, for example, he saw Bret Harte's new play *Sue*, with Annie Russell in the title role, at the Museum Theatre. He was not particularly impressed. "The plot is faulty," he remarked candidly to Irving Blake a few days later. "Some of the minor characters are quite picturesque, especially those who take part in a lynching court scene. I don't think, however, the piece can on the whole be regarded as a success."[45] Alger was also fascinated by such musical prodigies of his day as the Brazilian violinist Maurice Dengremont, who toured the United States in 1881 at the age of fifteen ("I became acquainted with Degremont with whom I could converse a little in French").[46] On April 23, 1890, he attended the farewell concert at

Alger working at his desk.
From *Frank Leslie's Pleasant Hours*, n.s. 1, March 1896.

Steinway Hall in New York of the young German pianist Otto Hegner ("He has promised to write to me").[47] On December 11, 1896, he heard the thirteen-year-old Polish violinist Bronislaw Huberman play a classical program at the Music Hall in Boston ("He is not good looking but in his childish costume he produced a pleasing impression").[48]

In short, despite the fragility of his health, Alger remained reasonably active until he was long past sixty, He wrote four serials a year as late as 1895, though he had begun to exploit opportunities to escape his desk. He attended the forty-year reunion of his college class at Young's Hotel in Boston on July 21, 1892,[49] and, as Class Odist, he once more penned a lamentation on lost youth for the occasion:

> Grown older now, we will not mourn
> Those exhalations of the dawn;
> The heroes that we hoped to be
> Will never live in History.
> No knights or paladins are we,
> Plain toilers only in the mart;
> Yet let us hope on Life's broad stage
> That we have played a worthy part.[50]

In the early 1890s, he began to spend more time each summer in Natick and at the coastal resorts of Maine and Massachusetts. He quit working for months at a time to relax in the sun. He had not written a word for publication in two months, he wrote Blake from Natick in August 1894, and he was about to leave to rusticate further at Old Orchard Beach and Martha's Vineyard.[51] He thought the sea breezes cleared his lungs and restored his strength, and he certainly ranked his health above the stories he might have wrung from a more active career.

He centered his life no less than his stories on boys during these years, but he still experimented with adult fiction. Frank Munsey had serialized *Helen Ford* in *Golden Argosy* in 1885–86 under the title "A Child of Fortune" and the old pseudonym "Arthur Hamilton." Early in 1889, Alger contributed a series of new adult short stories to the *Yankee Blade* which were subsequently syndicated in newspapers throughout the country. Munsey reprinted a slightly revised version of *The New Schoolma'am* in *Munsey's Magazine* in March 1892 under the title "A Fancy of Hers."[52] In short, Alger found the urge to write for adults difficult to suppress, especially when he read popular fiction by writers, such as Beatrice Harraden and Florence Marryat, who were no more talented than he. In fact, the idea for a new adult novel, *The Disagreeable Woman*, occurred to him as he read Harraden's *Ships That Pass in the Night* in the spring of 1895. The more telling influences on this story, however, were Holmes's Breakfast Table books and Longfellow's "Evangeline." Narrated by a young physician who has lately moved to New York from the country, the plot involves a menage of characters at a boarding house who try to cope with the economic depression of the mid-1890s. One of them, whom the others call the Disagreeable Woman, seems callous and indifferent, though the doctor understands that she merely disdains frivolities. In the final chapter, he tells her the whereabouts of her long-lost fiance and she hurries to his sickbed. She nurses him back to health, and the story concludes, like most of Alger's adult romances, with a long-deferred marriage on the threshold of consummation.[53] Because Porter & Coates had exclusive rights to Alger's fiction, this novel, published in July 1895 by G. W. Dillingham of New York, appeared under the new pseudonym "Julian Starr."

Though it retailed for only seventy-five cents per copy, the novel was Alger's personal worst seller. Dillingham issued it in attractive hardcover, and even the author admitted he "hardly thought this story worth such a setting."[54] Henry B. Blackwell in the *Woman's Journal* commended the feminist overtones of the "bright, lively, charming book," and Munsey loyally plugged it as "good, easy reading for a summer's day," but a reviewer for the *New York Times* intimated that the story was more disagreeable than the title-character.[55] By any measure the novel was a resounding flop. Only two copies of the original edition are known to exist, one of those deposited for copyright in the Library of Congress.

In June 1895, Alger declared a moratorium on work and left New York for New England "a little earlier than I intended. I find the rest and quiet very grateful."[56] He loafed around his sister's house in Natick for several weeks, gave his niece Annie away in marriage to the submaster of the Chapman School in East Boston on July 1, and left for Peak's Island on July 7.[57] "I have done no work since I've been away," and "I do not expect to do anything till fall," he wrote Blake from the Aldine Hotel, Old Orchard Beach, on July 11.[58] "Horatio Alger, Jr., is staying on the Maine coast during the summer, making his headquarters at Old Orchard and Peak's Island," the *Critic* reported later that month.[59] "The paragraph in the Critic may convey the misleading impression that I have given up work," Alger reassured a friend. "I do not propose to do this however, only to work less."[60] He returned to Natick via Manchester and Gloucester towards the end of the month, and left for two weeks in the Catskills on August 5 in company with his sixteen-year-old cousin, Frank Cushman, who also was descended "from Rev. Robert Cushman of Mayflower memory." They cruised down the Hudson to New York, where Alger took young Cushman to Central Park and the Statue of Liberty, before they returned to Natick on the 24th. Alger spent another week in Maine in early September and at last returned to New York and to work on October 9.[61]

The winter of 1895–96 would be his last season in the city. He was besieged by a nagging case of bronchitis, complicated by overwork, which lingered for weeks. In January, fearing an onslaught of fever, he hurried to Natick to be near his sister. "I considered myself in imminent danger of the *grip*," he wrote Blake on February 5. "I have staved it off, but still have a bad cold. . . . I may stay here some weeks."[62] Though nearly exhausted, Alger pushed his pen to finish *A Cousin's Conspiracy*, eventually serialized in the *New York Weekly* between April and August 1896. "I took special pains with it," he admitted later, because "I hope to leave a good impression on the readers, should that [story] be my last."[63] "I have been working very hard," Alger told a reporter in the lobby of the Adams House in Boston on April 9, "and it is a pleasure to be able to rest a little. I am staying out at Natick with relatives now. . . . I do not feel as energetic as I used to."[64] The reporter noted that Alger's closely cropped moustache was gray and his complexion "rather florid." Two weeks later, Alger wrote that his "general health is fair, but I find it difficult to rally from mental overwork."[65] For all practical purposes, he had retired, though not formally or voluntarily. He would never again work more than a day or two at a stretch. Eventually, he would realize that, at the age of sixty-four, he was past trying.

III

I wonder, Irving, how it would seem to be as young and full of life and enthusiasm as you are. I shouldn't dare to go back to 19 again, lest my share of success should prove to be less than it has been.

—HORATIO ALGER, JR.,
12 May 1897

At first, Alger treated his retirement as a period of recuperation. At the invitation of his sister Augusta, he recited a poem at a meeting of the Natick Woman's Suffrage League.[66] He still traveled occasionally—to New York in May 1896 on business; a day journey to Marblehead in late May with A. K. Loring, seventy years old and in straitened circumstances; several days on the Maine coast in August and two weeks at Woodstock, Connecticut, in September.[67] "My summer travel is doing me good," he reported to Blake. "I feel brighter & better than I did."[68] But early in November he took another brief business trip to New York—it would be his last visit to the city—and he "contracted so severe a cold that I thought it the part of prudence" to return to Natick earlier than planned.[69]

Predictably, he had begun to worry about how he might live on a reduced income. Soon after he moved to Natick, he bemoaned the fact that "There are plenty of good writers for boys. If there were not I should occupy a larger field & have more abundant sales." Early in 1897 he expressed the vain hope that "my books have sold well."[70] He was expecting any day to receive a royalty check from Henry T. Coates & Co., successor to the firm of Porter & Coates. When it arrived, it was not as large as he would have liked, though he presently concluded that his income was "adequate" to meet his reduced expenses.[71] In each of the last four years of his life, he sold book rights to two of his old serials to Coates at the flat rate of five hundred dollars per serial—this in addition to his royalties on earlier books still in print.[72] He had also become a silent partner in a small business in Boston to supplement his income.[73] "I still find writing up hill work," he complained to Blake in February, "and if things go well I shall not write any this year." "On account of overwork," he explained a week later in reply to an inquiry from an editor, "I shall not *for some time* be able to undertake any new work."[74] Though his health improved slightly over the summer, especially while he was at Old Orchard Beach in August, he continued to fret about the future.[75] He had earned, by his own estimate, about $100,000 as a writer during his thirty years in New York, but he had earned little money since moving to Natick.[76] "My royalties this year have been less than usual," he diplomatically observed in a letter to Coates in September, "but I hope we shall do better in the coming year."[77]

Unfortunately, Alger's anxieties, both financial and physical, only grew worse over the next twelve months, aggravated by a sluggish economy and a palpitating heart. "I suppose Coates is to publish a book or two for me this fall but I don't think any have appeared," he carped to Blake in October 1897.[78] His sales were still slow, and Coates was unwilling to saturate the market with more than two new Algers a year. Meanwhile, his health continued to fail. He cancelled a business appointment in New York in December because he was "afraid of taking cold" on the trip.[79] His precautions merely postponed the inevitable. The winter in Massachusetts was unusually severe that year, and in early February 1898 he suffered another attack of bronchitis, a fulminating infection "which to one of my physique would probably have been fatal" had it settled in the lungs.[80] "My bronchitis still hangs on," he wrote Blake on March 21, "and probably will for a week or two yet. The worst feature of it is the difficulty of breathing."[81] His condition was complicated by atherosclerosis, hardening of the arteries around the heart, which caused severe anginal pain. In May he took to his bed and wrote letters in a crabbed scrawl. "My most serious trouble is a too rapid heart," he complained in early June. "I have always been short breathed."[82] He tried to recuperate that summer in Nantucket and Old Orchard Beach, but to no avail. In October his eyesight began to fail as the flow of blood to his head was occluded. "I am not at all well," he admitted to Blake on October 21. "I am quite lacking in strength."[83] He still maintained a lively correspondence—he wrote or dictated as many as thirty letters a week to Blake, John Trowbridge, Edward S. Ellis, Louise Chandler Moulton, and others.[84] He still tried to read the *Atlantic Monthly* and other magazines, but he was merely marking time.[85] Even his sister thought he had aged beyond his years.[86]

"It is more than two years since I broke down in New York from over-work and removed to Natick, Mass.," he wrote his cousin Russell Alger on November 10, 1898. "I have been able to do little since then, and it has been somewhat discouraging, particularly as it has cut down my income considerably."[87] Most disturbing to him was his inability to support his eighteen-year-old ward, Tommy Downie, who had gone to work for a magazine dealer in New York. Alger was determined to send him to the Brooklyn Business College, the same school his brother John had attended, so that he might enter a profession and earn a good living. "I may not be able to leave Tommy much," he grieved, "but I want to leave him a better education at any rate."[88] "With such means as I had I have been able to do a good deal of charitable work," he added in his letter to Secretary of War Alger, "but I doubt if I shall be able to [do] very much more."[89] He was not penniless—he owned a lot in North Chicago and had over a thousand dollars in the bank[90]—but on Tommy's account he needed extra cash. When he left New York in 1896, he had written over half of a juvenile novel entitled *Out for Business*.[91] He had been unable to finish the story during his illnesses, however, so in the fall of 1898 he began to search for a ghostwriter who might complete it for him.

He settled on Edward Stratemeyer. Alger had corresponded with Stratemeyer, a sometime editor who had serialized his novel *The Young Acrobat* in the magazine *Bright Days* in 1896, for over two years. "He is an enterprising man and his stories are attractive and popular," Alger thought. "Under favorable circumstances I think he will win a book reputation."[92] In November 1896, during his last trip to New York, he had called on Stratemeyer and found him both polite and personable.[93] When he decided to recruit a ghost to round out his manuscript, he thought first of Stratemeyer, who had completed William T. Adams's last manuscript a few years before. On October 26, 1898, Alger wrote to solicit the help of the younger writer. He was "in a state of nervous prostration," he began,

> and not only can't write, but can't invent the rest of the story for some time to come. I think of all the juvenile writers you can write most like me. Of course I want this help to be *sub rosa*. Can you take my story and finish it in my style? You will be left to your own discretion pretty much. By way of compensation, if satisfactory to you, you shall take the story & sell it to some periodical under *my name*. You will divide the proceeds *equally* with me but I shall retain the copyright and it will appear as my book. . . . Do you think you could easily find a market for a *new book of mine*? Of course we can't get a high price but whatever you can get that is reasonable will satisfy me. You can collect the money & pay me.
>
> If this proposal suits you I will send [the manuscript] out by express. I fancy it would be *easy* work for you as you have a fluent & facile style.[94]

Alger quickly concluded negotiations with Stratemeyer and, on November 21, mailed him two hundred manuscript pages.[95] The story "*is a good deal below my average*," he confessed, "having been written when I was in a state of nervous depression" back in New York.[96] Barely three weeks later, Stratemeyer returned an outline of his projected final chapters. His suggestions pleased Alger, though he admitted he had "only taken a casual glance at the M.S. my eyes being a good deal affected by my illness." In a brief note on December 18, he promised to get back to Stratemeyer when he had a chance "to go through it" in greater detail. "Go ahead with any other work," he added. "Will communicate with you as soon as ready."

He did not write Stratemeyer again, despite the best of intentions. His health steadily deteriorated through the winter. In February 1899, perhaps the last time he touched pen to paper, he scribbled a request to Blake to send him an account of the latest Harvard Club dinner.[97] In April, he was permanently confined indoors. During his final illness he expressed a wish to his sister Augusta that as little publicity as possible attend his death—he did not even want his true age reported—and he acquiesced to her suggestion that his remains be cremated before burial.[98] He died in her home on Florence Street in Natick shortly after midnight on July 18. His physician listed heart disease as the cause of death.

The funeral on the 20th was a quiet, modest affair in keeping with Alger's wish.[99] In the morning his body lay in a plain coffin at Augusta's home, and, early in the afternoon, it was carried to the Eliot Church in South Natick, "one of those huge, shapeless, barn-like structures," as Harriet Beecher Stowe had described it, lit on the interior by "two staring rows of windows, which let in the glare of summer sun."[100] The Reverend George F. Pratt, the elder Horatio's successor in the pulpit, officiated at the service and delivered a brief eulogy. Both A. K. Loring and Henry Denny, the secretary of his college class, sat quietly in the pews. Four Natick boys, among them Arthur Burks and Eugene Sweetland, served as pallbearers. After cremation, his ashes were interred at Glenwood Cemetery, South Natick.

Alger's will contained no surprises.[101] Seventeen months before his death, he had decided to leave bequests of cash totaling $950 to young friends and family members, his calendar gold watch to a grandnephew in California, his lot in North Chicago to his niece Annie, his library to

Alger's funeral, Eliot Unitarian Church, South Natick, Massachusetts, July 20, 1899.
Courtesy of the Harvard University Archives.

Annie's and Augusta's husbands. He willed his copyrights and future royalties to Annie, Augusta, and the Downie brothers, and he directed his sister, as executor of the will, to sell as part of the estate any manuscripts or serials not yet published as books. "All the rest and residue of my estate"—including his private papers—"I bequeath to my sister to be used at her discretion in the furtherance of my wishes, privately communicated to her," he concluded. The files were to be destroyed. The long-kept secret of Brewster was not even to be divulged posthumously.

Augusta did her part to protect her brother's legacy and reputation. On the day he died, she explained to a reporter from the *Boston Post* that, although "he enjoyed ladies' company very much," he had never married because he "apparently never found one whom he particularly fancied."[102] She sold the fragment of *Out for Business* outright to Stratemeyer for $150.[103] "By arrangement with a friend, the book is to be finished and published," she announced.[104] In fact, Stratemeyer would divide the two hundred pages of Alger's manuscript between *Out for Business* and a sequel largely of his own invention, *Falling in with Fortune*.[105] He would rewrite the unpublished "Mabel Parker" for juvenile readers and publish it under the title *Jerry the Backwoods Boy*.[106] Over the next decade, he would complete eight more novels published under Alger's name. These stories were genuine collaborations, based at least in part on Alger's notebooks and other material which Augusta sent him. With her help, Stratemeyer became Alger's official literary heir.

Outside the immediate circle of his friends and family, Alger's death was not much noticed. There were no public outpourings of grief, though his college roommate George Cary visited Augusta to extend condolences on behalf of the Class of '52.[107] "He was continually doing some kind act to assist the boys," Augusta observed. "I never walked down town with him but that some boy or other would have something to say to him."[108] The published tributes to his memory were gracious but few in number. In a brief obituary he prepared for the *New York Tribune*, Irving Blake described him as "a short, stout, bald-headed old gentleman with cordial manners and whimsical views."[109] Stratemeyer wrote a memoir of Alger published in the October 1901 issue of *Golden Hours Junior*, a promotional supplement to *Golden Hours*. Though Augusta thought it "the most satisfactory article about him which has yet appeared," no known copy of it survives.[110] In 1907, eight years after Alger's death, Frank Munsey apotheosized his old friend and contributor in a privately-printed history of his publishing company. "He was one of the most human men I have ever known," Munsey declared, "a man with the simplicity of a child and the sweet, pure soul of God's best type of woman."[111] *De mortuis nil nisi bonum.* Alger was gone and, but for his books, mostly forgotten.

In addition to his books and the bequests in his will, Alger left another legacy of boys whose lives he had influenced as tutor, father, and friend. In most cases the boys did well by him. Joseph Dean became a banker in Palatka, Florida. Isaac Seligman succeeded his father and uncle as head of J. & W. Seligman Co. Edwin Seligman became, at the age of thirty, Professor of Political Economy at Columbia and spent a distinguished career in the study of public finance. In 1885, he helped organize the American Economic Association, and, in 1902, he was elected its president. Gilbert Hitchcock, to whom Alger dedicated a novel in 1878, subsequently succeeded his father in the Congress of the United States, served as wartime spokesman for the Wilson administration as chairman of the Senate Foreign Relations Committee, and was a dark-horse candidate for President in 1920. Alger's pupil Benjamin Cardozo became one of the outstanding jurists of his generation, and, in 1932, he was appointed by Herbert Hoover to the U. S. Supreme Court. Alger's pupil Lewis Einstein enjoyed an eminent career as an American diplomat in France, England, China, Turkey, and Czechoslovakia. Alger's ward John Downie served honorably on the New York Police Department for nearly forty years until his retirement in 1935. Alger's friend Irving Blake served as private secretary to Whitelaw Reid, editor of the *New York Tribune* and ambassador to the Court of St. James. Edward Stratemeyer went on to write the Tom Swift and Rover Boys books and hundreds of other juveniles.[112]

But the ledger was not filled entirely with credits to his memory. In 1871, Alger had dedicated a novel to Washington and Jefferson Seligman, nephews of Joseph, "in the hope that they may emulate the virtues of the distinguished men whose names they bear."[113] As an adult, Washington gambled heavily, concealed a mistress in his room, and subsisted mostly on whiskey, pieces of cracked ice he carried in a zinc-lined pocket, and chunks of charcoal which blackened his teeth. When he was broke he extorted money from his father, Jesse, by threatening to kill himself if refused. In 1903, he attempted suicide by slashing his wrists, and, in 1912, he succeeded with a gun. In 1886, Jefferson Seligman married for money, and, in 1915, he separated for love. He spent the rest of his life and most of his fortune giving fur coats to young women and advocating the kiss as social ritual. In 1889, Alfred

Seligman, the youngest of Joseph's sons, married Florine Arnold, a young family friend to whom Alger had once dedicated a novel. Through the years they conducted a salon for Bohemian artists. Their marriage nearly ended in divorce in 1901 when Florine confessed to an affair. A. Florine ("Boisie") Henriques, the son of the vice-chairman of the New York Stock Exchange, to whom Alger dedicated a novel in 1873, became as an adult a notorious *bon vivant*, and, in 1892, he was arrested and jailed for passing a bad check. Lorin Bernheimer, another friend of the Seligmans to whom Alger dedicated a novel in 1879, suffered a nervous breakdown in 1906; began to claim he possessed incredible wealth; was declared mentally incompetent two years later; and was committed to a sanatorium, where he boasted continually of his fabulous, albeit nonexistent, fortune until his death in 1913.[114] It was an insidious delusion Alger would have understood and perhaps perversely appreciated.

AFTERWORD

Upon Alger's death, one obituarist observed that he had been "perhaps better known to the boys of thirty years ago than to the present generation."[1] Sales statistics tend to support the assertion. A few months before his death, Alger estimated his total sales at about 800,000 volumes.[2] His popularity soared only when his books were reissued in cheap editions after the turn of the century. By 1910, his novels were enjoying estimated annual sales of over one million—that is, more were sold in a year than were sold in total during his life.[3] Alger's books remained popular until about 1920, when sales plummeted. By 1926, the circle of his readers had so shrunk that the leading publisher of his books discontinued them.[4] By 1932, less than twenty percent of seven thousand surveyed New York boys recognized Alger's name and only about fourteen percent admitted to having read even one of his books.[5] He was described that year in the pages of one magazine as "forgotten" and two years later in the pages of another as "extinct."[6] In 1947, a poll of twenty thousand New York children revealed that ninety-two percent of them had "never heard of Alger. Less than one percent had read any of his books."[7]

On the crests and troughs of this sales curve may be graphed two critical questions: If Alger's tales were more popular in 1869 than in 1899, why did he enjoy such astounding posthumous celebrity? And, more importantly, if Alger was virtually forgotten by the late 1920s, how did he acquire renown as a success ideologue? As Malcolm Cowley has complained, "I cannot understand how [Alger] should come to be regarded as the prophet of business enterprise; nor why the family melodrama that he wrote and rewrote for boys should be confused with the American dream of success."[8] As long ago as 1945, Cowley detected a broad discrepancy between what Alger actually wrote and what he is popularly believed to have written.[9] The Alger hero, he noted, was a poor boy who rose to middle-class respectability as a reward for his filial piety, not a poor boy who became a millionaire by dint of honesty and industry. Ironically, Alger's unearned reputation as a success mythmaker was institutionalized only two years later with the inauguration of the Horatio Alger Awards.

During the heyday of his popularity early in this century, Alger acquired a reputation as a champion of Uplift whose formulaic fiction blended moral heroism with economic success. As early as 1898, he was praised in the *Independent* for his "clever trick of turning incidents to account," a new twist on the old complaint about his contrived plots; and his latest hero was touted as "an admirable boy with wonderful ability to take care of himself." Three years later, Carolyn Wells publicly celebrated Alger for teaching "bravery, courage, and pluck through the medium of such characters as newsboys, shoe-blacks, match-sellers and luggage boys, who almost invariably rise to fame and fortune by their own persevering efforts." Similarly, in 1906, the ambitious hero of his *The Young Musician* was praised in the *New York Times*.[10] Alger's original reputation as a writer of simple moral tales for boys had begun to blur. When he was criticized, he was less liable to be charged with writing unwholesome or sensational fiction than reprimanded for emphasizing the accretion of material rewards. Whatever the personal taste of the reader, when read according to the canons of taste which were observed early in this century his moral tracts seemed to celebrate entrepreneurs who earned and spent their wealth honestly. His books were popular during the Progressive period, an era of intense nostalgia for an imaginary olden time of equal opportunity and equitable trade, because they satisfied the popular desire to reform institutions of business and government through a "return to fundamental morality." As Richard Weiss has noted, Alger became "a nostalgic spokesman of a dying order. Of middle-class rural origins, he was always an alien in the industrially dominated society of his adulthood. . . . Alger's work reflects an attempt to re-create the more harmonious society in which he was raised."[11] Because he idealized in his juvenile fiction the moral certainties of a preindustrial order, Alger ironically enhanced his appeal among a later generation of readers for whom he was reinvented as a type of Progressive prophet. Significantly, some of his books were packaged for sale as Progressive reform tracts. At least two editions of his novels issued during the first decade of the new century—a New York Book Company edition of *Joe's Luck* and a Street and Smith edition of *Tom Brace*—pictured Theodore Roosevelt on the cover, though Alger had died before the Great Trustbuster assumed the presidency and had not referred to him in any of his fiction. Unlike the more arcane preachments of "Oliver Optic," Edward Ellis, and other long-forgotten juvenile writers of the nineteenth century, in short, Alger's moral fables could be adapted to a new age.

Moreover, modern opinions of Alger doubtless have been affected by the confusing mass republication of his books early in this century. Cheap editions of Alger's novels were issued by approximately forty publishers between his death in 1899 and 1920. However, many of the earliest novels which conclude as the hero grasps the bottom rung on the ladder of respectability were rarely reprinted, and others were silently abridged, often by deleting as many as seven of the original chapters in which the hero performs virtuous deeds for which he is later rewarded. Thus the most popular editions of Alger's books garbled the moral message of the original versions. In effect, Alger's work was editorially reinvented to appeal to a new generation of readers. Whereas in his own time Alger was credited with inventing a moral hero who becomes modestly successful, during the early years of this century he seemed to have invented a successful hero who is modestly moral. The moral uses of money, not moral behavior *per se*, seemed to have been the focus of the stories.

Many American writers popular during this period adapted Alger's fiction formula, at least as it had been skewed, to their own versions of the success story. Alger's most direct successor, Edward Stratemeyer, who also blended moral heroism and economic success in his fiction, dominated the juvenile market for over two decades before his death in 1930. As early as 1902, Stratemeyer was commended for writing "the sort of book that used to come from the pen of Horatio Alger, Jr."[12] One of the most popular adult westerns ever published, Owen Wister's *The Virginian* (1902), sold an estimated two million copies during this period and owed at least part of its appeal to its assimilation of the Alger pattern. The hero begins a poor cowboy, becomes the ranch foreman, invests his wages in land, and by the end of the novel has become one of the chief citizens of Wyoming. Similarly, Gene Stratton-Porter tapped the wellsprings of Progressive sentiment in her best seller *Michael O'Halloran* (1915) by copying "the Horatio Alger formula, taking a little newsboy up the success ladder on the wings of determination and pluck."[13] The novel might well have been entitled "Ragged Dick Redux."

The most radical transformation in Alger's reputation, his canonization as an American success mythmaker, occurred largely after 1920 as his books declined in popularity and eventually lapsed from print. Much as his novels seemed to endorse Progressive reform when read in the benign spirit of the Progressive period, these same novels, no longer submitted to readers or to the bar of critical opinion, were recollected a generation later in the acquisitive spirit of the prosperous 1920s. Just as Bruce Barton reinvented Jesus of Nazareth as a business leader in *The Man Nobody Knows* (1924), Alger's stock hero was reinvented during this decade as a business tycoon. As *Time* magazine declared in 1928, "Ragged Dick, Phil the Fiddler, and the heroes of every one of his books survived adversity, invariably achieved fame and fortune at the end of the last chapter."[14] Obviously not so. Simply stated, Alger's moral tracts had acquired new meanings in a new context. The author had been transformed into a popular symbol of economic triumph. No longer considered a mere writer of didactic fiction, he became, according to the *New York Times*, a mythologizer who created "successful protagonists, ambitious boys who, through one variation or another of an ever-efficient formula, found their way up the ladder of achievement."[15] The phrase "Horatio Alger hero" obtained popular currency in the language during the 1920s—its first appearance in print may have occurred as late as 1926, even as more libraries were removing Alger's books from their shelves.[16] By 1928, only the frequent invocation of Alger's name reminded people of his earlier popularity. As one critic asked rhetorically that year, "Everyone knows Alger—and yet, do they? To most people Alger is just a name."[17]

During the depression of the 1930s and the world war that followed, Alger was at last transformed into a patriotic defender of the social and political *status quo* and erstwhile advocate of *laissez-faire* capitalism. The characteristics which had come to be associated with the Alger hero—the potential greatness of the common man, rugged individualism, economic triumph in a fabled land of opportunity—seemingly summarized the American way of life threatened by the depression and preserved by the war. Significantly, whereas Samuel Eliot Morison and Henry Steele Commager, in the original edition of *The Growth of the American Republic* in 1930, did not mention Alger at all, in the second and third editions published in 1937 and 1942 they asserted that Alger probably had exerted more influence on the national character than any other writer except perhaps Mark Twain.[18] The *Reader's Guide to Periodical Literature*, an index to articles published in popular magazines since 1892, finally catalogued its first item about Alger in 1932, the centenary of his birth—a revealing indicator of his enshrinement as a cultural hero long after his sales popularity had waned.

Read or selectively remembered during the depression and the war, Alger's novels seemed not to be merely moral tracts or simple success stories, but popular political propaganda. As the economy collapsed, Alger's ostensible celebration of the merits of free enterprise was acclaimed in the general press. In 1932, both the *New York Times* and the *Herald Tribune* editorially hailed him for propagating a philosophy of self-help.[19] In 1934, the *Christian Science Monitor* assured its readers that despite hard times "the Alger pattern still persists."[20] Over the next few years, hymns to Alger steadily crescendoed. In 1938, Frederick Lewis Allen reinforced the shared assumption that Alger had "had a far-reaching influence upon the economic and social thought of America" and had helped "to determine the trend and tradition of American business life."[21] In 1939, on the fortieth anniversary of his death, Alger was eulogized in the *New York Times Magazine*: "His imprint on American life is still clear after forty years; the papers almost every week report the success of some 'typical Alger hero' of the present."[22] The next year, Street and Smith published a comic-book version of *Mark the Match Boy* and NBC radio broadcast a dramatization of *From Farm Boy to Senator*.[23] The governor of New York, Herbert Lehman, declared at the end of this program that as a boy he had been an ardent reader of Alger's fiction and that "I was particularly interested because he showed in his books that the United States was a country of great opportunity for all and he was always a steadfast advocate of the democratic principles on which our nation was created and which have made it great." Rather than despair during the depression, Lehman adjured his listeners to affirm with him that, as in Alger's day, "Broad and unrestricted opportunities for success exist for those who have the vision, the equipment, the industry and the courage to seize them." The *New York Times* editorially commended Lehman for "rallying to the defense of Horatio Alger, and confessing without shame that he was 'an Alger fan when a boy.' It was Alger's comforting thesis that virtue and industry are always rewarded. . . .Hard times come and go, but America is not going to shut up shop. We expect the country to prosper." In a sense, Lehman had prescribed Alger as a home remedy for the economic ills afflicting the nation, reassuring a patient with a strong constitution of her eventual complete recovery.

With the advent of world war, Alger's nomination to symbolic office was ratified. Hardly a month after the bombing of Pearl Harbor, his birthday was celebrated by the Children's Aid Society—an annual event by this time, after the date had been ignored for decades—and the ceremony was duly reported and applauded by the *New York Times*.[24] In the popular motion picture *Yankee Doodle Dandy* (1942), a wartime biography of the patriotic playwright George M. Cohan, the protagonist describes his life to President Franklin Roosevelt as a Horatio Alger story. In 1943, the *Atlantic Monthly*, a magazine which had not reviewed a single Alger book during Alger's life, featured an article about his still-pervasive influence entitled "They Made Me What I Am Today." Because "the generation that grew up . . . before the last war" had, as boys, been inspired by Alger, the argument went, his "faith in *laissez-faire*, in the best of all possible worlds, in the inevitability of rags to riches" served the nation well in the prosecution of the new war.[25] In 1944, Stewart Holbrook, a popular historian, discussed Alger's influence in still more grandiose terms:

> With "Ragged Dick" Alger founded a new school of American literature, the Work and Win, Upward and Onward story; and no matter that today he is unread, Alger was a man of destiny. At exactly the right moment he put into simple words and a standard plot the hopes and beliefs of a nation, and by the sheer power of reiteration caused them to congeal into a national character, the Horatio Alger hero. . . . For the next half century and more nearly everyone in the U.S. believed that every bootblack was a potential capitalist with plug hat and gold-headed cane.[26]

As a wartime gesture in 1945, a publisher reissued four Alger novels that had been out of print for a generation. Copies of this anthology were still available for purchase in 1970, however, so it would seem that the stories were hardly more popular in than out of print. Yet the impression that Alger was enjoying a revival and that his novels remained influential was reinforced by favorable reviews of the omnibus in the *Saturday Review*, the *New Yorker*, the *New York Times*, the *New Republic*, *Time*, and *Commonweal*. The title of the review by William Rose Benét for the *Saturday Review*, "A Monument to Free Enterprise," suggests the slant adopted by them all.[27]

After the war, as the rest of the country demobilized, Alger retained his appointive political office. In 1947, the *New York Times* again cited him on the editorial page, contending that only disillusioned historians "who wrote, or may still be writing, in strong disapproval of America as a whole" dared to criticize Alger and his gospel of success,[28] and *Advertising Age* called for a latter-day Alger to inspire self-reliance among postwar American youth and to counteract "government interference" with private industry.[29] Spotting a trend, meanwhile, Holbrook suggested that Alger had

> put free and untrammeled competition on the side of the angels. . . . Though the 1870s and the eighties and nineties saw dismal and widespread poverty in the United States, and though anarchists and socialists fomented strikes and riots, the Red Dawn never came up over the horizon. Too many Americans held the vision of Upward and Onward.[30]

No longer perceived as merely moral fables, Alger's novels seemed more like tools of social control wielded by an entrenched ruling class. Basking in popular esteem like a decorated war hero, this mythical Alger in 1947 lent his name and reputation to the Horatio Alger Awards, a vehicle for recognizing meritorious service to the causes of political or religious conservatism and economic orthodoxy.[31] Sponsored by the American Schools and Colleges Association, Inc., which had become "concerned about the trend among young people towards the mindpoisoning belief that equal opportunity was a thing of the past," the Alger Awards Committee selects annually several "living individuals who by their own efforts had pulled themselves up by their bootstraps in the American tradition." Past recipients include Dwight Eisenhower, Ronald Reagan, Billy Graham, and W. Clement Stone. Transformed into an American mythmaker, Alger was viewed in a new light which distorted his original moral purpose. His novels were no longer considered literary documents, but evaluated according to the social and political ends they seemed to serve.

More recent invocations of the Alger myth, as in Garry Wills's *Nixon Agonistes* (1970) and John Seelye's *Dirty Tricks, or Nick Noxin's Natural Nobility* (1974), suggest that Alger's popular image crystallized with his institutionalization in 1947 and that his utility as a political symbol has remained essentially unchanged since the 1930s. The metamorphosis of his reputation—from didactic writer for boys, to Progressive moralist, economic mythmaker, and finally political ideologue—seems to have been dictated less by the content of his books than by the context in which the books were read or remembered. An economic and political symbol today more by accident of birth than by deliberate design, Alger has become, with the features of his mutation complete, the victim of mistaken identity.

In his juvenile stories, to be sure, Alger influenced a generation of young Americans early in this century. As one familiar only with his modern reputation might expect, many of his readers, such as Ben-

jamin Fairless of U. S. Steel, James A. Farley of Coca-Cola, FBI director
J. Edgar Hoover, and Presidents Gerald Ford and Ronald Reagan,
became real-life counterparts to the mythical Alger heroes.[32] But to
consider Alger simply as an apologist for capitalism and the political
right is to overlook his basic humanitarian impulse. As one familiar only
with his modern reputation might *not* expect, many well-known American writers on the political left, including not only Theodore Dreiser
and Jack London, but also Richard Wright and Upton Sinclair, read
Alger's books as youngsters and were not stirred to embrace capitalism
as adults.[33] Alger himself hardly could have imagined that he would be
long remembered, much less celebrated as an American mythologizer a
half-century after his death. As he wrote Irving Blake in 1897, "If I
could come back 50 years from now probably I should feel bewildered in
reading the New York Tribune of 1947."[34] He wrote with a soothsayer's
foresight, for one of the items in the news that year which doubtless
would have perplexed him beyond his wildest flights of fancy publicized
the inauguration of the annual Horatio Alger Awards. After fifty years,
Alger could not have recognized his offspring.

NOTES

The following abbreviations are used in the citations:

AAS   American Antiquarian Society, Worcester, Mass.

A-H   Andover-Harvard Theological Library, Harvard Divinity School, Cambridge, Mass.

"AMBR"   Horatio Alger, Jr., "Are My Boys Real?" *Ladies Home Journal*, 7 (Nov. 1890), 29.

AS   *Alger Street: The Poetry of Horatio Alger, Jr.*, ed. by Gilbert K. Westgard II (Boston, 1964).

AU   *American Union*

BA   *Boston Advertiser*

BDG   *Boston Daily Globe*

Bennett   Bob Bennett, *Horatio Alger, Jr.: A Comprehensive Bibliography* (Mt. Pleasant, Mich., 1980).

BET   Boston *Evening Traveller*

BP   *Boston Post*

BPL   Boston Public Library, Copley Square, Boston, Mass.

Brown   Addison Brown, *Autobiographical Notes for His Children* (Boyce, Va., 1972).

BT   *Boston Transcript*

CB   Class Book of 1852, University Archives, Pusey Library, Harvard Univ., Cambridge, Mass.

CI   *Christian Inquirer*

CR   *Christian Register*

CU   Edwin R. A. Seligman Papers, Rare Book and Manuscript Library, Columbia Univ., New York.

Edes   Grace Williamson Edes, *Annals of the Harvard Class of 1852* (Cambridge, 1922).

EI   Essex Institute, Salem, Mass.

GA   *Golden Argosy*

Gardner	Ralph D. Gardner, *Horatio Alger, or The American Hero Era* (Mendota, Ill., 1964).
Gen.Hi.	Arthur M. Alger, *A Genealogical History . . . of the Alger Family* (Boston, 1876).
Gruber	Frank Gruber, *Horatio Alger, Jr.: A Biography and Bibliography* (West Los Angeles, 1961).
HA	Horatio Alger, Jr.
HGM	*Harvard Graduates' Magazine*
Hoyt	Edwin P. Hoyt, *Horatio's Boys* (Radnor, Penn., 1974).
HU	Houghton Library, Harvard Univ., Cambridge, Mass.
HUA	Harvard Univ. Archives, Pusey Library, Cambridge, Mass.
Hunt	The Huntington Library, San Marino, Cal.
HW	*Harper's Weekly*
Knox	Seymour Collection, Knox College Library, Galesburg, Ill.
LC	Manuscript Division, Library of Congress, Washington, D.C.
LChr	*Liberal Christian*
LJ	*Library Journal*
Mayes	Herbert R. Mayes, *Alger: A Biography Without a Hero* (New York, 1928; reprinted with a new introduction by Mayes, Des Plaines, Ill., 1978).
Mich	Russell A. Alger Collection, William L. Clements Library, Univ. of Michigan, Ann Arbor, Mich.
MM	*Marlborough Mirror*
MPL	Marlborough Public Library
Munsey	Frank A. Munsey, "Two Veteran Authors," *Munsey's*, 8 (Oct. 1892), 58–61.
N	*Newsboy*, publication of the Horatio Alger Society
NEHGS	New-England Historic Genealogical Society, Boston, Mass.
NHS	Natick Historical Society, Natick, Mass.
NL	Malcolm Cowley Papers, Newberry Library, Chicago, Ill.
NYEP	*New York Evening Post*
NYS	*New York Sun*
NYTi	*New York Times*
NYTr	New York *Tribune*
NYHS	New-York Historical Society, New York.
NYPL	Manuscript and Archives Division, New York Public Library, Astor, Lenox and Tilden Foundations, New York.
NYW	*New York Weekly*
PML	Pierpont Morgan Library, New York.
PT	*Portland Transcript*
S&B	Gary Scharnhorst and Jack Bales, *Horatio Alger, Jr.: An Annotated Bibliography of Comment and Criticism* (Metuchen, New Jersey, 1981).
SFMC	*San Francisco Morning Call*
Shur	Benjamin Shurtleff, *The History of the Town of Revere* (Boston, 1938).
SS	Stratemeyer Syndicate, Maplewood, New Jersey.

Tebbel	John Tebbel, *From Rags to Riches* (New York, 1963).
TF	*True Flag*
UUA	Archives, Unitarian Universalist Association, Boston, Mass.
UV	Horatio Alger Collection (#6325-a), Clifton Waller Barrett Library, Univ. of Virginia, Charlottesville, Va.
"WSfB"	Horatio Alger, Jr., "Writing Stories for Boys," *Writer*, 9 (Feb. 1896), 36–37.
YB	*Yankee Blade*
YU	Beinecke Rare Book and Manuscript Library, Yale Univ., New Haven, Conn.

Preface

1. HA to Irving Blake, 16 July 1896 (Hunt).

2. In his will, HA specified he had "privately communicated" to his sister O. Augusta Cheney his wishes regarding the disposition of his papers. According to Stanley Pachon, a long-time HA researcher, Cheney later acknowledged destroying them. Certainly none have come to light.

3. Anna Alger Richardson to Frank Millner, [9?] Aug. 1942, quoted in Millner to Mabel Parmenter, 12 Aug. 1942 (NHS).

4. W. R. Alger letter: Carl Seaburg to Scharnhorst, 8 June 1981.

5. Mayes's hoax: Mayes's own discussions of his hoax appear in "After Half a Century," the new introduction (pp. i-xxxv) he prepared for a reissue of his HA biography; letters reprinted in *N*, 12 (Jan.–Feb. 1974); and his autobiography, *The Magazine Maze* (Garden City, 1980), 184–186.

6. Reviews: S&B, 65–67.

7. *Time*, 13 Aug. 1945, p. 98 and *passim*; *New Republic*, 10 Sept. 1945, pp. 319–320.

8. Mayes to Cowley, 15 Jan. 1958 (NL).

9. Cowley to Mayes, 19 Feb. 1958 (NL).

10. Cowley to Scharnhorst, 28 July 1973.

11. Mayes to Bales, 9 April 1978.

12. *Horizon*, 12 (Summer 1970), 62.

13. Mayes, 220.

14. *Time*, 10 June 1974, p. 18.

15. *The Dream of Success* (Boston, 1955), 4–10 and *passim*.

16. *Hudson Review*, 19 (Winter 1959), 549–557.

17. Gruber, esp. 13, 16, 26–27.

18. Tebbel, esp. v; Tebbel to Scharnhorst, 2 Jan. 1973; *Who's Who in America 1980–81*, 41st ed. (Chicago, 1980), II, 3662; S&B, 151.

19. Exchange of letters: Gardner to Mayes, 11 April 1975 (Mayes, xxiii); Mayes to Gardner, 24 June 1975.

20. Gardner, 13.

21. Gardner to Scharnhorst, 16 March 1976.

22. Reviews: S&B, 68–72, 79.

23. Hoyt, 214, 252.

24. Mayes to Gardner, 24 June 1975.

Interlude

Like most events in his life, HA's resignation from the ministry and his early years in New York have been grossly misrepresented by his biographers. According to Mayes (p. 98), HA simply grew dissatisfied with preaching and resigned his pulpit. Gruber (p. 22) and Tebbel (p. 66) state matter of factly that HA "resigned his ministry" or "his pastorate" and "moved to New York." According to Gardner (p. 183), HA "wasn't able to continue as pastor and writer and properly handle both jobs," so he welcomed the vote of the church deacons not to extend his contract and, after a terminal period of three months, headed for New York, where he would spend his future years as a writer. Only Hoyt (pp. 1–7) mentions the accusation of pedophilia that precipitated HA's sudden resignation from the ministry and his flight to New York.

The records of the Unitarian Church and Society in Brewster regarding the termination of HA's ministry there have been frequently reprinted, though rarely in their entirety. They were first excerpted in detail by Richard Huber in *The American Idea of Success* (New York, 1971), 42–61. They have been fully reprinted in *N*, 18 (Dec. 1979), 5–7. The other correspondence in the records of the American Unitarian Association, cited below, has been reprinted in its entirety in *N*, 19 (Dec 1980), 8–13.

1. Lowe to Brewster committee, 21 March 1866 (A-H).
2. George Copeland to Lowe, 23 March 1866 (A-H).
3. Lowe to Brewster committee, 21 March 1866 (A-H).
4. Brewster committee to Lowe, 19 March 1866 (A-H).
5. Alger to Lowe, 22 March 1866 (A-H).
6. Solomon Freeman to Lowe, 24 March 1866 (A-H).
7. Copeland to Lowe, 23 March 1866 (A-H).
8. Lowe to Brewster committee, 21 March 1866 (A-H).
9. Freeman to Lowe, 1 Sept. 1866 (A-H).
10. Lowe to Freeman, 22 March 1866 (A-H).
11. *CR*, 24 March 1866, 3.

1. The Odds Against Him (1832–1860)

I

Earlier biographers have known next to nothing about HA's childhood. As Mayes recounts the story, HA's early growth was stunted by a puritanical father, a soldier in the Church Militant, who drilled his son in the niceties of doctrine and prevented his marriage to a childhood sweetheart named Patience Stires. Mayes attributes to HA "a speech defect—a stutter—he never had" and has his schoolmates nickname him "Holy Horatio"—a detail which was "altogether a figment of my imagination," as he recently admits (Mayes, vii–viii). Unfortunately, HA's next four biographers depend almost exclusively on two sources— Mayes and their own imaginations—for data about the early years. Consider the following excerpt from Mayes's original biography (p. 19):

> Mr. Alger dressed his boy in dignity and was proud to see him stand, as he supposed, aloof from other children of his age. In reality it was the children who sedulously avoided him when play time came. They were not favorably impressed

with his grave demeanor or the immaculate clothes in which, even for interludes of leisure, he inevitably appeared. They teased him, mocked him, made him the butt of pranks, and called him Holy Horatio.

This paragraph, with minor revisions, appears in each of the four subsequent biographies.

Despite his professed repudiation of Mayes, Gruber borrows liberally from his biography on the subject of HA's childhood. The "greatest desire" of the elder Alger, he asserts (p. 18):

was that Horatio, Jr., should follow in his footsteps and from infancy he tried to influence him. Young Horatio rebelled frequently, but always his father brought him back in line. Young Horatio had an unhappy childhood; his father was severe and his domination almost broke young Horatio's spirit. His playmates called him by the alliterative nickname of "Holy Horatio" and he detested it.

Despite Gruber's protestations, he writes in Mayes's shadow. This paragraph contains not a word of truth.

On his part, Tebbel slips into the trap of pyschoanalyzing HA on the basis of specious sources. As a child, he explains (pp. 24–25), HA exhibited "an early symptom of personality disorganization: he stuttered badly." Young HA "was excluded from games, teased, made to suffer indignities large and small, poked fun at, and of course given an odious nickname—'Holy Horatio.'" According to Tebbel, his domineering father marked the distinction with pride: "Alger Senior considered that he had created a superior child, and he enjoyed seeing him stand grave and aloof from the others, always immaculately dressed." Indeed, Tebbel follows Mayes's lead so closely he even paralleled his prose, as the following passages from their respective biographies reveal:

Until he was seven he had mute companions—only colored, wooden blocks—to play with. Yet the little mind, already impinged upon by ministerial data, found solace in those hours when, alone, he could squat upon the floor and build. . . . Horatio specialized in towers. Over and over he built a tower of the same design, anticipating always a structure that would stand straight and proud, higher than his head, an impressive architecture. When the tower crumbled to the floor before its tall destiny was accomplished, the boy would gather the scattered segments and begin again, uncomplainingly [Mayes, pp. 17–18].

Horatio was unutterably lonely. He spent much of his early childhood building with large blocks, and no doubt a psychiatrist studying him at that stage would have derived further clues from the fact that he built the same structure again and again—towers which he erected block upon block until they toppled, whereupon he would quietly, unemotionally, start building them up again [Tebbel, p. 24].

Though Tebbel paraphrases the anecdote, he simultaneously invests it with psychoanalytical significance. His biography is virtually a pathological case study. Whereas Mayes invented incidents, Tebbel examines syndromes.

Gardner also repeats Mayes's fable of HA's childhood. He reports (pp. 58, 90, 92) that young HA "stuttered badly." He likewise mentions (p. 61), without attribution, the derogatory nickname:

Unlike [his] classmates, [HA] always wore Sunday clothes, which his father considered proper attire for a minister's son. For this he was teased and ridiculed, until he tearfully persuaded Mother that he must be allowed to dress like the others.

"I cannot go back to school, Mother," he cried. "They laugh at my clothes and call me 'Holy Horatio, the parson's son.'"

"I haven't re-read my book," Gardner protests in his letter to Mayes in April 1975, "but it seems to me that someplace in it I, too, used 'Holy Horatio.'" Yet he tries to avoid personal responsibility for the error: "I know I did not take it from your book," he writes (Mayes, p. xxv). Gardner misses the point with this curious defense. Would he be less culpable had he taken it from another source?

At a loss for hard data, Gardner resorts to lifting characters and long passages directly from HA's fiction. He apparently considers this permissible biographical method. As he asserts in his preface (p. 13), "Much childhood biography exists in [HA's later] writing. . . . Careful checking discloses" that there are "similarities of occurrences" between HA's art and HA's life. So Gardner justifies copying an entire chapter—without so identifying it—from HA's little-known *nouvelle* "A Fancy of Hers." HA had written as follows (*Munsey's*, 6 [March 1892], 736):

> At four o'clock in the afternoon people began to arrive. The parsonage had been put in order, and the minister and his wife awaited their visitors.
> "Is it necessary for me to be here?" asked Ralph.
> "It would hardly look well for you to be away, my son."
> "I will stay if you wish it, of course, father; but it always humiliates me. It looks as if we were receiving charity."

Rather like a college freshman hard-pressed to finish a term paper, Gardner writes (p. 74):

> At four o'clock on the afternoon of the party, guests began to arrive. The house had been arranged for the gathering, and The Rev. and Mrs. Alger awaited their visitors.
> "Is it necessary for me to be here?" asked Horatio.
> "It would hardly look well for you to be away, my son."
> "I'll stay if you wish, father, but it humiliates me. It looks as if we were receiving charity."

In his introduction to *A Fancy of Hers* and *The Disagreeable Woman* (New York, 1981), p. 17, Gardner reiterates that the former story contains "generous dollops of Alger's own childhood." Nathanael West, who plagarized HA in his novel *A Cool Million*, at least labeled his work a fiction.

Hoyt neatly assimilates "facts" he culled from Gardner to "prove" HA's homosexuality was the result of a pathetically unhappy childhood (pp. 10, 15, 21):

> The Reverend Horatio Alger worked to bring his son up as a God-fearing boy who would join the church. . . . It was only proper, said the Reverend Alger, for a boy who was going into the church to be trained carefully from his earliest youth. In school they called him Holy Horatio, and he was the butt of the jokes of the ruder, bigger boys, so much so that he complained tearfully to his mother. . . . He was, in any case, hardly fitted for the rowdy world of business, for in his teens he still stuttered and was uncomfortable in any public role. . . . From the early days his rejection by roughneck boys hurt him. By the time he was in college he had all the makings of a homosexual: a domineering father, a weak and patient mother, a strong and not very attractive sister and a grave feeling of inferiority in the world of men.

Like an armchair psychologist, Hoyt scratched around until he found "facts" to

fit his conclusion. He might have avoided these mistakes had he better researched his subject. Mayes had admitted months before that "it was I, without
any basis, who wrote that the senior Alger wanted his son to follow in his
footsteps. . . . I created the alliterative nickname Holy Horatio. . . . I created
that stammer."

1. *Gen.Hi.*, 2, 9, 15, and *passim*; Kate Caffrey, *The Mayflower* (New York,
1974), 37, 154, 355–56; William Bradford, *Of Plimouth Plantation* (New York,
1975), 54.

2. *Gen.Hi.*, 28–29; *MM*, 18 Feb. 1860, 1:1–3; *BT*, 10 Nov. 1881, 2:5.

3. *CR*, 5 Sept. 1829, 142:4–5.

4. *Unitarian Advocate*, 4 (Sept. 1831), 112–121; 5 (Jan. 1832), 21–28; 6
(Sept. 1832), 113–118; 6 (Oct. 1832), 178–185.

5. Alger to first religious society in Chelsea, 5 Nov. 1838 (Bales).

6. Shur, 150; Francis Parkman to Alger, 24 Jan. 1830 (BPL).

7. *AS*, 93.

8. Shur, 120; *MM*, 18 Feb. 1860, 1:1–3.

9. *Gen.Hi.*, 28.

10. Shur, 276–78, 291.

11. Alger to first religious society in Chelsea, 5 Nov. 1838 (Bales).

12. *TF*, 25 March 1854, 1.

13. Shur, 384.

14. *MM*, 18 Feb. 1860, 1:1–3.

15. *Gen.Hi.*, 29.

16. Shur, 277.

17. Alger to first religious society in Chelsea, 3 April 1844 (BPL).

18. Shur, 277, 291, 433.

19. *TF*, 22 Oct. 1859, 2:2.

20. CB, 101.

21. Joshua Chapin, *Asthma, Its Causes and Treatment* (Boston, 1843),
13–16.

22. CB, 101.

23. *MM*, 18 Feb. 1860, 1:1–3.

24. *Gen.Hi.*, 15; Shur, 150; CB, 101.

25. Classified ad in *MM*, Feb. 1861 (MPL).

26. *Monthly Religious Magazine*, 2 (March 1845), 105; *CR*, 25 Jan. 1845,
14:2; *CR*, 15 March 1845, 42:5–6.

27. CB, 101–102.

28. *Bound to Rise* (Boston, 1873), 188.

29. Alger to Rev. Mr. Holland, 10 Oct. 1848 (A-H).

II

While acknowledging the significance of HA's undergraduate education at
Harvard, past biographers fail to describe it fairly. Mayes invents ten pages on
the subject (pp. 50–60), but most of them merely describe the "pathetic,
shrivelled" young scholar's futile search for suitable lodgings in Cambridge.
Gruber dismisses HA's college years in two brief paragraphs (pp. 15–16).
Tebbel paraphrases Mayes's ten pages in eight (pp. 32–41). Gardner dilutes his
twenty pages (pp. 98–117) with contrived conversations and an irrelevant aside

about a sensational murder which occurred in Cambridge in 1849. HA was not involved in the intrigue even tangentially. But it was one of the few events between 1848 and 1852, HA's years as a Harvard undergraduate, which Samuel Eliot Morison mentioned (p. 284) in *Three Centuries of Harvard* (Cambridge, 1936), so Gardner borrowed and embellished the reference. Little wonder that Hoyt, in the midst of his Gardner rehash, admits that "the facts of Horatio's college life are sparse" (p. 19). A critical assessment of the other biographies would lead to that unfortunate conclusion.

30. CB, 102.

31. Albee: *Historical Catalogue of Brown University 1764–1894* (Providence, 1895), 108–109; CB, 102; Charles Hudson, *History of the Town of Marlborough* (Boston, 1862), 284; *MM*, 22 Sept. 1860, 1:2. Gates Academy: CB, 102; *The Church Record . . . of the West Church in Marlborough* (Boston, 1850), 3.

32. *Gen.Hi.*, 46; *SFMC*, 9 Nov. 1890, 12; *GA*, 17 Oct. 1885, 365.

33. *TF*, 15 Oct. 1853, 2:1–3.

34. HA to Irving Blake, 12 Nov. 1898 (Hunt).

35. CB, 102.

36. College catalogue for the Class of 1852, 39–40; *The Life of Joseph Hodges Choate* (New York, 1920), I, 58; *HGM*, 8 (Sept. 1899), 112.

37. CB, 102.

38. *Life of Choate*, I, 69–70; *Harvard and Its Surroundings* (Cambridge, 1882), *passim*.

39. *TF*, 21 Jan. 1854, 4:2.

40. Edes, 6.

41. Aid from Cyrus Alger: *HGM*, 8 (Sept. 1899), 112. Tuition and room rent: *Life of Choate*, I, 62; Jim Dan Hill, *The Civil War Sketchbook of Charles Ellery Stedman* (San Rafael, Cal., 1976), 9. College commons: *Life of Choate*, I, 61. After commons closed: *Sam's Chance* (Boston, 1876), 237.

42. College catalogue for the Class of 1852, 41–44; *Life of Choate*, I, 74; Hill, 7; Brown, 60.

43. *Luck and Pluck* (Boston, 1869), 132; *Tom the Bootblack* (New York, 1889), 188.

44. Academic record (HUA).

45. Edes, 6; Brown, 62, 65; *GA*, 17 Oct. 1885, 364; CB, 103.

46. Holograph MS (HUA).

47. *Life of Choate*, I, 76, 77.

48. Herbert Baxter Adams, *The Life and Writings of Jared Sparks* (Boston and New York, 1893), II, 466; James Bradley Thayer, *Letters of Chauncey Wright* (Cambridge, 1878), 23, 28; *Life of Choate*, I, 59; Edes, 6; Brown, 72.

49. CB, 102–103.

50. Bennett, 192, 199.

51. Library charging lists for 1848–52 (HUA); *From Farm Boy to Senator* (New York, 1882), 23–24.

52. *New York Railroad Men*, 9 (March 1896), 142.

53. HA to J. F. Cooper, 12 Sept. 1850 (Yale).

54. HA to H. W. Longfellow, 16 Dec. 1875 (HU).

55. Holograph poem, 18 Dec 1882 (UV). Copy also in NYPL.

56. *Life of Choate*, I, 67–68; Brown, 73.

57. *From Farm Boy to Senator*, 5, 274.

58. *Life of Choate*, I, 68–69; Brown, 70–71; Donald Spencer, *Louis Kossuth and Young America* (Columbia and London, 1977), 154–159.

59. *Gleason's Literary Companion*, 24 July 1869; reprinted in *N*, 17 (Dec. 1978), 12–14.

60. Brown, 64.

61. Edes, 6; Hill, 16; Thayer, 24; William T. Washburn, *Fair Harvard* (New York, 1869), 132.

62. *Walter Sherwood's Probation* (Philadelphia, 1897), chap. 1.

63. Indexed MS, now lost (HUA).

64. *TF*, 12 Nov. 1853, 4:6.

65. Brown, 64, 66; Albert Poole Jacobs, *The Psi Upsilon Epitome* (Boston, 1884), 35–36.

66. *Sam's Chance*, 230–233.

67. *AS*, 78.

68. *Annals of Psi Upsilon 1833–1941* (New York, 1941), 168, 170.

69. *AS*, 79.

70. *TF*, 19 Jan. 1856, 4:5.

71. Edes, 6; *AS*, 81.

72. CB, 103.

73. *BT*, 20 July 1852, 1:6.

74. Holograph MS (HUA).

75. *Life of Choate*, I, 74.

III

76. George Norris to J. H. Choate, 2 Aug. 1853 (LC).

77. Edes, 5; Brown, 64.

78. *Gen.Hi.*, 43–44; *CR*, 18 Sept. 1847, 151:4.

79. E.g., *Monthly Religious Magazine*, 5 (1849), 397, 488; 6 (1849), 337; *CR*, 19 Jan. 1850, 9; and 9 Aug. 1851, 125.

80. *Monthly Religious Magazine*, 8 (1851), 167–76.

81. *N*, 20 (Aug.–Sept. 1981), 30–31; 21 (Oct.–Nov. 1982), 33.

82. Loose notes in HA file (HUA).

83. Bennett, 193, 199; *N*, 20 (Oct.–Nov. 1981), 4; CB, 103.

84. *N*, 22 (March–Apr. 1983), 20–23.

85. *N* (March–Apr. 1983), 19.

86. Bennett, 173–191; Frank Luther Mott, *A History of American Magazines 1850–1865* (Cambridge, 1938), 10, 35, 409–412.

87. *TF*, 20 Aug. 1853, 4:6.

88. Loose notes in HA file (HUA); CB, 104; Edes, 6.

89. *N*, 21 (Oct.–Nov. 1982), 37. Some of these stories were subsequently reprinted in such New England papers as *PT* (*N*, 21 [Dec. 1982], 7).

90. CB, 104.

91. HA to Robert Bonner, 21 Nov. 1879 (PML).

92. *TF*, 9 April 1853, 4:1; and 10 Sept. 1853, 4:1.

93. CB, 104; Edes, 6–7.

94. *John Godfrey's Fortunes* (New York, 1864), 182.

95. HA to Robert Bonner, 21 Nov. 1879 (PML).

96. CB, 104; HA to Irving Blake, 28 April 1896 (Hunt).

97. *BA*, 10 April 1896, 9.

98. CB, 103.

99. *TF*, 13 March 1858, 2:3.

100. *TF*, 21 Jan. 1854, 4:2.

101. CB, 104.

102. E. W. Cobb, *A Memoir of Sylvanus Cobb, Jr.* (Boston, 1891), 283.

103. *My Own Story* (Boston, 1903), 135.

104. HA to Robert Bonner, 21 Nov. 1879 (PML).

105. "WSfB."

106. *YB*, 11 March 1854, 2; 24 Sept. 1853, 2; 20 Nov. 1853, 2; *AU*, 1 July 1854; reprinted in *N*, 16 (Dec. 1977), 3–9.

107. *YB*, 1 April 1854, 2.

108. *TF*, 14 Oct. 1854, 2:6.

109. CB, 104.

110. Louise B. Clarke, *The Greenes of Rhode Island 1534–1902* (New York, 1903), 413–414.

111. *John Godfrey's Fortunes*, 221.

112. *Paul Prescott's Charge* (Boston, 1865), v.

113. HA to J. H. Choate, 29 Nov. 1854 (LC).

114. Adams, *Jared Sparks*, II, 476–77.

115. *N*, 20 (Oct.–Nov. 1981), 4–8.

116. *AS*, 49–50.

117. *BT*, 8 Nov. 1855, 2:1; and 27 Nov. 1855, 2:2.

118. *Bertha's Christmas Vision* (Boston, 1856), v.

119. *John Godfrey's Fortunes*, 226–27.

120. Reviews: *BT*, 7 Dec. 1855, 2:1; *BP*, 17 Dec. 1855, 1:7; *BA*, 19 Dec. 1855, 2:4; *Providence Daily Journal*, 25 Dec. 1855, 1:6; *S&B*, 27; *YB*, 5 Jan. 1856, 3:5; *CR*, 2 Feb. 1856, 19:1.

121. *John Godfrey's Fortunes*, 227–28.

122. The book is still owned by the Harvard libraries.

123. CB, 104; David R. Proper, "Horatio Alger in Deerfield," *Historic Deerfield Quarterly*, 13 (Jan. 1974), 8–9.

124. CB, 104.

125. W. R. Alger presented HA with an inscribed copy, now owned by PML, of his first book *The Poetry of the Orient*, published in late 1855.

126. *N*, 12 (Aug. 1973), 8–9; *Dime Novel Roundup*, 15 Sept. 1973, 98–104.

127. Scharnhorst, "Good Fortune in America" (Ph.D. dissertation, Purdue Univ., 1978), 354–355; *Putnam's* 9 (March 1857), 235–243.

128. *Graham's*, 52 (Jan. 1858), 30–32; *Harper's* 18 (Dec. 1858), 43–46. See also *TF*, 11 Dec. 1858, 2:4–6.

129. Quoted in Mott, *A History of American Magazines 1850–1865*, 472.

130. *AS*, 15–24.

131. HA to W. A. Wheeler, 2 Jan. 1869 (UV).

132. HA to Irving Blake, 10 Nov. 1896 (Hunt).

133. *BT*, 30 July 1857, 3:2.

134. Reviews: *BT*, 10 Aug. 1857, 2:3; *CR*, 15 Aug. 1857), 130:6; *PT*, 22 Aug. 1857, 155:2; NYS, 5 Sept. 1857, 1:4; *TF*, 8 Aug. 1857, 3.

135. Tebbel, 153.

136. *CR*, 12 Sept. 1857, 148.

137. Brown, 65.

138. The book, dated 15 Sept. 1857, is still owned by the Harvard libraries.

139. Washburn, *Fair Harvard*, 111.

140. Quoted in Morison, *Three Centuries of Harvard*, 395.

141. *N*, 12 (Aug. 1973), 8–9; *Dime Novel Roundup*, 15 Sept. 1973, 98–104; Frank O'Brien, *The Story of the Sun* (New York, 1918), 194–95.

142. Bennett, 174–191, 194.

143. Bennett, 173–191.

144. *The Church Record . . . of the West Church in Marlborough*, 3–5; John A. Bigelow to Frank Millner, 11 Feb. 1940 (HUA).

145. *MM*, 18 Feb. 1860, 1:1–3.

146. Senior Alger to Samuel Johnson, 28 Sept. and 22 Nov. 1855 (EI); senior Alger to R. W. Emerson, 28 Dec. 1853 (HU); *Journals and Miscellaneous Notebooks of Ralph Waldo Emerson*, ed. R. H. Orth and A. R. Ferguson (Cambridge, 1977), XIII, 510.

147. HA to Irving Blake, 18 Dec. 1896 (Hunt).

148. *BA*, 24 Aug. 1855, 2:4.

149. B. E. Hazard, *The Organization of the Boot and Shoe Industry in Massachusetts Before 1875* (Cambridge, 1921), 103 and *passim*.

150. Senior Alger to Rev. Dr. Miles, 15 March 1858 (A-H).

151. John A. Bigelow to Frank Millner, 11 Feb. 1940 (HUA).

152. *The Church Record . . . of the West Church in Marlborough*, 11–22.

153. *MM*, 18 Feb. 1860, 1:1–3.

154. *CR*, 16 Feb. 1861, 27:1; and 28 Sept. 1861, 154.

155. *MM*, 18 Feb. 1860, 1:1–3.

156. *Ibid.*; Hudson, *History of Marlborough*, 284.

157. *MM*, 18 Feb. 1860, 1:1–3.

158. *TF*, 18 Sept. 1858, 4:4–5.

159. *MM*, 5 May 1860, 1:2–4.

160. *Natick Observer*, 16 June 1860, 2:3; *Gen.Hi.*, 28; NEHGS *Register*, 36 (Oct. 1882), 415.

161. *MM*, 14 July 1860 (NHS).

162. Classified ad in *MM*, 4 Aug. 1860 (NHS).

163. *MM*, 15 Sept. 1860, 2:2.

164. *CR*, 13 Oct. 1860, 163:2; *MM*, 27 Oct. 1860, 1:3.

165. *CR*, 10 March 1860, 39:3.

166. Hudson, *History of Marlborough*, 495, 508–509.

167. *AS*, 89.

168. *CR*, 21 July 1860, 115:1–2; *MM*, 21 July 1860 (HU).

169. *Abraham Lincoln, the Backwoods Boy* (New York, 1883), 120.

170. *MM*, 18 Aug. 1860, 2:3.

171. CB, 104; *MM*, 1 Sept. 1860, 2:1; *BET*, 5 Sept. 1860, 3:3; E. W. Smith, *Trans-Atlantic Passenger Ships* (Boston, 1947), 43.

172. *MM*, 1 Sept. 1860, 2:1.

2. Bound to Rise (1860–1866)

I

Past biographers agree HA sailed to Europe in 1860 with two male companions. This point of concurrence is the only one they get right. Mayes (pp. 68–83) has HA, on the eve of his graduation from Divinity School, escape the clutches of his reproving father to take a moral holiday abroad with two libertine friends, Gilbert Ramsbotham and Martin Embry. Once he reached the continent, according to Mayes, HA wrestled with his conscience and lost. He took two mistresses in quick succession before a letter from his mother recalled him to his senses, his filial duty, and Massachusetts. As usual, Tebbel (pp. 44–54) solemnly repeats this drivel point by point. Gruber (p. 17) dismisses HA's trip in a paragraph, though he purports to correct Mayes's fiction: "Alger was accompanied on his European tour by his Harvard and Cambridge Divinity School classmate Vinal and his cousin, one of the numerous Fenno family." Gruber guesses on the latter point. In fact, HA had merely indicated in his Harvard Class Book (p. 104) that he had sailed to Europe in 1860 with Charles Vinal "and a cousin" whom he did not further identify. At a loss for this detail, Gardner embellishes Gruber's guess, confident he could not be easily contradicted. Thus, in his biography (pp. 141–148), HA and Vinal were accompanied by George Fenno, whose name Gardner gleans from a genealogical history of HA's maternal ancestors. "Horatio, Charley Vinal and George Fenno slowly covered miles of narrow roads bordered by mossy piled-rock fences," he writes, for example. "Horatio and Charley Vinal were amenable to George Fenno's urging, early in January, 1861, that they continue on their journey to Italy," he adds two pages later. The evening before they embarked on their return voyage, he avers still later, Horatio and Charley "strolled along the left bank of the Seine" while "George Fenno . . . preferred to finish packing and get to bed." Hoyt (pp. 37–39) also mentions that George Fenno accompanied HA to Europe. Unfortunately, Gruber, Gardner, and Hoyt fail their homework. None of the Fennos—much less cousin George—accompanied HA and Vinal to Europe. According to a published passenger log, they were joined by Cyrus Alger Sears, son of one of HA's second cousins.

Fortunately, HA described the trip in detail in travel letters he mailed to the NYS and *BT*, though past biographers fail to cite these sources. The letters have been reprinted in their entirety in *N*, 19 (April 1981), 7–26; and 20 (Dec. 1981), 11–14.

1. CB, 104.

2. Leon Edel, *Henry James, The Untried Years* (Philadelphia and New York, 1953), 159.

3. NYS, 24 Dec. 1860, 1:2; *Shenstone Laurel*, 18 Dec. 1860.

4. NYS, 10 Nov. 1860, 4:1; *Continental Monthly*, 3 (June 1863), 730–733.

5. *BT Supplement*, 3 Nov. 1860, 2:4; NYS, 24 Dec. 1860, 1:2; *GA*, 14 April 1883, 148; *New York Railroad Men*, 9 (March 1896), 141.

6. NYS, 7 Nov. 1860, 1:3; and 30 Nov. 1860, 1:3; *Ragged Dick* (Boston, 1868), 77; *Bernard Brook's Adventures* (New York, 1903), 177; *Frank Hunter's Peril* (Philadelphia, 1896), 143. The hero of the latter novel tours Europe along the same route taken by HA and his companions in 1860–61.

7. CB, 104; *Frank Hunter's Peril*, 186, 284.

8. NYS, 22 Jan. 1861, 1:4; *Frank Hunter's Peril*, 224; CB, 104; *A Boy's Fortune* (Philadelphia, 1898), 202–203.

9. NYS, 22 Jan. 1861, 1:4.

10. *BT*, 26 Feb. 1861, 1:1; *AS*, 48.

11. NYS, 22 March 1861, 1:6.

12. CB, 104.

13. NYS, 22 March 1861, 1:6.

14. NYS, 12 March 1861, 1:4–5; and 18 March 1861, 1:3–4; *BT*, 26 Feb. 1861, 1:1.

15. *BT*, 26 Feb. 1861, 1:1; NYS, 12 March 1861, 1:4–5; and 18 March 1861, 1:3; Stowe, *Agnes of Sorrento* (Boston, 1862), 331; Mark Twain, *The Innocents Abroad* (Hartford, 1869), chap. 30.

16. NYS, 22 March 1861, 1:6. HA may have been reading *The Marble Faun*, in which Hawthorne also complains about "beggar-haunted" and "priest-ridden" Rome.

17. NYS, 20 March 1861, 1:5; 25 March 1861, 1:5; 4 April 1861, 1:5; and 15 April 1861, 1:3; *Ben Bruce* (New York, 1901), 238; *North American Review*, 97 (Oct. 1863), 325–326; *Continental Monthly*, 730–33.

18. CB, 104.

19. *NYW*, 5 Aug. 1872, 4.

20. BET, 16 May 1861, 3:4.

21. *The Education of Henry Adams* (Boston, 1961), 112.

22. *NYW*, 5 Aug. 1872, 4.

23. *BP*, 13 June 1861, 3:4; BET, 12 June 1861, 3:2–3.

24. *BT*, 12 June 1861, 1:4.

II

No prior biographer reports accurately the circumstances of HA's exemption from service in the Union army. According to Mayes (pp. 91–97), HA tried twice to enlist, but both times broke an arm en route to the recruiting station. When he later contracted a severe case of pneumonia, he relinquished his dream of glory on the battlefield. Tebbel (p. 63) in turn finds in Mayes's account evidence of psychic conflict in HA, "his conscience propelling him toward the war and his natural timidity making him shrink from it in horror." Tebbel may be right, but for the wrong reasons. Gruber tactically retreats: He ignores the subject altogether. Gardner reports (pp. 151–153, and "Foreword" to *Silas Snobden's Office Boy* [Garden City, 1973], p. 7)—and Hoyt repeats (p. 39)—that HA volunteered twice for militia duty in the spring and summer of 1861 but was rejected each time when his chronic asthmatic condition was discovered during medical examination. HA ostensibly grew despondent at the thought he had been deprived of a great adventure. This account is not even close to the truth.

25. *CR*, 4 Oct. 1845, 157; Edward F. Hayward, *History of the Second Parish, Marlborough* (Marlborough, 1906), 20; *National Era*, 26 April 1855, 68; "W. R. Alger: Forgotten Man of Letters," *American Transcendentalist Quarterly*, 53 (Winter 1982), 5–23.

26. *HW*, 8 Aug. 1863, 507.

27. CB, 104; senior Alger to "Bro. Sewall," 7 March 1867 (A-H).

28. CB, 104; HA to E. R. A. Seligman, 14 July 1885 (CU).

29. CB, 104; *Try and Trust* (Boston, 1873), viii.

30. *AS, passim; N,* 20 (Oct–Nov 1981), 4–8; *Our Daily Fare,* 10 June 1864, 21; Bennett, 193–199.

31. *HW,* 1 Nov. 1862, 694; MS in NYPL.

32. *TF,* 22 Oct. 1859, 2:2–3; 55 holograph letters from Dean to his mother, 3 Sept. 1862–31 May 1863 (BPL); *Record of the Service of the Forty-Fourth Massachusetts Volunteer Militia* (Boston, 1887), 240, 309; *Massachusetts Soldier, Sailors, and Marines in the Civil War* (Norwood, Mass., 1932), IV, 291.

33. HA to Robert Bonner, 21 Nov. 1879 (PML).

34. HA to William C. Church, 20 April 1866 (NYPL).

35. CB, 104; *BT,* 10 July 1863, 2:2; *BA,* 11 July 1863, 1:7; NYEP, 11 July 1863, 2:2.

36. *HW,* 8 Aug. 1863, 507; and 25 July 1863, 174.

37. CB, 104; B*ET,* 30 July 1863, 3:2; Roll of Drafted Men, 4th Congressional District, Mass. (National Archives, D.C.).

38. *BT,* 18 Aug. 1863, 4:1.

39. CB, 104; *BA,* 2 July 1863, 1:6; and 6 Aug. 1863, 1:7; *Roll of Membership 1844–1890* (Boston, 1891), 26.

III

40. *BA,* 10 April 1896, 9.

41. HA to E. C. Stedman, 29 Nov. 1875 (YU).

42. "WSfB."

43. NYEP, 20 Jan. 1864, 4:1; *AS,* 53.

44. Bennett, 133.

45. *The Selected Letters of Mark Twain,* ed. Charles Neider (New York, 1982), 55.

46. *N,* 15 (Jan.–Feb. 1977), 5–6.

47. *BT,* 13 July 1864, 1:2.

48. HA to E. C. Stedman, 29 Nov. 1875 (YU).

49. "WSfB."

50. *Frank's Campaign,* iii; Joseph Dean to his mother, 16 March 1863 (BPL); *NYTi,* 18 Dec. 1864, 3:5.

51. *Frank's Campaign,* v.

52. "AMBR."

53. *Frank's Campaign,* 174; Dean to his mother, 21 Dec. 1862 (BPL).

54. *TF,* 2 April 1859, 2:5–6; *Frank's Campaign,* chap. 19.

55. Madeleine Stern, *Imprints on History* (Bloomington, Indiana, 1956), 181, 186.

56. "WSfB."

57. Reviews: *BT,* 17 Nov. 1864, 2:1; NYEP, 29 Dec. 1864, 1:2; *CI,* 31 Dec. 1864, 3:2; S&B, 28.

58. "AMBR."

59. *BT,* 10 Dec. 1864, 3:2.

60. "WSfB."

61. *Paul Prescott's Charge,* vii.

IV

Mayes depicts HA as a promiscuous heterosexual (pp. 74–76, 81–83, 169–195). Gruber skirts the subject entirely. On the basis of Mayes's fabrications, Tebbel suggests that HA lived "a kind of existence which was homosexual in nature, if not in fact" (p. 69). Again he is right, but for the wrong reasons. The news Charles Lowe successfully contained in 1866 was not leaked to the press until 1971, eight years after the publication of Tebbel's biography.

Gardner's shortcomings as a biographer are well illustrated by his suppression of evidence about the Brewster affair. Gardner claims that he examined the Brewster church records when he was preparing his biography and learned that HA had been charged with pedophilia. Indeed, in his letter to Mayes in the spring of 1975 he purports to be "the first to discover" these records (Mayes, p. xxv). So as to depict HA as a respectable mid-Victorian, however, he fails even to mention their existence in his book. He tries to rationalize this omission with a recent public explanation that seems both pretentious and, in light of his other errors, utterly ludicrous. "I am an old newspaperman," he writes in 1981,

> and, as great as was the temptation to evaluate this material in my Alger biography—especially as I would have been the first Alger biographer to do so—I felt obligated to put the accusations to normal tests of verification, corroborative evidence, and reliability. This could not be done satisfactorily at that time and—despite much that has by now been written about these findings—no new *facts* to clarify the events of March, 1866, have, to date, been uncovered. ("Introduction" to *A Fancy of Hers* and *The Disagreeable Woman*, p. 10)

This is sheer sophistry. Corroborative evidence *was* available in the letterbooks of the American Unitarian Association, stored in the early 1960s at Unitarian Universalist Association offices in Boston and, more recently, in the library of the Harvard Divinity School. Though Gardner asserts that "there exists no record" that a report of HA's indiscretions "ever reached the American Unitarian Association," such records *do* exist. Unfortunately, no past HA biographer has sought access to these records. Gardner not only did not check, he later pretended he did. Even Hoyt, in his haste to reach print with his "tells all" biography, failed to check the most likely source for evidence corroborating the Brewster records.

62. *N*, 18 (Dec. 1979), 5–7.
63. HA to W. S. Sargent, 14 Oct. 1884 (Knox).
64. NEHGS *Register*, 19 (April 1865), 185.
65. HA to George L. Chaney, 25 Nov. 1864 (HU); *BT*, 12 Dec. 1864, 2:4; *CI*, 17 Dec. 1864, 3:3; *CR*, 17 Dec. 1864, 203; *N*, 22 (July–Aug. 1983), 11.
66. Freeman to Lowe, 24 March 1866 (A-H). For additional details of HA's routine in Brewster, see his letter to "My dear Claire," dated 25 Jan. 1866, described in David Holmes's *Catalogue Seven: Autograph Letters* (Philadelphia, 1984), item 7.
67. *N*, 18 (Dec. 1979), 6.
68. Bennett, 173–191.

69. HA to John Ward Dean, 23 June 1865 (NEHGS). HA apparently wished to avoid any association with two Confederate generals surnamed Preston and perhaps wished to exploit the reputation of Capt. George Lincoln Prescott, who had recently led the 32nd Mass. Regiment in a famous charge on a Confederate stronghold at the Battle of Petersburg. Unfortunately, the working title was publicized before HA changed it. As a result, he is still listed occasionally as the author of the ghost title *Paul Preston's Charge.*

70. *CI*, 2 Sept. 1865, 3:1.

71. Reviews: *CI*, 21 Dec. 1865, 4:1; S&B, 27–28.

72. S&B, 145.

73. HA to E. A. Duyckinck, 28 Jan. 1866 (NYPL).

74. *BT*, 1 Feb. 1866, 1:3.

75. Freeman to Lowe, 24 March 1866 (A-H).

76. *N*, 18 (Dec. 1979), 5–7.

77. *CI*, 8 Feb. 1866, 5:1.

78. Brewster census records for 1860, 228, 266; *N*, 18 (Dec. 1979), 5–7; Brewster standing committee to Lowe, 19 March 1866 (A-H).

79. Brewster committee to Lowe, 19 March 1866 (A-H).

80. Freeman to Lowe, 24 March 1866 (A-H).

81. Brewster committee to Lowe, 19 March 1866 (A-H).

3. *Adrift in New York* (*1866–1873*)

I

1. Munsey.

2. HA to W. C. Church, 20 April 1866 (NYPL); Adrift in the City, 120.

3. *John Godfrey's Fortunes*, 182.

4. HA to W. C. Church, 20, 23 April 1866 (NYPL).

5. *John Godfrey's Fortune*, 183.

6. *AS*, 34–35.

7. "WSfB."

8. Henry James, *Notes of a Son and Brother* (New York, 1914), 275.

9. Bennett, 173–191.

10. *Seeking His Fortune and Other Dialogues* (Boston, 1875), 11–26.

11. *N*, 12 (Aug. 1973), 8–9.

12. *BT*, 7 Aug. 1866, 2:3.

13. Reviews: S&B, 28; NYS, 12 Dec. 1866, 2:7; *BT*, 10 Aug. 1866, 3:6; *BT*, 24 Dec. 1866, 2:3; *CI*, 30 Aug. 1866, 3:3; *LChr*, 29 Dec. 1866, 3:3.

14. Freeman to Lowe, 1 Sept. 1866, (A-H).

15. *CR*, 21 April 1866, 2:6.

16. Lowe to Freeman, 7 Sept. 1866 (A-H).

17. Reviews: *BT*, 5 Oct. 1866, 1:4; *CI*, 25 Oct. 1866, 5:1; *CR*, 3 Nov. 1866, 1:7; S&B, 29; NYEP, 5 Oct. 1866, 1:3.

18. *CR*, 25 Jan. 1845, 14.

19. Samuel B. Stewart, "Necrology of the Divinity School, 1904–1905" (HUA).

20. HA to E. R. A. Seligman, 6 Aug. 1877 (CU).

21. *Writer*, 8 (Dec. 1895), 182–183; *Adrift in the City*, 120. In a later novel, HA observed that "Time was when St. Mark's Place had some pretension to gentility, but now it is given up to lodging and boardinghouses." In the same novel, a character who writes for story papers—an HA persona—lives in the third-story, rear room of a brick house on East 8th between 1st and 2nd avenues in St. Mark's Place (*A Boy's Fortune*, 12).

22. HA to Henry Denny, 6 March 1893 (HUA).

23. *Philadelphia Public Ledger*, 18 May 1868, 1:8.

24. *AS*, 77–78.

25. *Merry's Museum*, 59 (March 1871), 144–146; *Writer*, 8 (Dec. 1895), 182–183. Mark Twain almost certainly parodied the ballad in "The Aged Pilot Man," first published in chapter 51 of *Roughing It* (1871).

26. NYS, 9 Jan. 1867, 2:7.

II

All earlier biographers agree that HA virtually lived in the Newsboys' Lodging House when he settled in New York. As Mayes wrote (pp. 101–102), "The Newsboys' Lodging House became Alger's New York home. . . . Gradually he made it a practice to stay for supper with the boys and, like them, paid the necessary pennies. When there was room he occupied a bed." Gruber echoes this claim (p. 23): "The House became Alger's second home. He ate most of his meals there, sometimes slept in the dormitories with the boys." Tebbel concurs (pp. 68–69): "Alger became virtually an inmate of the House. . . . He began to stay on for supper, paying his pennies with the others, and if there was a bed available, he paid the fee and slept in it." Gardner embellishes the assertion by providing HA with his own room (p. 198): "After his first visit, Horatio returned almost daily to the Newsboys' Lodging House. It became his office, workshop and laboratory. Charles O'Connor set up a spare chamber where Horatio could write, and a bed was soon installed so he could remain overnight." Hoyt follows Gardner's lead and reports (pp. 88, 90, 97) that HA "had the run" of the lodge. "A bed was put there for him, and he had a desk where he could write when he chose," he adds. In 1869, "Horatio spent much of his time at the Newsboys' Lodging House lounging around in carpet slippers and an old sweater." Though HA doubtless became a frequent visitor to the lodge after he moved to New York, not a scrap of evidence actually indicates he ever ate a meal, spent a night, or wrote a sentence within its walls.

27. "AMBR."

28. *GA*, 17 Oct. 1885, 364.

29. *BDG*, evening ed., 18 July 1899, 10:6.

30. *GA*, 17 Oct. 1885, 364.

31. "AMBR."

32. *CI*, 9 Aug. 1866, 2; *LChr*, 30 Nov. 1867, 6; *NYEP*, 13, Nov. 1867, 1:3–4; 23 Jan. 1868, 1:2; and 3 Nov. 1868, 2:2–3; NYS, 4 Feb. 1867, 4:1; 16 Feb. 1867, 4:1; and 20 June 1868, 1:7.

33. *BT*, 18 April 1855, 1:4.

34. *LChr*, 20 April 1867, 6.

35. *21st Annual Report of the Children's Aid Society* (New York, 1873), endpage.

III

HA's work on the MS of *Ragged Dick* has also been consistently misrepresented by his biographers. According to Mayes (p. 101), HA outlined the story while he was still in Brewster, and, after he moved to New York and the tale began to appear serially in *The Schoolmate*, he was sought out by the administrators of the Newsboys' Lodging House. Tebbel detects a possible discrepancy in this account (p. 67): If it were accurate, "it would be difficult to explain Alger's introduction" to the later book version of *Ragged Dick*, in which the author expressed his indebtedness to Charles O'Connor for some of the data used. "This would indicate," Tebbel deduces, "that Alger was already familiar with the House" before he wrote the story. However, Tebbel quickly papers over the apparent problem. Because "the published book was a rewritten and expanded version of the magazine serial," perhaps "the serial was written from observation outside the House, and the book had the benefit of his new acquaintance with the institution." The logical gymnastics betray Tebbel's failure to test the thesis. In fact, HA does mention the lodge in the serial version.

In each case, these biographers aver that HA submitted the MS of the story to William T. Adams, editor of *The Student and Schoolmate*. Mayes (p. 98): "Adams invited him to write" for the magazine. Gruber (p. 29): "Adams was the editor" of the magazine in 1867, when *Ragged Dick* appeared in it. Tebbel (p. 65): "Adams invited Horatio to contribute" to the magazine. Gardner extrapolates a new composition history (pp. 21–22), which Hoyt later recapitulates (pp. 73–74), from this point. Gardner opens his biography by quoting a long letter HA purportedly wrote in November 1866 to Adams in which he reports his progress on the MS of *Ragged Dick*. "Early next week," HA ostensibly wrote,

> I intend to send you the remaining parts of my story. I hope they are as acceptable to you as the first chapter, which you already received.
>
> Your encouragement is most welcome, and I share your eagerness awaiting Loring's decision whether to publish the story as a book.

This letter to Adams is spurious. HA could not have written it, for W. T. Adams was no longer editor of *The Schoolmate* in November 1866. He had resigned in October to edit a rival magazine. Indeed, as HA later explained, the story of Ragged Dick was not originally planned as a book at all, but was expanded and sold to Loring only after it generated reader interest several months into the serialization.

36. *BT*, 12 Oct. 1866, 1:4.
37. *Ragged Dick*, v, vii–viii.
38. *CI*, 25 Oct. 1866, 5:2.
39. Synopsis: *Ragged Dick*, 15, 21, 91, 124–26, 132, 146–47, and *passim*.
40. "AMBR."
41. *Ibid.*
42. *Ibid.*
43. "WSfB."
44. S&B, 28–29.

45. *Frank Leslie's Pleasant Hours*, NS 1 (March 1896), 354.

46. *LChr*, 20 April 1867, 7.

47. *GA*, 17 Oct. 1885, 364.

48. *Frank Leslie's Pleasant Hours*, NS 1 (March 1896), 354; *Ragged Dick*, vii.

49. Stern, *Imprints on History*, 182–184.

50. *Ragged Dick*, vii–viii.

51. *BT*, 5 May 1868, 3:6.

52. S&B, 30.

53. Mott, *Golden Multitudes* (New York, 1947), 309.

54. *Bookman*, 42 (Nov. 1915), 11.

55. S&B, 140.

56. Reviews: *BT*, 12 May 1868, 3:7; *BT Supplement*, 16 May 1868, 2:2–3; S&B, 30–31; *CR*, 27 June 1868, 1:8.

57. *Fame and Fortune* (Boston, 1868), vii.

IV

58. Synopsis: *Fame and Fortune*, 276–77 and *passim*.

59. *Ibid.*, v.

60. *BT*, 8 Dec. 1868, 3:7.

61. *BT Supplement*, 12 Dec. 1868, 1:2.

62. *BT*, 16 Dec. 1868, 1:3.

63. *BT*, 10 April 1869, 3:7.

64. *Mark the Match Boy* (Boston, 1869), 276.

65. Reviews: NYEP, 22 April 1869, 1:1; quoted in *NYW*, 5 Aug. 1872, 4. See also *Peterson's*, 56 (July 1869), 75.

66. *Ben the Luggage Boy*, v–viii.

67. Reviews: S&B, 31; *Nation*, 30 Dec. 1869, 587; *BT*, 18 Nov. 1870, 1:3.

68. *NYW*, 5 Aug. 1872, 4; HA to R. A. Alger, 2 May 1888 (Mich); S&B, 112.

69. *GA*, 17 Oct. 1885, 364.

70. *Student and Schoolmate*, 23 (Feb. 1869), 100.

71. HA to George A. Bacon, 26 Jan. 1874 (UV); *N*, 19 (March 1981), 10.

72. HA to W.A. Wheeler, 2 Jan. 1869 (UV).

73. HA holograph (HUA).

74. HA to Irving Blake, 10 July 1896 (Hunt).

75. *Luck and Pluck*, v.

76. *Peterson's*, 57 (Feb. 1870), 165.

77. *BT Supplement*, 25 Nov. 1871, 1:2; S&B, 33; *BT*, 19 May 1873, 6:1.

78. Clarence Day, *Life with Mother* (New York and London, 1937), 70.

79. *BT*, 22 April 1871, 1:1. See also *BT*, 21 April 1871, 2:2.

80. *Tattered Tom* (Boston, 1871), vii, 10.

81. S&B, 32.

82. *Paul the Peddler* (Boston, 1871), v; Scudder, *Hand-book for Young Men* (New York, 1892).

83. *Slow and Sure* (Boston, 1872), 278.

84. *NYW*, 5 Aug. 1872, 4.

85. Henry Nash Smith, *Virgin Land* (New York, 1950), 115.

86. F.S. Smith, *Gems for All Generations* (New York, 1913), 14.

87. Joseph to Babet Seligman, 26 June 1872 (NYHS); HA to Edward Stratemeyer, 18 Dec. 1898 (SS).

88. William W. Ellsworth, *A Golden Age of Authors* (Boston and New York, 1919), 92.

89. *NYTi*, 16 April 1883, 5:2; *Jack's Ward* (Boston, 1875), iii.

90. Quentin Reynolds, *The Fiction Factory* (New York, 1955), 82.

91. *Gems for All Generations*, 6, 25.

92. Bennett, 194.

93. Synopses: *Brave and Bold* (Boston, 1874), chap. 35 and *passim*; *Tom the Bootblack*, 141 and *passim*.

94. Bennett, 119–120.

95. HA to Robert Bonner, 21 Nov. 1879 (PML).

96. S&B, 158.

97. *Prairie-Town Boy* (New York, 1932), 141; *Twentieth Century Journey* (New York, 1976), 109.

98. S&B, 34.

99. HA to Lee & Shepard, 21 may 1872 (AAS).

100. Raymond Kilgour, *Lee and Shepard* (Hamden, Conn., 1965), 144–146.

101. HA to Lee & Shepard, 15 Nov. 1872 (AAS).

V

HA falsely claimed that his novel *Phil the Fiddler* had been instrumental in outlawing the padrone system in New York and other major American cities. Unfortunately, HA's biographers bought and embellished the claim. According to Mayes (pp. 131–148), a dry-goods merchant in Newark named George Nelson Maverick—a figment of his imagination, he recently admits—initiated the anti-*padroni* campaign and enlisted HA in the cause. "It was Maverick who raised the flag, Horatio who waved it," Mayes writes. The two men called mass protest meetings. HA memorized a speech which "evoked storms of applause wherever delivered." The *padroni* began to harass HA with threatening letters and several times attempted to assault him, so he began to carry a pistol for self-defense. "Oh, yes, Horatio Alger was militant then," Mayes adds. In a fever of indignation, HA penned *Phil*, a work of "explosive propaganda" which established him "once and for all as a force to be reckoned with. . . . Almost a thousand messages poured in on the author after its publication." Within six months or so, the padrone system was abolished, a happy ending Mayes attributes "almost wholly to what Horatio Alger bravely brought to light."

Tebbel repeats this gibberish point by point (pp. 86–96). "George Nelson Maverick, who operated a department store in Newark," sought out HA's help on behalf of the Italian children. Maverick and HA organized mass meetings. HA often delivered a set speech "which never failed to bring down the house." Eventually the "real operators of the padrone system, probably the Mafia," got tough, but still HA "persisted. He carried a pistol to protect himself." He wrote *Phil* and the "result was gratifying. . . . Letters poured in from everywhere, nearly a thousand of them; sermons were preached; editorials were written; Alger was hailed as a crusader for morality." When the abuses were curtailed a few months later, it represented "a clear-cut victory for Alger."

Incredibly, Gardner's version of HA's anti-*padroni* campaign is even more fanciful (pp. 207–226 and "Foreword to *Cast Upon the Breakers* [Garden City, 1974], pp. 32–33). One day an abused Italian boy was brought to the Newsboys'

Lodge, as he tells the story. HA, who "was writing in his corner room" (*sic*), "opened his door to investigate" the commotion and overheard a delirious child "whisper in Italian, 'No, padrone, no! Don't beat me, padrone!'" as he died. His compassion aroused, HA "was determined to track the story to its source." That he did, in a neat bit of investigative reporting, even after a stink bomb exploded in the Lodge and his apartment was ransacked. Gardner's HA was not a man easily intimidated. He wrote continuously for three months on the MS of *Phil.* "When it appeared, the following spring," Gardner concludes,

> it caused an uproar in New York and other metropolises, and reaction was immediate. Newspapers began paying special attention to crimes against "the little white slaves," and day after day quoted Horatio Alger as their authority. . . . It took Horatio only six months, after publication of 'Phil the Fiddler,' to spell out the end of this criminal traffic. His life was threatened and he even was mauled by irate padrones, but the little minister stuck to his guns, and won.

Even Hoyt admits doubts about this tale (p. 256). "I have played down the Alger part in the destruction of the padrone system," he writes, "because much of the material comes from suspect sources and Gardner's manufacture of conversations does not lend itself to total belief."

Unfortunately, Hoyt fails to trust his intuition. In his biography, he blends and abbreviates Mayes's and Gardner's equally unfounded accounts (pp. 115–116). "Early in the 1870s a Newark department store owner named George Nelson Maverick" turned to HA for help in publicizing the cruelties of the *padroni*, he writes. HA wrote *Phil*, "which in its own way was a major exposé of a vile social ill." The novel "created a considerable stir in New York and other cities." Public opinion was mobilized, and, he concludes, "Half a dozen years after Horatio's book was published, the padrone system was outlawed and came to an end." It would make a better story if only it were true.

102. NYEP, 23 March 1868, 2:3.
103. *Phil*, vi–vii.
104. *N*, 14 (April 1976), 17.
105. *American Notes* (London, 1957), 88–89.
106. *Phil*, vi–vii.
107. "AMBR."
108. *New York Railroad Men*, 9 (March 1896), 142; *Slow and Sure*, 24.
109. Synopsis: *Phil*, 255 and *passim*.
110. Reviews: S&B, 33; *BT*, 11 May 1872, 6:3.
111. *GA*, 17 Oct. 1885, 364.
112. *Frank Leslie's Pleasant Hours*, NS 1 (March 1896), 354–355.
113. *NYTi*, 17 June 1873, 1.

VI

For over thirty years, even while writing three or four juvenile novels per year, HA tutored privately. His biographers mostly guess about such details as the identities of his students, however. According to Mayes (p. 88), HA taught French and Greek to the young Wilbur Cross, future governor of Connecticut. Gruber (p. 16) and Tebbel (p. 56) echo the claim, which has no basis in fact.

Gardner (pp. 200–202) correctly identifies the children of Joseph Seligman as HA's pupils—that much could have been gleaned from the dedications of several HA novels and published sketches of several Seligman sons—but other details of his account are unreliable. "At least once each week," he writes, HA would stroll with his charges "through nearby streets, or Madison Square Park, after which they adjourned to an ice cream parlor." There is no evidence for so sentimental an assertion. Gardner continues: HA "moved to 26 West 34th Street—a fashionable neighborhood conveniently near the Seligman home." Though he here correctly specifies HA's address between 1869 and 1875—that much could have been gleaned from city directories for the period—Gardner once more betrays his ignorance about his subject. The house where HA lived was not "conveniently near" the Seligman home. It *was* the Seligman home. Fortunately, many details of HA's employment as tutor of the Seligman sons are preserved among the family papers in the New-York Historical Society.

114. HA to W. A. Wheeler, 2 Jan. 1869 (UV).

115. George Hellman, "The Story of the Seligmans" (unpub. MS, NYHS, 1945), unpaginated notes and 182–183, 236–237; Linton Wells, "The House of Seligman" (unpub. MS, NYHS, 1931), 307.

116. Joseph to Babet Seligman, 24 June 1872 (NYHS). I have freely translated the quotation from German: "Mr. Alger war Samstag in der Office, und sagte dass Ike George & Eddie ihre Prüfung wie er glaubt gut bestanden. . . . George war oben an in Latin, Eddie in Mathematic, auch Ike soll gut bestanden."

117. *Die Volkswirtschaftslehre der Gegenwart in Selbstdarstellungen*, ed. Felix Meiner (Leipzig, 1929), 117. The quotation is a retranslation into English of this German translation of the original: "Bis zum Alter von 11 Jahren wurde ich zu Hause unterrichtet und hatte das Glück, Horatio Alger jr. als Erzieher zu haben. . . . Ihm verdanke ich den Sinn für gute Literatur und die solide Grundlabe in den klassischen Sprachen."

118. Hellman, "Story of Seligmans," 235–236. Ironically, Gardner has had the temerity to complain in print about distortions in the record of these pranks. No doubt Stephen Birmingham embellishes Hellman's account of HA's years as friend and tutor of the Seligmans. In *"Our Crowd"* (New York, 1967), p. 133, Birmingham contends HA

> was a timid, sweet-tempered little man who, in his nonteaching hours, practiced his ballet steps. He was easily cowed, and his customary cry of alarm was "Oh, Lordy-me!" Ten lively Seligman boys were clearly too much for him, and he was forever having to rush to Babet or James' wife, Rosa, for assistance. Once, when he cried out for help, the boys jumped on him, tied him up, and locked him in a trunk in the attic. They refused to let him out until he promised not to tell their mothers. . . . After lessons, such as they were, he liked to play billiards with the boys. He was extremely nearsighted, and when it was his turn at the cue, the boys substituted red apples for the red balls. Alger never caught on, and, as each new apple was demolished with his cue, would cry, "Oh, Lordy-me, I've broken another ball! I don't know my own *strength*."

As Birmingham tells the story, the J. & W. Seligman Co. invested HA's royalties "and made him a wealthy man"—a claim for which there is absolutely no evidence. In later years, he avers, the practical jokes continued.

> There was one favorite. . . . After dinner one of [Helene's] brothers would steer Mr. Alger into the library and into a sofa next to Helene. There he would artfully drape one

of Mr. Alger's tiny arms around Helene's rather ample waist while another brother ran from the room shouting, "Mr. Alger is trying to seduce Helene!" Helene's husband would then rush into the room brandishing a bread knife, crying, "*Seducer!*" The first three times this happened, Horatio Alger fell to the floor in a dead faint.

Similarly, in *The Grandees* (New York, 1971), pp. 296–297, Birmingham asserts that HA "was flutily effeminate, with mincing ways and a fondness for practicing ballet positions in his spare time, crying out such exclamations as 'Oh, lawsy me!' or bursting into wild tears when things went wrong. . . . As a teacher he was hopelessly ineffective . . . [and] healthy boys kept him perpetually cowed. They locked him in closets and tied him to chairs." Birmingham clearly cannot keep his own story straight, and Gardner rightly objects to such liberties with the record. "Birmingham told me," Gardner declares in his introduction to the recent reprinting of *A Fancy of Hers* and *The Disagreeable Woman*, p. 13, that "he got his information from the late author and editor, Geoffrey T. Hellman." (Who can say whether Birmingham misremembers or Gardner misreports the name?) With good reason, Gardner doubts the accuracy of warmed-over hearsay repeated at third hand. He thus observes a double standard. He fails to apply to Mayes's "facts" the same standards of reliability he expects Birmingham to observe. No less than Birmingham, he has embroidered documents with dialogue and with his own invention.

119. Joseph to Babet Seligman, 26 June 1872 (NYHS). I have freely translated the excerpt from German: "Ich sagte Alger gestern Abend dass ich mich erst mit dir benehmen würde ehe ich ihm Bescheid über seinen (groben) Antrag wegen Preis erhohung von 600 auf 1200 Dl, nebenbei nach 3 Monate ferien von July bis Oct 1873 und das beste noch das doppelte für die vergangenen 3 Monate. Dabei schrieb er dass er \$3000 vom schreiben seiner Bücher im letzten Jahr erübrigte. Ich will deine Meinung entgegen nehmen, bin aber beriet jeder Zeit einen andern Tutor zu nehmen, der mehr energy [*sic*] hat."

120. Hellman, "Story of Seligmans," 182–183.
121. *Life of Choate*, I, 319; *From Farm Boy to Senator*, 5.
122. NYEP, 24 Feb. 1869, 2:4; *NYTi*, 24 Feb. 1869, 8:2.
123. AS, 82.
124. NYTr, 12 Feb. 1870, 7:2; *NYTi*, 12 Feb. 1870, 5:2.
125. AS, 83.
126. NYEP, 23 Feb. 1871, 3:8; NYTr, 23 Feb. 1871, 5:2–3.
127. NYEP, 2 Feb. 1872, 1:5.
128. NYEP, 22 Feb. 1873, 1:2 and 2:2; NYTr, 22 Feb. 1873, 12:1–2.
129. AS, 84–86.
130. HA to J. W. Dean, 26 Feb. 1873 (NEHGS).
131. *NYTi*, 8 June 1873, 8:6.

4. Facing the World (1873–1887)

I

1. GA, 14 April 1883, 148.
2. HA to Robert Bonner, 21 Nov. 1879 (PML).
3. *Bernard Brooks' Adventures*, 168.

4. *Bound to Rise*, v-vi; *Frank Hunter's Peril*, 194.
5. *Young Israel*, 4 (Jan. 1874).
6. HA to Irving Blake, 10 July 1896 (Hunt); *Frank Hunter's Peril*, 164.
7. NY*Tr*, 13 Oct. 1873, 7:6.
8. *Julius* (Boston, 1874), iii.
9. *BDG*, evening ed., 18 July 1899, 10:6.
10. CB, 104; *Woman's Journal*, 5 Aug. 1899, 245.
11. S&B, 172–73.
12. Chicago *Times*, 13 Aug. 1875, 6:6; and 20 Aug. 1875, 2:6; *Luke Walton* (Philadelphia, 1889), 1.

II

In the diaries Mayes invents, HA strikes one note so often it becomes his magnificent obsession: to write the Great American Novel. Mayes has HA wonder again and again (pp. 112, 120, 188–89) whether the time is ripe to forsake juvenile fiction forever and begin the book "that will endear him to posterity." HA first considers depicting Chinatown—"its dirt, disease, chaos, brawls, crimes, passion, lust, viciousness." He will entitle the tale *Opium, the Story of a Dream*. Later he sets to work on a novel which slowly evolves into *Struggling Upward*, just another juvenile. He begins a masterpiece entitled *Tomorrow*, only to abandon it when he realizes he plagarized the premise from Dickens's *A Tale of Two Cities*. According to Mayes, HA was so inept he could not appreciate his own shortcomings. Even on his deathbed, HA prays for strength enough to try his hand at the *magnum opus* that will ensure his literary immortality.

Ironically, Mayes is not wrong except in details. His fabrications bear an uncanny resemblance to HA's all too real ambition to write for adults. Every subsequent biographer, influenced by Mayes, agrees HA aspired to write fiction for adult readers. Gardner allows (pp. 286–87, and "Introduction" to *A Fancy of Hers* and *The Disagreeable Woman*, p. 17) that HA was "eternally driven to create a significant reputation as a serious novelist." Perhaps overstated, but true enough. No less than Mayes, however, Gardner errs in details. For example, he alleges that HA wrote an adult story entitled "A Fancy of Hers" in South Natick during the summer of 1891, using as a model for the heroine his 21-year-old niece, Annie. According to Gardner, Frank Munsey, to whom HA submitted the MS, abridged the romance before featuring it in *Munsey's Magazine* in 1892. Unfortunately, Gardner did not know the tale had in fact been written in 1877—thus the heroine could not have been modeled on his niece—and originally appeared unsigned under the title *The New Schoolma'am*. Fifteen years later, Munsey merely reprinted a slightly revised, certainly unabridged, version of the story. Equipped with only half the facts, Gardner plastered the holes with pretense.

13. HA to E. R. A. Seligman, 6 Aug. 1877 (CU).
14. *Mark Twain Journal*, 20 (Winter 1981), 16–17.
15. S&B, 34.
16. *Journal of American Culture*, 5 (Summer 1982), 91–95.
17. Bennett, 95, 173–191.
18. *Fitzgerald/Hemingway Annual* (1978), 161.
19. *Theatre Studies*, no. 23 (1976–77), 53–55.

20. *Notes of a Son and Brother*, 271–275; *Life of Edwin Forrest* (Philadelphia, 1877), I, 141.

21. *From Canal Boy to President* (New York, 1881), 175.

22. *Notes of a Son and Brother*, 275.

23. *Life of Edwin Forrest*, I, 140. Compare the excerpt with the following passage from one of HA's juveniles (*The Store Boy* [Philadelphia, 1887], 299):

> On the eighteenth of December Ben arrived from Pentonville. It was his first visit since he went up to New York for good. He reached home without observation, and found his mother overjoyed to see him again.
>
> "It has seemed a long, long time that you have been away, Ben," she said.
>
> "Yes, mother; but I did a good thing in going to New York."
>
> "You are looking well, Ben, and you have grown!"
>
> "Yes, mother; and best of all, I have prospered. Squire Davenport can't have the house!"
>
> "You don't mean to say, Ben, that you have the money to pay it off?" asked his mother, with eager hope.
>
> "Yes, mother, and, better still, the money is my own."

24. S&B, 35.

25. HA to W. R. Alger, 7 Dec. 1875 (YU).

26. HA to E. R. A. Seligman, 9 Nov. 1876 (CU).

27. Richard Moody, *Edwin Forrest* (New York, 1960), 373, 390.

28. HA to Henry Denny, 6 March 1893 (HUA).

29. HA to E. C. Stedman, 29 Nov. 1875 (YU). See also HA to Stedman, 9 Jan. 1888 (NYPL). In 1911, the copy of *Grand'ther Baldwin* which HA sent Stedman was included in a lot of several books and letters which sold at auction for $1.25 (*Catalogue of the Library, Autograph Letters and Prints of Edmund C. Stedman* [New York, 1911], item 93). A copy of this auction catalogue in the Univ. of Oregon library lists sale prices.

30. HA to H. W. Longfellow, 16 Dec. 1875 (HU). The Houghton Library at Harvard still houses the inscribed copy of *Grand'ther Baldwin* which HA sent Longfellow.

31. This book is owned today by Prof. Emeritus John Hepler of Central Michigan Univ., Mt. Pleasant, Mich.

32. Reviews: *BT*, 27 Nov. 1875, 6:1, S&B, 34–35.

33. HA to E. R. A. Seligman, 6 Aug. 1877 (CU).

34. *The New Schoolma'am* (Boston, 1877), 7.

35. Reviews: S&B, 35–36.

36. HA to E. R. A. Seligman, 3 Jan. 1878 (CU).

37. S&B, 36.

38. HA to E. R. A. Seligman, 15 July 1878 (CU). There is extremely fragile, circumstantial evidence that HA wrote the unsigned novel *How We Saved the Old Farm*, issued by Loring early in 1879. This book was deposited for copyright on 15 Feb. 1879, the same day as *Grand'ther Baldwin*, and it recapitulates a genealogical history similar to the Alger family history.

III

HA went to California: The more his biographers write about the trip, however, the less they get right. According to Mayes (pp. 156–165), HA traveled west in an unspecified year, paused in Cincinnati for a few days where he was involved in a *ménage à trois*, met two dilettantish spinster sisters in San Francisco who soon threw him over for Bret Harte, and moved "to a settlement in the shadow of the Rockies, there fitting up a hut in which he mourned." Tebbel adds (p. 108) that the fickle sisters' rejection "was apparently the final turn of the screw in Alger's personality disorganization," for HA soon "left San Francisco and stayed for a time in a small town in the foothills of the Rockies, living by himself in a hut, like a hermit." Gruber summarizes (p. 23) the trip in one sentence as inaccurate as it is straightforward: HA went "to California, where he lived for a few weeks in a miner's shack to get material for The Pacific Series."

Though Gardner correctly identifies 1877 as the year HA journeyed west, his dime-novelized account of the trip (pp. 239–253) is no more reliable than the Mayes/Tebbel/Gruber fantasy. In his version, HA is urged by Bret Harte, no less, to "go to California and write stories with a western setting." "Harte's suggestion appealed to Horatio," Gardner writes, whereupon he left for the West, trekking through Injun territory by wagon train, horseback, and stagecoach. While on the West Coast, he spent much of his time in the gold fields talking with miners and gathering material for stories. After several months of this routine, HA decided to return to New York via the sea route around Cape Horn.

> Learning that a magnificent four-masted schooner was leaving almost immediately, he booked passage, and sailed with the evening tide. He had a splendid cabin, dined at the captain's table and looked forward to some months of relaxation, interrupted only by infrequent calls at strange, enchanting South American ports.

Suntanned and fit, Gardner reports, HA sailed into New York Harbor in September. Gardner has recently reiterated his version of these events in an essay prepared for *Publishers for Mass Entertainment in Nineteenth Century America*, ed. Madeleine Stern (Boston, 1980), p. 288: HA "dashed westward with the homesteaders, traveled alone through wild Indian territory, visited lawless mining camps in the California Sierras, and sailed around Cape Horn in a four-masted schooner. These exploits . . . are fairly well documented." Predictably, Hoyt (pp. 187–88) paraphrases Gardner. In his account, HA travels the same routes to and from California on the same horse, stagecoach, and schooner.

In truth, there is no evidence HA ever met Harte. His letters reveal he was whisked to California, with brief layovers en route, on the Union Pacific railroad. He spent most of his time on the Coast holed up in hotels and visiting friends in various cities. He subsequently based his western stories more upon his reading than upon his experiences or personal observations. He returned east in late spring, not the fall of 1877, and he traveled once more by rail across the continent, not by steamer around the Horn.

39. Merle Curti, "Dime Novels and the American Tradition," *Yale Review*, 26 (Summer 1937), 761–778; Smith, *Virgin Land*, (New York, 1950), 99–135; Edmund Pearson, *Dime Novels* (Boston, 1929), 131; J. C. Derby, *Fifty Years Among Authors, Books and Publishers* (New York, 1884), 525.

40. *Julius*, 276.

41. *The Young Adventurer* (Boston, 1878), v.

42. HA to E. R. A. Seligman, 21 Feb. 1877 (CU). See also *The Young Adventurer*, 241.

43. HA to E. R. A. Seligman, 15 Feb. 1877 (CU). See also *The Train Boy* (New York, 1883), 263.

44. *From Canal Boy to President*, 163.

45. *The Young Adventurer*, iii.

46. *The Train Boy*, 230.

47. HA to E. R. A. Seligman, 15 Feb. 1877 (CU); S&B, 150; Salt Lake City *Daily Tribune*, 16 Feb. 1877, 4:6.

48. SFMC, 17 Feb. 1877, 1:7; *Alta California*, 17 Feb. 1877, 1:4; *The Young Explorer* (Boston, 1880), iii; HA to E. R. A. Seligman, 21 Feb. 1877 (CU).

49. *The Young Explorer*, 112.

50. Guillermo Prieto, *San Francisco in the Seventies*, trans. Edwin Morby (San Francisco, 1938), 20–21; HA to E. R. A. Seligman, 21 Feb 1877 (CU); *Joe's Luck*, 211.

51. HA to E. R. A. Seligman, 21 Feb. 1877 (CU); *Silas Snobden's Office Boy*, 135–141.

52. HA to E. R. A. Seligman, 21 Feb. 1877 (CU).

53. HA to Harriet Jackson, 3 March 1877 (UV).

54. HA to E. R. A. Seligman, 13 March 1877 (CU); "AMBR"; SFMC, 9 Nov. 1890, 12.

55. HA to E. R. A. Seligman, 13 March 1877 (CU).

56. HA to Elsie Leslie Lydes, 24 April 1890 (PML).

57. "AMBR"; *Illustrated London News*, 11 June 1887.

58. *BSU Forum*, 21 (Autumn 1980), 58–65; S&B, 89.

59. HA to E. R. A. Seligman, 13 March 1877 (CU).

60. San Francisco *Daily Examiner*, 26 March 1877, 3:6; SFMC, 26 March 1877, 4:1.

61. *The Young Adventurer*, v.

62. *The Young Miner* (Boston, 1879), 11, 250–54; *Joe's Luck*, 90.

63. Portland *Daily Standard*, 30 April 1877, 3:1; Portland *Oregonian*, 30 April 1877, 3:2; HA to E. R. A. Seligman, 7 May 1877 (CU).

64. Portland *Daily Standard*, 3 May 1877, 3:1; Portland *Daily Bee*, 9 May 1877, 4:1.

65. HA to E. R. A. Seligman, 7 May 1877 (CU).

66. Portland *Oregonian*, 4 May 1877, 3:2.

67. HA to E. R. A. Seligman, 4 May 1877 (CU).

68. *Abraham Lincoln, the Backwoods Boy*, 145–46.

69. *Alta California*, 25 May 1877, 4:4; San Francisco *Chronicle*, 25 May 1877, 4:4.

70. N, 17 (June-July 1979), 5; *The Young Explorer*, 195.

71. *Omaha Republican*, 22 June 1877, 4:1.

72. HA to E. R. A. Seligman, 6 Aug. 1877 (CU).

73. HA to E. R. A. Seligman, 1 April 1878 (CU); *Cincinnati Enquirer*, 22 March 1878, 8:2; Cincinnati *Daily Gazette*, 23 March 1878, 8:1; *Missouri Republican*, 26 March 1878, 8:1.

74. HA to E. R. A. Seligman, 1 April 1878 (CU); *Rocky Mountain News*, 2 April 1878, 4:2; and 7 April 1878, 4:2; *Do and Dare* (Philadelphia, 1884), 181.

75. HA to E. R. A. Seligman, 22 April 1878 (CU).
76. *Natick Bulletin*, 24 Jan. 1902, 1:4; *Woman's Journal*, 22 Feb. 1902, 63.
77. HA to E. R. A. Seligman, 15 July 1878 (CU).
78. Anna Alger Richardson to Frank Millner, 27 Sept. 1943 (NHS).
79. HA to E. R. A. Seligman, 19 Aug. 1878 (CU).

IV

HA's biographers also speculate wildly about his popularity. Mayes contends (pp. 39, 213) that "No matter how strange it may seem now, Horatio Alger, Jr., was the most widely read writer of the ages. . . . His name in America is better known than Shakespeare's, his writings more widely read. Some of his contemporaries acquired fame; he acquired popularity." Gruber agrees (pp. 11, 27, 40) that the most interesting fact about HA is that "He was the greatest selling author of his time, of all time. . . . More of Alger's books have been sold than of Dickens, Thackeray, Hemingway, Faulkner and Lloyd C. Douglas, combined." Though estimates of HA's total sales "range from one hundred to three hundred million copies," according to Gruber, he is "inclined to favor the latter figure." Gardner raises the ante (pp. 356, 378). He asserts without any explanation that "some 400,000,000 copies" of HA's books were sold. More recently, however, he hedges ("Introduction" to *The Erie Train Boy* [Leyden, Mass., 1975], p. v, and "Foreword" to *Cast Upon the Breakers*, pp. 12–13):

> There are estimates [*sic*: his own] of up to 400 million copies of his books having been printed. That's more than those of Mark Twain, Louisa May Alcott, John Steinbeck and Ernest Hemingway combined. There are skeptics who claim Alger's total couldn't have been more than 250 million, but even at the lower figure, his sum was phenomenal!

Similarly, Hoyt reports (p. 235) that estimates of HA's aggregate sales "range from 100,000,000 to half a billion."

Nonsense. In 1947, in *Golden Multitudes*—a work Gardner elsewhere cites in his biography (p. 349)—Frank Luther Mott, dean of the University of Missouri School of Journalism, realistically estimates (pp. 158–59) HA's total sales at approximately 17 million copies.

80. "Eight Cousins," *St. Nicholas*, 2 (Aug. 1875), 616–17. See also Gene Gleason, "Whatever Happened to Oliver Optic?" *Wilson Library Bulletin*, 49 (May 1975), 647–650.
81. "What Our Boys Are Reading," *Scribner's*, 15 (March 1878), 681–85; reprinted in *Earth-Hunger and Other Essays*, ed. Albert Galloway Keller (New Haven, 1914), 367–377.
82. Arthur L. Vogelback, "The Publication and Reception of *Huckleberry Finn* in America," *American Literature*, 11 (Nov. 1939), 260–272.
83. Richard L. Darling, *The Rise of Children's Book Reviewing in America 1865–1881* (New York, 1968), 39.
84. S&B, 113.
85. *LJ*, 6 (1881), 182.
86. S&B, 135.
87. Dee Garrison, "Cultural Custodians of the Gilded Age: The Public Librarian and Horatio Alger," *Journal of Library History*, 6 (Oct. 1971), 331.

88. HA to Victor H. Wolff, 23 July 1879 (Ill. St. Historical Society).

89. *LJ*, 4 (1879), 341–350.

90. *Christian Union*, 24 May 1883, 420; S&B, 135.

91. *LJ*, 19 (Dec. 1894), 83.

92. S&B, 137.

93. Worcester *Evening Gazette*, 8 Aug. 1907, 1:3–4; and 10 Aug. 1907, 1:6–7.

94. "WSfB."

95. Stern, *Imprints on History*, 187–89.

96. HA to Henry T. Coates, 11 June 1881 (Haverford Coll.).

97. *From Canal Boy to President*, 307.

98. HA to Mr. Elderkin, 2 Aug. 1884 (YU). HA later was unsuccessfully sued for copyright infringement by James A. Gilmore ("Edward Kirke"), author of one of the Garfield biographies he consulted. See *American Bookseller*, 15 Feb. 1887, 30; *Publishers Weekly*, 8 Feb. 1889, 101; and *Dime Novel Roundup*, 53 (June 1984), 38–43.

99. *From Canal Boy to President*, 309.

100. S&B, 155.

101. HA to Mr. Elderkin, 2 Aug. 1884 (YU).

102. Reviews: S&B, 36–37.

103. *Abraham Lincoln, the Backwoods Boy*, 5–6.

104. HA to Irving Blake, 7 April 1894 (Hunt).

105. HA to Mr. Elderkin, 2 Aug. 1884 (YU); HA to Porter & Coates, 19 Aug. 1884 (UV).

106. HA to Irving Blake, 21 March 1898 (Hunt).

107. HA to Edward Stratemeyer, 3 Feb. 1897, (SS).

108. HA to Edward Stratemeyer, 11 Nov. 1898 (SS).

109. *The Young Circus Rider* (Philadelphia, 1883), 3.

V

Though he never married, HA became a foster father: Again, his biographers agree on the point, however inaccurately they report the details. According to Mayes (pp. 108–111), HA first met a Chinese orphan he named Wing in the winter of 1873. He rescued the ten-year-old boy from a mob of urchins who held him face down in snow,

> took him in his arms and carried him to the lodging house, there to have him dried and fed. That night Wing slept in the lodging house, and the night following, and on every night for three years after that. Wing became in effect Horatio Alger's son.

However, one evening in August 1877, as Mayes tells the story, Wing was trampled to death by a runaway horse. "A part of the good" in HA "was swept away and something like a tinge of spleen usurped its place. The fringes of his hair turned white that day."

Incredibly, Tebbel, more resolute than accurate, repeats this bunk (pp. 73, 75). "Alger first saw Wing in Chatham Square on a cold winter evening in 1873," he begins. "A small gang of assorted children" had attacked a "small ten-year-old boy" whose face they washed with snow when HA came upon the scene.

> Horatio carried him in his arms to the House, where O'Connor helped dry him out and feed him. He slept there that night, and every night for more than three years.

HA "was idyllically happy" until he learned of Wing's death beneath the hooves of the horse. "Overnight Alger was a changed man," Tebbel adds. "What hair he had remaining turned white, and a flood tide of bitterness washed out most of what religion remained in him."

Gardner invents an alternative account (pp. 12, 281–282). First, he changes the surname of HA's wards John and Edward Downie to Down, arguing for no good reason that he does so "to eliminate possible embarrassment to descendants." Inexplicably, Hoyt (pp. 229–232) follows Gardner's spelling, even though he examined original documents with the correct spelling. Moreover, Gardner invents details which are demonstrably untrue. The Down brothers, he writes, came with their widowed mother Kate

> from Ireland in 1885, when John was fourteen and Edward twelve. John arrived first, and Horatio met him at the Lodging House, where he stayed, getting started as a messenger while finding a room for his mother and brother, who reached America two months later.
>
> Both boys were slender and dark-haired with blue eyes and rich brogue. Their mother was a handsome woman in her mid-thirties, with freckles, auburn hair and the lilting voice of her County Kerry people, where she was raised on a hillside farm.

Later, Gardner avers that HA "legally adopted" the boys, "naming them among his heirs" ("Foreword" to *Silas Snobden's Office Boy*, p. 26). In fact, he errs in the ages he assigns to the brothers, misreports the year HA met them, and overlooks HA's reference to them in his will as "my two informally adopted boys." Worse yet, Gardner fabricates the character of Kate Down from whole cloth, much as Mayes did Wing. The boys were orphaned three years before HA met them.

110. After moving from the Seligman home in 1875 and before moving to Natick in 1896, HA lived in nine different New York boarding houses, as follows: 111 East 46th (1875–79); 107 West 44th (summer 1879–fall 1879); 210 West 34th (fall 1879–1882); 52 West 26th (1882–87); 36 West 33rd (1887–1890); 249 West 34th (1890–91); 223 West 34th (1891–95); 227 West 34th (1895–winter 1896); 44 West 10th (March 1896).

111. HA to E. R. A. Seligman, 5 Sept. 1879 (CU).

112. Between 1874 and 1892, HA attended eight of the annual dinners of the Club, as well as dedication ceremonies in 1887 for the clubhouse at 11 West 22nd, and in 1875 he served briefly as the club secretary *pro tem.* See the *NYTr,* 19 Feb. 1876, 7:5; *NYTi,* 22 Feb. 1881, 5:3; *Harvard Register,* 3 (March 1881), 145; *NYTi,* 22 Feb. 1882, 2:1, and 22 Feb. 1883, 5:4; *NYTr,* 22 Feb. 1885, 2:6; *NYTi,* 21 Feb. 1886, 2:3; *NYTr,* 22 Feb. 1887, 5:2; *NYTi,* 10 June 1887, 5:1, and 20 Feb. 1892, 3:1. See also Harvard Club of New York minutes book for 18 Dec. 1875.

113. HA to E. R. A. Seligman, 5 Sept. 1879 (CU).

114. HA to Irving Blake, 2 Aug. 1895 (Hunt).

115. HA to Robert Bonner, 21 Nov. 1879 (PML).

116. *Gen.Hi.,* 28; Shur, 140; Annie Alger Richardson to Frank Millner, 13 March 1943 (NHS); *Denver Tribune,* 21 June 1884, 8:1.

117. HA to E. R. A. Seligman, 5 Sept. 1879 (CU).

118. NEHGS *Register*, 36 (Oct. 1882), 414–15; *Addresses Delivered by Rev. J. P. Sheafe Jr. and Rev. Horatio Alger at the Semi-Centennial Celebration of the Dedication of the First Unitarian Church, South Natick, November 20, 1878* (Natick, 1879), 33–34 and *passim*.

119. HA to Irving Blake, 14 Dec. 1897 (Hunt).

120. Mabel Parmenter to Frank Millner, 22 May 1940 (HUA).

121. "AMBR"; *The Young Circus Rider*, 25–27 and *passim*; HA to E. R. A. Seligman, 14 July 1885 (CU); HA to Mr. Elderkin, 2 Aug. 1884 (YU); *GA*, 17 Oct. 1885, 364; Annie Alger Richardson to Frank Millner, 13 March 1943 (NHS).

122. *NYTi*, 8 Dec. 1945, 17:2; HA to Russell Alger, 2 May and 4 July 1888 and 10 Nov 1898 (Mich); *Mark Manning's Mission* (New York, 1905), 48; *Chester Rand* (Philadelphia, 1903), 258–59; HA to Blake, 1 Jan. 1898 (Hunt); *GA*, 17 Oct. 1885, 364.

123. HA to Blake, 1 Jan. 1898 (Hunt); HA to R. Alger, 10 Nov. 1898 (Mich); *The Odds Against Him* (Philadelphia, 1890), 99.

124. Samuel C. Beane, "Necrology of the Harvard Divinity School, 1900" (HUA).

125. HA to R. Alger, 2 May 1888 (Mich).

126. *The Young Adventurer*, 167; *Chester Rand*, 313; *Lester's Luck* (Philadelphia, 1901), 256; *Forging Ahead* (Philadelphia, 1903), 37–38.

127. HA to E. R. A. Seligman, 1 July 1885 (CU); HA to E. C. Stedman, 9 Jan. 1888 (NYPL); Drew Pearson and R. S. Allen, *The Nine Old Men* (Garden City, 1936), 215; S&B, 150; *Scribner's*, 14 (Nov. 1893), 560; *Cosmopolitan*, 17 (1894), 450; *Century*, 46 (July 1893), 479; *Critic*, 8 April 1893, 226; *New England Magazine*, NS 7 (Sept. 1892), 92.

128. HA to E. R. A. Seligman, 1 July 1885 (CU).

129. *New-England Galaxy*, 16 (Summer 1974), 7; HA to "dear Percy," 19 Aug. 1886 (LC).

130. "AMBR"; *GA*, 5 Nov. 1887, 776.

5. Cast upon the Breakers (1887–1899)

I

Previous biographers sing one note in the same key: HA preached a gospel of wealth. Mayes claims (pp. 214–15) that the "most omnivorous readers of Horatio Alger were poor boys" or "boys who wanted to grow rich." He suggests that HA aimed his pitch at incipient robber barons. Like a catalyst in a chemical reaction, according to Mayes, HA's stories inspired entrepreneurs to join the scramble for wealth and prestige. Gruber chimes in (p. 11) that "Generations of successful men read Alger in their youth and many, many hundreds, thousands of them give Alger at least partial credit for their success." Gardner asserts (p. 346) that "Innumerable American leaders of today—and of recent memory—once read Alger and believed in him." The folklore of rags to riches, the celebration of free enterprise—HA's critics and his admirers alike agree to debate his merits in these terms. Unfortunately, his stories, especially those he wrote after 1880, harp on different themes—especially the rascality of the rich and the potential of money and power to corrupt.

1. *Number 91* (New York, 1887), 181–82.
2. Matthew Josephson, *The Robber Barons* (New York, 1934), 198.
3. *The Store Boy*, pp. 279–80.
4. *Luke Walton*, 115, 117.
5. *Paul the Peddler*, 9–48.
6. *Luke Walton*, 18, 35.
7. HA to E. R. A. Seligman, 14 Nov 1885 (CU).
8. *Tom Tracy* (New York, 1888), 42. Luke Walton, 246.
9. HA to E. R. A. Seligman, 9 Nov. 1876 (CU); to R. Alger, 4 July 1888 (Mich); to Blake, 9 Sept. 1896 (Hunt).
10. HA to Blake, 12 Dec. 1896 (Hunt).
11. Anti-Tammany: HA to Blake, 7 Nov. 1897 (Hunt). Pro-civil service: *From Canal Boy to President*, 293, 300. Pro-tariff: *Abraham Lincoln, the Backwoods Boy*, 117. "Sound" money: *From Canal Boy to President*, 251–252; *From Farm Boy to Senator*, 175.
12. HA to Blake, 26 June 1896 (Hunt).
13. HA to Blake, 9 Sept. 1896 (Hunt).
14. HA to R. Alger, 2 May 1888, 28 June 1888, (1 July?) 1888, 4 July 1888, 10 Nov. 1898 (Mich).
15. *NYTi*, 22 Feb. 1881, 5:3; HA to Blake, 23 Dec. 1895, 5 Feb. and 3 Dec. 1896 (Hunt); HA to R. Alger, 10 Nov. 1898 (Mich).

II

16. Mott, *A History of American Magazines 1885–1905*, 419.
17. "WSfB."
18. "Could enjoy": HA to Blake, 7 Sept. 1895, 3 Jan. 1896.
19. Route west: *Chester Rand*, 335. Jackson Park: *Rupert's Ambition*, 260. Reached Helena: *Helena Herald*, 28 Oct. 1890, 5:2. Passed Arlee: Portland *Oregonian*, 30 Oct. 1890, 6:6. Reached San Francisco: *Alta California*, 3 Nov. 1890, 5:4.
20. SFMC, 9 Nov. 1890, 12.
21. HA to Blake, 2 June 1896 (Hunt).
22. Reviews: S&B, 39–43; *Dial*, 16 Dec. 1896, 391–92; and 1 Dec. 1899, 434.
23. SFMC, 9 Nov. 1890, 12.
24. *Frank Leslie's Pleasant Hours*, NS 1 (March 1896), 354.
25. *BDG*, evening ed., 18 July 1899, 10:6.
26. HA to C. T. Scott, 25 March 1895 (LC).
27. "AMBR."
28. *Writer*, 6 (Jan. 1892), 16.
29. *N*, 23 (Nov.-Dec. 1983), 10.
30. *Chester Rand*, 117; *The Young Salesman* (Philadelphia, 1896), 15; *Rupert's Ambition*, 285; *Out for Business* (New York, 1900), 73–77.
31. HA to Blake, 27 Feb. 1897 (Hunt).
32. *BP*, 19 July 1899, 5:4.
33. *Roses and Buckshot* (New York, 1946), 52.

34. *N*, 23 (Nov.-Dec. 1983), 10.
35. E. W. Burks to Frank Millner, 27 June [1939?] (LC).
36. HA to Ernest Burks, 23 Nov. 1892 (Hunt). HA also mentioned young Trott by name in *Walter Sherwood's Probation*, 232–33.
37. HA to Blake, 14 March 1898 (Hunt).
38. HA to Blake, 17 March 1896 (Hunt).
39. HA to E. R. A. Seligman, 1 July 1885 (CU).
40. HA to Blake, 17 Sept. 1896 (Hunt); *Rupert's Ambition*, 206, 228; *A Boy's Fortune*, 69; *TF*, 1 May 1858, 2:5.
41. HA to E. R. A. Seligman, 3 Jan, 1878 (CU).
42. HA to Blake, 28 April 1896 (Hunt).
43. HA to Elsie Leslie Lydes, 24 April 1890 (PML).
44. HA to Blake, 28 April 1896 (Hunt).
45. HA to Blake, 3 Dec. and 12 Dec. 1896 (Hunt).
46. *NYTi*, 12 Jan. 1881, 4:7; HA to Blake, 12 Dec. 1896 (Hunt).
47. HA to Elsie Leslie Lydes, 24 April 1890 (PML).
48. HA to Blake, 12 Dec. 1896 (Hunt).
49. *HGM*, 1 (Oct. 1892), 157.
50. *AS*, 87–88.
51. HA to Blake, 7 Aug. 1894 (Hunt).
52. Munsey reprints: Bennett, 88, 130. Adult syndication: Bennett, 173–191; *N*, 22 (May–June 1983), 21–23.
53. Synopsis: *The Disagreeable Woman* (New York, 1895), v and *passim*.
54. HA to Blake, 4 April 1895 (Hunt).
55. Reviews: S&B, 41–42; *Woman's Journal*, 3 Aug. 1895, 247.
56. HA to Blake, 13 June 1895 (Hunt).
57. HA to Blake, 7 July 1895 (Hunt).
58. HA to Blake, 11 July 1895 (Hunt).
59. *Critic*, 27 July 1895, 61.
60. HA to Blake, 26 Aug. 1895 (Hunt).
61. Returned to Natick: HA to Blake, 2 Aug. 1895 (Hunt). Visit to New York: HA to Blake, 26 Aug. 1895 (Hunt); *The Young Salesman*, 72. Maine and return: HA to Blake, 7 Sept. 1895 (Hunt).
62. HA to Blake, 5 Feb. 1896 (Hunt).
63. HA to Blake, 2 June 1896 (Hunt).
64. *BA*, 10 April 1896, 9.
65. HA to Blake, 28 April 1896 (Hunt).

III

Mayes and Gardner offer two contrasting views of HA in his sixties. According to Mayes (pp. 167–195)—and, of course, Tebbel as well (pp. 110–122)—HA had an affair with a middle-aged, married woman named Una Garth whom he pursued all the way to Paris. The waning of her affection caused him to return to New York sadder, wiser, and temporarily insane. His health broken, his ambition to write the Great American Novel turned to ashes, he died an invalid in his sister's home, destitute of money but rich in dreams. According to Gardner, on the other hand (pp. 289, 303), HA was infatuated late in life with the widowed mother of John and Tommy Down. Gardner explains in detail how HA, in the spring of 1891, bought a house in a quiet Brooklyn neighborhood, where he and the three Downs lived together in middle-class respectability. "Kate Down made for Horatio a snug home in Brooklyn," he writes, and as in most fairy tales they all lived happily ever after. Unfortunately, there is not a scrap of evidence to indicate that HA ever lived in Brooklyn or that "Kate Down" ever lived at all. Consider too the closing sentences of Gardner's biography:

> Still holding the letter, appearing tiny and childlike on the large bed, he closed his eyes to slumber, nevermore to awaken. But on Horatio Alger's face was a relaxed expression of contentment, for he went to sleep knowing that when he joyously greeted his Kate, the first thing he would tell her was that he loved her.

Not only does Gardner invent the character of Kate Down, not only does he presume to read the mind of a man who would die in his sleep, he clearly suggests that HA had formed a heterosexual attachment, an unconscionable distortion of the Brewster records he claims to have examined.

Gruber, Gardner, and Hoyt are also misinformed about the so-called "Stratemeyer Algers." After HA's death, eleven novels were published under his name with the stipulation, at first explicit and later implied, that they had been completed by "Arthur M. Winfield," a pseudonym of Edward Stratemeyer. Gruber argues (p. 45) that all eleven "were actually written" by Stratemeyer. Gardner concurs (pp. 364–68; "Foreword" to *Cast Upon the Breakers*, p. 30): The novels "were actually written by Edward Stratemeyer." Hoyt echoes Gardner (p. 248): "They were books written by Edward Stratemeyer." Unfortunately, no earlier biographer checked with Stratemeyer's heirs. The MS of *Out for Business*, the first Stratemeyer completion, started in HA's hand and finished on Stratemeyer's typewriter, as well as HA's scrawled plea to finish the story for him, are still owned by the Stratemeyer Syndicate in Maplewood, New Jersey.

66. HA to Blake, 26 Oct. 1896 (Hunt).
67. To New York and Marblehead: HA to Blake, 2 June 1896 (Hunt). Maine coast: HA to Blake, 7 Aug. 1896 (Hunt). Woodstock: HA to Blake, 9 Sept. 1896 (Hunt).
68. HA to Blake, 22 Aug. 1896 (Hunt).
69. HA to Blake, 10 Nov. 1896 (Hunt).
70. HA to Blake, 6 April 1896, 14 Jan. 1897 (Hunt).
71. HA to Blake, 3 Feb. 1897 (Hunt).
72. O. A. Cheney to Edward Stratemeyer, 2 Nov. 1899 (SS).
73. HA to Blake, 16 Feb. 1897 (Hunt).
74. HA to Edward Stratemeyer, 26 Feb. 1897 (SS).
75. HA to Blake, 15 Aug. 1897 (Hunt).
76. HA to Edward Stratemeyer, 18 Dec. 1898 (SS).
77. HA to Henry T. Coates & Co., 24 Sept. 1897 (Bob Bennett).
78. HA to Blake, 17 Oct. 1897 (Hunt).
79. HA to Blake, 1 Jan. 1898 (Hunt).
80. HA to Blake, 14 Feb. 1898 (Hunt).
81. HA to Blake, 21 March 1898 (Hunt).
82. HA to Blake, 2 June 1898 (Hunt).
83. HA to Blake, 21 Oct. 1898 (Hunt).

84. HA to Blake, 2 Feb. 1897 (Hunt).

85. HA to Blake, 7 Nov. 1897 (Hunt). HA had been reading the excerpts of Mark Twain's *Following the Equator* published in *McClure's*.

86. *BDG*, evening ed., 18 July 1899, 10:6.

87. HA to R. Alger, 10 Nov. 1898 (Mich).

88. HA to Blake, 1 Jan. 1898 (Hunt).

89. HA to R. Alger, 10 Nov. 1898 (Mich).

90. *N*, 18 (Jan.–Feb. 1980), 4.

91. *BP*, 19 July 1899, 5:4.

92. HA to Blake, 25 Sept. 1896 (Hunt).

93. HA to Blake, 10 Nov. 1896 (Hunt).

94. HA to Edward Stratemeyer, 26 Oct. 1898 (SS).

95. HA to Edward Stratemeyer, 21 Nov. 1898 (SS).

96. HA to Edward Stratemeyer, 18 Dec. 1898 (SS).

97. HA to Blake, 24 Feb. 1899 (Hunt).

98. *BP*, 19 July 1899, 5:3–4.

99. Death and funeral: *BT*, 21 July 1899; *Natick Bulletin*, 21 July 1899, 1:4–6; S&B, 152–53.

100. *Oldtown Folks* (Boston and New York, 1869), 2, 49–50.

101. *N*, 18 (Jan.–Feb. 1980), 4–5.

102. *BP*, 19 July 1899, 5:4.

103. O. A. Cheney to Edward Stratemeyer, 2 Nov. 1899 (SS).

104. *BP*, 19 July 1899, 5:4.

105. *N*, 21 (May–June 1983), 5; 22 (July–Aug. 1983), 12.

106. *Jerry the Backwoods Boy* (New York, 1904).

107. *HGM*, 9 (Sept. 1900), 111.

108. *BP*, 19 July 1899, 5:4.

109. NY*Tr*, 19 July 1899, 7:3. Blake had prepared the copy 3 years before (HA to Blake, 16 July 1896 [Hunt]).

110. *Golden Hours*, 28 Sept. 1901, 16:4; O. A. Cheney to Edward Stratemeyer, 11 Nov. 1901 (SS).

111. *The Founding of the Munsey Publishing-House* (New York, 1907), 5–6.

112. Joseph Dean: *Record of the Service of the Forty-Fourth Massachusetts Volunteer Militia*, 309. Isaac Seligman: *DAB* (New York, 1935), VIII, 570–71. E. R. A. Seligman: *Who Was Who in America* (Chicago, 1943), I, 1102–03. Gilbert Hitchcock: *NYTi*, 3 Feb. 1934, 13:1. Benjamin Cardozo: George Hellman, *Benjamin N. Cardozo: American Judge* (New York, 1940). Lewis Einstein: *Who Was Who in America* (Chicago, 1950), II, 171. John Downie: *NYTi*, 8 Dec. 1945, 17:2. Irving Blake: *NYTi*, 18 Nov. 1940, 19:4. Edward Stratemeyer: Russel Nye, *The Unembarrassed Muse* (New York, 1970), 76–84.

113. *Strong and Steady* (Boston, 1871), v.

114. Washington Seligman: *NYTi*, 13 Feb. 1912, 7:5; Peggy Guggenheim, *Confessions of an Art Addict* (New York, 1960), 19. Jefferson Seligman: *NYTi* 6 Aug. 1915, 18:5; Guggenheim, 19. Alfred Seligman and Florine Arnold: *The Telegraph Boy* (Boston, 1879), iii; Hellman, "The Story of the Seligmans," 296–301. A. F. Henriques: *Try and Trust*, iii; *NYTi*, 8 March 1892, 3:6; *GA*, 25 April 1885. Lorin Bernheimer: *The Telegraph Boy*, iii; *NYTi*, 30 Jan. 1913, 11:3.

Afterword

1. *HW*, 5 Aug. 1899, 761.
2. *S&B*, 147–48.
3. *World's Work*, 20 (June 1910), 13045.
4. A. M. Jordan, *Children's Interest in Reading* (Chapel Hill, 1926), *passim*.
5. *Nation*, 17 Feb. 1932, 186.
6. *Literary Digest*, 30 Jan. 1932, 20; *Christian Science Monitor*, 19 Nov. 1934, 7:1.
7. *NYTi*, 13 Jan. 1947, 23:2–3.
8. *Horizon*, 12 (Summer 1970), 65.
9. *Time*, 13 Aug. 1945, 98.
10. Reviews: *S&B*, 44, 48, 138.
11. *The Myth of American Success* (New York, 1969), 49, 59–60.
12. *Book Buyer*, 25 (Dec. 1902), 495.
13. John Cawelti, *Adventure, Mystery and Romance* (Chicago and London, 1976), 224; Roderick Nash, *The Nervous Generation* (Chicago, 1970), 138.
14. *Time*, 7 May 1928, 47.
15. *NYTi Book Review*, 22 April 1928, 2.
16. *Literary Digest*, 9 Jan. 1926, 48.
17. *Outlook*, 11 April 1928, 598.
18. *S&B*, 162.
19. *NYTi*, 13 Jan. 1932, 22:4.
20. *S&B*, 104.
21. *Ibid.*
22. *NYTi Magazine*, 16 July 1939, 11.
23. *NYTi*, 30 March 1940, 9:2; and 6 April 1940, 16:3.
24. *NYTi*, 14 Jan. 1942, 12:4.
25. *Atlantic Monthly*, 172 (Nov. 1943), 117.
26. *NYTi Book Review*, 2 July 1944, 9.
27. Reviews: *S&B*, 48–50.
28. *NYTi*, 16 Jan. 1947, 24:4.
29. *Advertising Age*, 1 Dec. 1947, 18–19.
30. *Lost Men of American History* (New York, 1946), 228, 238.
31. *Opportunity Still Knocks* (New York, 1971), 3 and *passim*.
32. *Opportunity Still Knocks, passim*; *N*, 9 (Feb.–March 1971), 1, 3–9; and 14 (March 1976), 13; *American Libraries*, 12 (Feb. 1981), 61.
33. *S&B*, 50, 155, 158–59.
34. HA to Blake, 12 May 1897 (Hunt).

INDEX